ESCAPING GOD'S CLOSET

ESCAPING
GOD'S
CLOSET

The Revelations of a Queer Priest

Bernard Duncan Mayes

UNIVERSITY PRESS OF VIRGINIA

CHARLOTTESVILLE AND LONDON

The University Press of Virginia
© 2001 by the Rector and Visitors of the University of Virginia
All rights reserved
Printed in the United States of America
First published 2001

Library of Congress Cataloging-in-Publication Data
Mayes, Bernard, 1929–
   Escaping God's closet: the revelations of a queer priest / Bernard Duncan Mayes
   p. cm.
   Includes index.
   ISBN 0-8139-2004-3 (cloth: alk. paper)
   1. Mayes, Bernard, 1929–   2. Episcopal Church—Clergy—Biography.   3.
Ex-clergy—United States—Biography.   4. Gay clergy—United States—Biography.   I. Title.

BX5995.M38 A3 2001
283'.092—dc21
[B]   00-043640

IN MEMORY OF THE DEAD

CONTENTS

ACKNOWLEDGMENTS

So much of what follows was made possible by many who are now dead that I have dedicated the result to their memory. I want also to thank those who encouraged me to begin and continue: my colleagues at the University of Virginia, especially Herbert Braun, whose careful criticism was most helpful; Ann J. Lane, whose support of lesbian and gay rights over the years has meant much to me and to others and whose comments were important and valuable; and Farzaneh Milani, whose enthusiasm continually urged me forward. I am also grateful to others at the University who gave me time and space in which to prepare the first drafts: Carl Trindle of Brown College, whose generosity was boundless; Ray Nelson, who allowed me to travel; Mel Leffler and my fellow College deans, who gave me valuable time away; Sherry Bullock, my admirable secretary; and Mary Creed, our network administrator, who took special care of the computer files for me. I thank these also: the librarians of the Library of Congress, Prints and Photographs Division, without whose assistance so many of the key illustrations could not have been included—Rosemary Hanes, Marilyn Ibach, Barbara Natanson, and especially Maja Keech, who to my great relief sorted out many intricacies; the librarians of the History Room of the San Francisco Public Library, especially Tim Wilson and Thomas Cary of the Lesbian and Gay History Collection, and David Ettinger of the Gelman Library at George Washington University, all of whom helped me find key material; Eve Meyer of the San Francisco Suicide Prevention Center for finding records from the past; James Day, Jeanne Alexander, Jo Anne Wallace and Carol Cicerone of KQED-FM, for their archive material; the Reverend John Rawlinson, archivist of the Episcopal Diocese of California, who spent much time with me sorting through church records; Ronald Bansemer and Ray Herth for making their facilities available and without whose help the Parsonage would have had no home; "Uncle Donald," whose wonderful website includes key pictures of gay history; Donald Quayle, Thomas Connors, and Karen E. King of the National Public Broadcasting Archives at the University of Maryland, who helped me find records of National Public Radio; Robert Newman, Nathan Shaw, Donald Johnle, and Peter Van der Kar for their immediate and generous help with photographs; John Fecondo, who made his home available, allowing me to spend a week of research in San Francisco archives; my dear friend John Horrex for his reliable memory; Christopher Prue and Thomas Edwards of the Office of Information Technology and Communication at the University of Virginia, who rescued my disks in time of trouble; Ron Taylor and Colin Tooke of the Great Yarmouth website; Malcolm Barr-Hamilton of the Tower Hamlets Bancroft Library; and especially Richard Holway and David Sewell, my editors, and the production staff of the University Press of Virginia, who thought this book was worth reading, made numerous helpful corrections and improvements, and saw it through to publication. I am also in debt to many friends and colleagues who made it possible to survive physical ordeals during the writing, especially Arthur Scott, Daniel Stern, Joyce Dudek, and Sandra Snyder. Of many others I cannot bring myself to name only a few, and they are all remembered with gratitude.

This is the story of a life and what it revealed, not only about the joys of the body and the problems posed by religion, but also about the nature of the universe itself. It starts where we all start, and it moves forward through the entanglements of a sophisticated culture already at odds with itself to an unequivocal explanation of existence. Down the ages, the search for such an explanation has engaged the attention and imagination not only of professional thinkers but also of most of humanity, and especially its outcasts. Many still hedge their bets in hopes that life leads somewhere after all. And as I suggest in this necessarily rambling account, it does, but not to where we have been led to expect. Life is not what it seems to be, and we are not what we think we are; none of us.

ESCAPING GOD'S CLOSET

GHOSTS

1929-1938

I survived the previous century and we have entered another. And because of what is happening to us all and to me in particular, I must make sense of it.

Early in life we sort experiences according to inherited beliefs and theories; later these are shaken when we discover unexpected facts, or ones that others have suppressed. Religions, for example, those supposed repositories of ultimate meaning, still claim the loyalty of millions even while the accelerating pace of discovery about the world around us forces many to rethink what once they took for granted. Each life, in fact, is a new exploration rather than a recapitulation of history.

What we discover is often upsetting. For gay people like myself the search for meaning has been a never-ending task. After all, we were once supposed not to exist, or to exist merely as curiosities who were misbehaving. Today, thanks to an increasing number of witnesses, many of whom are dead, we are no longer irrelevant. Not that we ever were. But now we and other marginalized people must be included in whatever explanation is arrived at. The task no longer belongs only to others.

As for myself, it took me several professions to find clues to a possible answer. The result is a story that has a surprisingly wide reach. The clues were well hidden, and even when I found them, it was, as you will discover, difficult to trace where they were heading. I was very busy. There was often little chance to work out directions. For some years I broadcast to millions on radio and television and was once even recognizable in the street. I felt what it was like to travel at great speed through the midst of cities on urgent assignments. I shook hands and chatted with astronauts and movie stars, and saw my work sold in stores, read in libraries, heard on the radio, and watched on television. I even bandied words with those at the top of the heap. When I was being bombed, beaten up, and nearly murdered, I found it difficult to accept what I was learning. Only toward the end did everything begin to make sense. I then became an anomaly, an eccentric, and finally an apostate.

Gay heretics were once boiled in oil, or hung and drawn and quartered like so many cattle, their pieces burned at the stake. Established authorities used to see a threat in us, and the stench of that cruel morality can still be detected. As a result I learned to take my chances with isolation. But I was not desolate, and so hardly ever lonesome. Being different from the rest in such a basic, physical way seemed to privilege my body, enlarge its significance, rescue it from artificial and intellectual constraints, and finally make it wholesome. Too often in those days, even among the rich and frivolous and especially among the disguised, the gay body became a shrunken, timid thing that found a furtive existence only in hidden holes and corners of the world. Bringing it to life and happiness, if this could be done, seemed to me worthwhile.

Meanwhile, my paths kept dividing and were marked with signposts that eventually pointed in different directions. Many times I suspected I might arrive back where I started, or else find myself confounded by a maelstrom of intellectual confusion, the horrors of genteel silence, or even physical violence. The Ku Klux Klan, for instance, well knew me for a revolutionary worth beating up. They smelled me from afar. And the stiletto at my throat, much later, whose fault was that?

It was my priesthood that caused the most trouble, as others had said it would and should. To doubt the Christian Church, a community so extensive, an edifice of such enormous pride and inertia, with its beauty, its monuments and palaces, its convoluted thought, its roots so deep and branches so extensive, was, as history testifies, a dangerous game. Eventually I triumphed—or I like to think I did—constructing from fragments gathered together from the wreck something that made more sense, that hung together and was all-inclusive.

But this took time and many unexpected turns.

I was born, if you can call it that, very early in the morning of October 10, 1929, in Middlesex Hospital, London, England. A pregnant woman, my mother, lies restless on a gurney and turns frightened eyes toward a nurse who wheels her into the operating theater. Her hands are bound to her side. An ugly brown rubber mask clutches at her nose and mouth, engulfing her in fumes, carrying her away.

"But I'm not Mrs. Deacon! My name is . . ." Chilling fear chokes her. She clutches at the thin hospital robe stretched over her enormous belly.

"What's that you say, Mrs. Deacon?"

Again she tries desperately to speak. Visions of being cut up, losing limbs, appal her. They have the wrong woman! But her mind is drowning fast; the deadly waves wash over her again. Still struggling against them, she is finally engulfed. Only a faint twitching of her hands betrays the terror of her unconscious mind. The surgeon slices in, and I am born.

That is how it was in many hospitals during the first third of the twentieth century. Ensuring that the patient was properly anesthetized was deemed paramount; the terror that accompanied the procedure was of secondary importance.

Terror, or the memory of it, had been on people's minds for many years. In those days, the effects of the Great War of 1914–18 were still very apparent. It had killed men by the millions, so that in Europe there were comparatively few left. A deadly flu epidemic had then carried off millions more women and children.

In 1929, the howitzers, the deadly machine guns, the huge unwieldy tanks, the screams of the dying, had been silent for only ten years. On Vimy ridge and in the fields of Flanders the trenches were still there, dug so close together the soldiers on each side could hear their enemies whispering. Only years later did tourists, I among them, come to gaze at the shell holes, by then grassy green, while children chased each other up and down, laughing and playing in total ignorance. Thousands had died on that very spot, winning and losing, losing and winning, only to be buried alive in the ghastly, stinking mud. It was along those terrible lines that my mother's first love had been mown down or blown to bits.

After being "untimely ripped" from my mother's womb and welcomed into this turbulent and unhappy world, I was sequestered for a month, and even when I regained my mother's breast I found its milk too thin and nearly died a second time. I am told that I was inconsolable and wept for weeks. I was, and I remained, a needy child, desperate for reassurance, in terror of rejection; but that is hindsight. At the time I was glad to be rediscovered, as it were. Being absurdly cosseted, I enjoyed myself. Without the warmth lavished on me then, I doubt if later I would have had the peace of mind to survive the rest of life.

I loved my dear mama, but didn't dote, or didn't think I did. She loved me not only because she nearly lost me but because she had a past. She wasn't young, was nearly forty in fact, the tallest of four daughters. She had attended both the jubilee and the death of Queen Victoria when all the world seemed draped in black. She was quiet and spare with overtones of passion forever unexpressed. Being a widow, she was required to wear mourning at her wedding to my father; her first husband, the tall, aristocratic red-haired young officer, was ever in her thoughts.

During the war in which she lost her love, my mother had worked as a key telephone supervisor at Allied HQ, sending and receiving messages to and from the European front. It turned out that her commanding officer was a spy who learned the battle dispositions by grabbing the earphones from her head and listening in. Perhaps he had been her husband's murderer. She was still working in communications when, ten years after the armistice, she met my father, a crippled artist with a shortened leg. He, too, though younger than my mother by ten years, had problems of his own. Hauled into existence on American Independence Day in 1900, he suffered the carelessness of some doctor, nurse, or midwife, who, in pulling him to life, wrenched and twisted one leg in such a way that—like his own father's total blindness in one eye—the injury went undetected until it was too late to remedy. The only nostrum the doctors of the time could offer was for him to massage the calf in warm water every morning of his life to stimulate circulation. To compensate for the abbreviated limb, he would lurch and lift the other leg, making his stride much longer than the steps of companions who would struggle to keep pace. It became a metaphor for both our lives, this struggle to keep up, he with his peers and I with him. He was always fearful of games that might bring attention to his weakness, and never drove a car. He volunteered for the trenches but was inevitably rejected, and so was left behind and lived.

My father had an eye for physical beauty. He was a painter of exceptionally fine watercolors. But he was a crypto-sensualist. His high school homework book is more a painter's sketchbook. The exercises in arithmetic, shorthand, or writing are elaborately illustrated or illuminated in chalk and paint. So prodigious was this talent that when he was fifteen he ran away to London and almost immediately made a living as a draftsman and later as chief artist, first of the London Midland and Scottish Railway, and then of British Railways itself.

At heart he remained a pietist. His family name was Duncan. The grave of King Duncan, once laird of that celebrated clan, is supposedly a broad flat stone on the tiny island of Iona beside the rocky sea coast of the Scottish Highlands. Worn smooth by North Atlantic storms that roar and crash around the shore, its only observers are the brothers of a Presbyterian foundation and screeching seabirds forever wheeling overhead. When I later looked at it, the stone face presented an austere front like the stern morality overlain with Calvinist leanings whose effects, handed down through the generations, might explain my father's fear of the very beauties he admired so much.

Tough as nails, self-disciplined, and (like many disabled people) desperate to outperform the rest, he lived on and on, opinionated and questioning all he met. He liked to grow flowers in his garden but planted them carefully in predetermined rows measured exactly with a ruler so as to leave no more than six inches between each plant. He dared to be adventurous only toward the century's end, when I felt nearly as old as he. To my cost, I learned his scorn of halfheartedness, and shared his dreams of an orderly existence. His violent temper and his intransigence, his intellectual snobbery and need to dominate, were as disagreeable as they were catching. Knowing earlier than I did myself that I was gay, both he and my mother seem to have secretly rejoiced in a son who stayed close and was not quickly lost to them. Not until I was nearly thirty did I escape.

Thus the tormenting shadows of the First World War reached across my childhood. The dead watched all of us. One of my mother's sisters had nursed soldiers brought back to hospitals in Cairo while Lawrence of Arabia was rampaging in the deserts. She lived alone and would rarely speak except in terms of war. She was not the only gay relative of mine. There were others, all with tales to tell, an uncle and two other aunts, all three on my father's side. (Not until much later did I learn about their lives.)

My mother's youngest sister married a former major of artillery who long remained for me a model of the intimidating heterosexual male. During the war, he had been gassed and seen men die for want of self-control. Understandably obsessed with preserving resources, he ruled his family with an iron hand. He liked to forbid mothers to attend to their crying babies. Like a walking propaganda poster, he commanded: "Babies must learn patience. Patience saves lives." He would stalk the dining table behind us, his guests, as if on duty in the mess, passing judgement on our eating habits and calling, "Any complaints?" One day he gathered us together for a tour. His tours began with, "Want to pee? You never know how long you have to hold it in." He made certain the advice held good. Forced marches followed through the town. Suddenly he'd call a halt and, while we gathered round, strike the pavement with his cane.

"At this point here, d'you see," he'd say, describing the line of our advance, "the main sewer from the north crosses the western subsidiary drain which reaches twenty meters to the south." Then, fixing us with narrowed eyes, he'd lift his cane from this significant spot, and thrusting through us, take aim at some manhole cover far off down the street.

"Follow!" he would bark, fingering his short red moustache and leading us in tight file towards the next bivouac, where once more he'd "put us in the picture" with location, volume, and direction of whatever noisome waters flowed beneath our feet.

This birth, this parentage and family, affected the outcome of my life. How could they not? I was being formed, shaped, led by the hand in certain unexplained directions. My experiences then, now burned in memory, provided me with evidence, at the time misunderstood, rich in contrasts and oppositions that forestalled any easy explanation of the world. I was, like most of us still, given only half an answer to questions I might have had about "existence." For example, everyone I knew believed we had immortal souls that would live forever, and, as they told me, this was why we must all be good, and even why we fought the First World War.

It appeared that there was evidence for this belief. Being heir to my father's family name, I was taken north in the early 1930s to stay for a time in a house my parents knew as Bailey Piers, my grandparents' home in Great Yarmouth, Norfolk, on the coast. This was no handsome, cozy country seat, but a tall, gaunt customs house that stood, as suited its lugubrious name, beside the dark, salt-ridden wharves along the river Yare leading to the grey North Sea. Yarmouth was where David Copperfield's Peggotty once lived, next to the threatening roar of crashing cold dark surf. It seems the building may have been erected in the 1700s on the foundation of a medieval "marthouse" which in 1332 was owned by Thomas de Drayton, a bailiff. It was constructed of mottled brown brick, and was said to be haunted by the spirits of men long dead. As if to prove this beyond doubt to us visitors, my cot was placed in a high-ceilinged room of bare whitewashed walls, its head against the marks of what was once a doorway leading to a stone stairwell bricked up long ago.

I was no more than three or four years old and the wharf to which I would be taken seemed always dismal, dank, and forbidding. Here the sea surge was tamed from its natural wildness to a slurp and slap against piers and pilings of tarred trees rammed into the sea bed. The deep brick sides of the quay, dark with weed and encrusted with shells, were slippery and descended, tomblike, into the reflecting black. Black, too, were the bows of the drifters—fishing boats tied up close as if fearful of being torn away and thrown back along the river and out to sea by the eddying squalls that scrape and tear at those frigid waters. The endless creak, rattle, and squeal of stays and lines reaching up from their decks into grey scudding clouds, the ubiquitous stench of rotting fish and dried blood, with fish scales still sparkling here and there among the cobblestones that lined the edges of the quay, made an ominous scene for the looming shape of Bailey Piers to brood upon.

Old Bailey Piers had a long memory. In a stone-flagged courtyard of the main house, protruding from one of its blank brick walls, was a cast-iron gibbet. From this, I was told, after their summary trial, smugglers were once hanged by the neck until they were dead, cut down and buried in unconsecrated ground. It seemed that this had been the fate of one of my cousins, so the family remembered. He would steal out at night along the coast, night lantern in hand, to guide Dutch barks across the shoals. The Dutch braved the British coast to smuggle in casks of illicit gin. They would find their way to shore by my cousin's light swinging to and fro at the edge of the marshland. On one such night the excise officers from Bailey Piers had met and arrested him, and in the morning, strung him up.

In the moonlight, the long shadow of the gibbet on the wall would reach across the flagstones and cobbles of the yard, a dark finger of despair. Was it my great-cousin's mother whose quiet figure my grandfather once saw sitting sadly in the bay window on a Monday morning and who, on his approach, slowly vanished from his sight without a whisper? Perhaps, too, it was his old sea chest which was discovered that same day resting on the cobbles beside the wall beneath the gibbet but which the family dared not tamper with, so ancient and forbidding were its locks, and which, during a horrendous night of banging doors and windows, disappeared, never to be seen again.

As if this was not enough, while I lay sleeping in my cot, my parents told me they could hear the heavy thud and scrape of old sea boots ascending the stone stairs toward the bricked-up door behind my head. Lamps within the house, well stocked with oil and even when later wired for electricity, would flicker, falter, and unaccountably die, or be blown out by strange breaths and breezes reaching up the ancient stairs and along the brown-walled corridors of the upper storeys. Doors, too, flew open in the darkness.

"Didn't you lock them?" my grandmother would complain.

"Of course I locked them. I always do. Here's the key!" granddad would reply. But then they'd bang, bang, bang again, sending so many shivers of fear down my grandmother's back that finally she refused to remain in "such a horrible place."

My grandfather would not speak of these forbidden things, but when I heard about them later I found them fascinating. This was the other world the preachers warned us of! What did it mean? Did these spirits have substance in this life?

Our family sold shoes, each member taking part, a rather boisterous crowd as I remember them. They used the old bay windows looking on the street across the quay to display their wares. Later, when the haunting had driven the family away, they took another shop in Regent Road, well named in honor of that prince of pleasures. Here during many a summer I would play with sand shoes and bathing suits hung before the doors, proud of such an enterprising family who could always, or so it seemed, be on holiday. My father's mother died and my grandfather married again and had many more children. The family was enlarged, with half-aunts, uncles, and cousins, but when the shoes had all been pulled inside the shop and the windows shuttered for the night I became the center of attention once again. My still young female aunts would dress me up in skirts, blouses, and high heels (and no doubt makeup too) to family applause, my parents' wonderment, and my own delight. Taboos were being broken, early on.

By the time I was five we were living on the northern outskirts of London, in Edgware, once a mediaeval village in the shire or section called "Middle" or Middlesex. Our connection with my grandfather's family remained and was marked by an annual generosity of toys sent for Christmas. On that wonderful morning I would wake before the sun was up to find that Father Christmas had called. (This mysterious figure we never called Santa Claus, it being the Catholic remnant of a popish title all good Protestants had long abjured.) My little bed was piled high with boxes and packages heaped all around as if the world had showered me with gifts. Wrapped in rough brown paper and covered in stamps of many colors, they were tied up with lengths of string held together by lumpy sailor's knots difficult for my fingers to untie. Clutching new toys I would run into my parents' room and crawl between their warm bodies. Then, fed with milk and cookies, and the music of carols reaching up to me from the miracle of wireless radio or the hand-cranked phonograph, I knew my Christmas had begun. The sparkle of frosty windows and the rich scent of the pine tree dancing with colored lights made that day, with its promise of still more gifts, candies, and pastries, the sweetest time, full of color, happiness, and love. The tiny Baby that we celebrated in its mother's arms, surrounded by animals as gentle and contented as he, seemed to join in my happiness.

Even now it needs no more than a chill wind with a touch of snow to revive those memories with their promise of everlasting joy. But the beauty of those special days and the evanescence of what had seemed so real, so inviting, now dismay me. That such experiences can mislead is difficult to accept. Their sweet allure beckons ever backward into a world which was, in reality, quite different from that of my memories. Not only because it was a narrow world, circumscribed and ignorant or careless of anything beyond itself, but also because it stood for beliefs and attitudes that themselves had long been undermined and discredited.

Those were also troubled years, years first of waste and then of want. A police sergeant lived next door and showed me how to make a radio using only a thread of wire and a tiny piece of sparkling rock. It was an introduction to another world, a revelation that has fascinated me ever since. I drew music from the air. But then, one morning in 1936, I heard the BBC broadcast no music, no talk, only the hollow ticking of a solemn clock to mark the final hours of the fifth King George's life, a sad time when all of us, parents too, wept in each others' arms. Then, not much later, we heard the abdication speech of his handsome, naive son who had dared to say he would "do something" for the coal miners, thus threatening the establishment with civil war. He was also in love with an American, a commoner and, worse, a divorcee, a triple shame. The beauty of his postage stamps, carefully portraying his better profile, were seemingly belied by his betrayal of the crown. Later still, infected by some nameless terror, I watched while groups of housewives gathered in the streets outside the shops and talked of war. Did we shake our heads at Chamberlain's promise of "peace in our time"? It may have been so, but I still remember the relief that people felt.

For twelve years Christmas remained for me preserved and safe, reinforcing a fairy tale of life whose pleasures my memory carried around with me. Yet I needed constant reassurance. I told myself, and my parents unconsciously reinforced the idea, that I was somehow "different." I thought about myself endlessly; other boys did not seem to do this, and it worried me. Accordingly, I struggled for acceptance and slowly became a mother's little gentleman, an "MLG," obedient, obsessional: a priggish prude. My obsessions took devotional form. I used secretly to beat my head on the floor an exact number of times in honor of Jesus before resuming whatever I was about. I was so "good" I was chosen to be head boy of my primary school, a school to which I had originally been dragged screaming by my mother at the age of five, and where at age ten I fell in love with a girl and wrote her love notes until I grew out of it. It was there that we sang hymns daily to Someone who made the world what it was, *The rich man in his garden, the poor man at his gate: God made them high and lowly, and ordered their estate*—followed by the chorus reinforcing this bitter message, larding it with glitter: *All things bright and beautiful, All things wise and wonderful, the Lord God made them all.* It was a world of law and order, imposed from the outside; a world in which spirits might wander unhappily, forever unredeemed. My attention had already been attracted by various so-called mysteries, sexual and spiritual: spirits that may be unhappy souls; the need to take thought for "the morrow," a formless threat that overshadowed all; and a curious unpredictable stir of my penis, an appendage for which I didn't even have a name because no one spoke of it. It was a morality so demanding that each step of the way was fraught with danger: a god existed who must be pleased, or the future would be jeopardized. My parents, constrained by the same tyranny, making what sense they could of it, bent to the threats and trusted always to the promises.

And, indeed, for a time, all seemed at peace, or at least under control. What did we know of the outside world? My father, for example, even refused to eat in foreign restaurants. The only other world was one we glimpsed in "the pictures," as we called the movies then. At first silent, and then increasingly glamorous, they told of a faraway place where anything was possible for good or ill. Americans were misty creatures who seemed to live apart, unconstrained by common morality, free to come and go as they pleased, and I was warned not to be taken in by them.

As for other countries, by 1938 we heard on the "wireless" a German named Herr Hitler, shouting with excitement. We saw him only occasionally on news films, for television was still no more than a tiny square flickering in enterprising shop windows. Our world was the British Empire, which filled the shops with fruits, vegetables, and cheap clothes. Moreover, London was not only our home but the home of our red, white, and blue royal family, and the enormously wealthy, sparkling, and endlessly privileged aristocracy whom everyone envied and admired. And Church was the home of that other white, English-speaking family called "God" who had created this arrangement and found it good. We middle classes never rocked the boat. We "knew our place" and kept to it. We lived our lives by kind permission, seemingly ignorant of the cruelty of privilege. We played a nineteenth-century game, detesting abstract modernism, refusing to talk to divorcees or to shop where our "betters" shopped. And I was being prepared for private school. A friend deserved this far more than I, but he was from the servant class and refused to compete. "That's for you," he told me ruefully, and to this day I feel the shame of it. When once I returned to see my school friends, they laughed at the new upper-class accent that I had unconsciously taken on. "La-di-da!" they crowed derisively. But this time, I was proud.

THE PIT

1939

Suddenly, one morning, this contented life changed forever. The Second World War began for Britain on September 3, 1939. We heard the saddened voice of Chamberlain warning us of our formidable foe. No sooner had he finished speaking than air-raid sirens, which we had never heard before, wailed their way into our lives for the first of many, many times. Bursting into tears of terror, I clutched and shook. Then all fell silent as we waited for catastrophe: the waves of bombers reaching toward us from the horizon, darkening the sky and bringing instant destruction and death to everyone.

We prepared for the end. Teachers held their classes in our homes. Thousands of children were evacuated to the country. Brick shelters were constructed overnight. There was a mass distribution of gas masks, with specially large ones to contain entire babies. Quickly, Hitler's blitzkrieg drove the British Expeditionary Force into the sea at Dunkirk and we awaited the first invasion of Britain since that of the Normans in 1066. We collected pitchforks and knives. That was all we had.

I was growing up and, as if I needed to know how to keep the family name alive before I was cut down, I was taken aside into the back sitting room by my father and the secrets of procreation were hesitatingly confirmed. He explained what my penis was capable of and how it worked. It was then my mother's turn. She took me to their bedroom, rummaged in her boudoir drawer painted shiny black, and withdrew a handful of medals, their ribbons still attached, and a wristwatch still with a well-worn strap and a special silver cover that was designed to prevent enemy observers from aiming at the light of the phosphorescent figures, and that sprang open at a touch. This cover was dented as if it had been struck. Handing them to me, she shyly told me about the man from whose body they had been taken; his life, their hopes of emigrating to New Zealand, and his death. As I stroked the smooth silver cover, and fingered the heavy round bronze medallions with their silken ribbons and shimmering rainbow colors, she grew still. Was she listening even then to the rattling guns, the screams of dying men? She turned her face to me, her only child.

"Never be an officer," she whispered. "They're the first to die."

It was more entreaty than command, though I took it for the latter, yet spoken without hope, for by then she saw the dreadful years ahead. She didn't weep. Her grief had already been composed long since. But she had still another secret she felt obliged to tell as part of my initiation into birth and death. When she was small, she told me, she had been raped. Not by anyone she knew, apparently, though that was never clear. The man, or boy, had been drunk. This, it seemed, explained the distance between my mother and her religious family. For only after she had not only been married but also given birth was the shame of her earlier deflowering "forgiven."

Was I receiving strong messages about sexuality—"Don't get married, you might lose him; don't trust sex, it's dangerous"? I was silent, almost stunned by these revelations. Momentarily I even wondered if I had been the rapist's or the first husband's child. For I knew what I'd been told had to do with me, with my future life and the behavior expected of me. I felt that a pall had fallen over precious things, one that could never be removed.

The Second World War had already begun when my father, earnest that I should shine like a guiding light amid the encircling gloom, enrolled me, much against my will, as a choirboy in the local Church of England church. Built of stone and dark blue flints, this was determinedly Protestant, seemingly built in Cromwell's time, a bastion of basic Christianity where Jews and Catholics were not well spoken of. On Saturdays I attended choir practice. Sundays included Sunday school, from which even at that age I fled in horror at its utter foolishness. Then for Morning Service at eleven I was bound about and robed in a long black cassock and flowing white surplice with an Eton collar starched shining hard and choking my young neck. In the late afternoon I returned for Evening Prayer, an offering even less appealing than that of the morning. Such lugubrious exercises were "worship" and implied a dour, unsmiling God.

Our voices had not yet broken. I was told mine was sweet enough to sing solos but I was soon discovered to be tongue-tied and was heard only by the organist who, unknown to us, was dying of cancer and who during the service would utter loud and seemingly inexplicable groans, interrupting and often drowning our performance. I was deputed to pump the bellows of the ancient organ and, standing by the organ bench, I would watch him in his agony while he struggled to keep up with his own music, nodding now and then at me to pump the big wooden handle harder when he played the chords.

The sermons were simple but interminable; while they droned on, glorious reds and blues sprang down from windows no doubt replaced when King Charles regained the throne and Cromwell died. The colors stained our surplices, transforming us into rows of resplendent angels. But I hated Sundays for their futility and learned only patience. I would sit, kneel, sing, think, and, bemused by the scent of slowly decaying prayer books, cast my eyes across to the cantoris side where sat a quiet, demure, diamond-faced boy whom I suddenly knew, without quite knowing why, I longed in vain to kiss. Nor was he the only one I loved as only twelve-year-olds can do. Taken from church to church by my doting papa, I fell for a choir boy at another church and would gaze at his handsome tanned face and blue eyes with terrible longing, taking his image home to bed with me. But I was no more than twelve, and my innocence remained intact until the great Campaigner outing. Until that time, and even later still, I wore the crotch of my pants away by endlessly picking at the fabric as if to reach the forbidden pleasures that lay curled up inside.

I received a scholarship to a private school of some repute in London, and there a friend invited me to join another church that was the home of a national organization calling itself the Campaigners. These were a group of eager Christians who had appropriated to themselves Scottish tartans, shorts and shirts of powder blue, and even more inappropriate tam-o'-shanters. Encouraged to join them by my parents, who perhaps feared as much for my loneliness as for my soul, I donned this outrageous outfit and was duly draped in a girdle of heavy rope, which was called the "Life-Line" and was bleached white for moral purity. This chastity belt was wound round our teenage bodies in a series of great knots, the complexity of which we were admonished, on pain of hellfire, to examine and learn so that when tested we could tie and untie them on command. It was my introduction to sadomasochism.

I can remember only the friend who brought me into the Campaigner fold. His name was Michael and he quickly became my constant companion. Intelligent and handsome, he was the son of a wealthy engineer.

The Campaigners, as is usual with religious youth organizations, was run like a holiday camp. Get-togethers, prayer meetings, and other persuasive ploys were organized to accommodate our energies without compromising the sect's pietistic doctrines. One Sunday we had been ordered to appear in full regalia at a local park for games and races to be conducted by our cadaverous, bible-thumping, tartan-wearing colonel-in-chief. The games being over, my friend and I shed our Life-Lines with relief and went off on our own. Running about in our powder-blue shorts we must have been quite fetching. I was apparently very much so, for my friend rolled me in the grass and tried to make love. I pushed him away but was flattered nonetheless. Not surprisingly, we both soon abandoned the Campaigners, and without compunction and for half price sold our Life-Lines back to the Colonel. It was our bodies we wanted, not moralizing.

In the evenings, after school, I would excuse myself from home to visit Michael. His mother would give me dinner and we would then be shown how to cut elaborate decorative chair legs and other phallic articles on his father's lathe. He would then take me upstairs to his bedroom for further physical enjoyments so delightful I would plead with him for more. He, being Jewish, had what I called a streamlined "American" circumcised penis, while mine was of the bulldog British variety and complete. He also enjoyed what are now described as "water sports" and would urinate onto my hand and body, which at the time I found strange but not altogether objectionable.

From these earliest years as a sexual being my loves were not only essential, they were glorious. I adored the boys who possessed splendid bodies and often tried to kiss and hold them close. I knew my feelings to be authentic, not assumed, and well worth sacrifice. I discovered in my young way that to be deprived of one's beloved is to die a thousand deaths. I was prepared for dislike, even hatred, but the need to hide my feelings, to pretend that my body was somehow wrong, and the knowledge that what I did with it was natural but forbidden, did not sit well with me. I hid from the guilt I did not really feel but thought I ought to, seeking out dark corners and only now and then being bold enough to throw caution to the winds. It was a delicious mixture of sex and what I assumed was sin.

It was during the early years of the war that I first perceived the unusual characteristics of some of my father's family members, nearly all of whom were now in some kind of military service and from time to time were posted near London. A sister who was usually loud and hearty returned from camp one day in tears. Breaking down, she told us of "Babs," another aircraftwoman at the same camp to whom she had been devoted and who had suddenly and unaccountably been transferred. Inconsolable, she wept throughout her leave, and then, as if in anger at the genteel silence of our home, and perhaps to force us into learning a few truths, left our toilet filled with menstrual blood. Her half-sister, with quite as loud a laugh, strong limbs, and a farmer's face, joined up to work the fields, married late, and never cast aside her mannish ways. Her brother, however, was what my parents described as "wet." Tall, handsome, and musically inclined, he was the only boy in my grandfather's large second family of daughters. An officer, he would arrive suddenly by jeep on his way to the front, accompanied by a batman whom he never introduced but kept waiting for hours at the curb. My father, to whom he was devoted, indulged him, but my mother openly despised him for his effeminate ways, his affected speech, and his flaunting of rank. After the war he went up to Oxford where, he told me once, his heart was broken by a "golden boy." He understood, he said, why I had not married: "Like myself, you have had your fill of domineering women."

During the first years of the war I traveled to school by underground train, fearing lest we be bombed each time we stopped. Green mesh covered the windows and partitions, leaving only diamond shapes to look through, and at night the train's lamps were shaded so as to throw only a thin bar of light along the passengers' thighs. My family spent nearly all our nights under the reinforced floorboards of a house belonging to a customs official who, like my parents, was too old to serve and had joined the militia known as the "Home Guard." My father, not knowing army ways, became an air-raid warden and my mother donned a uniform of Sherwood green to serve meals in the local "British Restaurant," a temporary building erected by the government in the middle of town to feed the poor and those whose homes had been destroyed, the "bombed out." All food was severely rationed, and some days, despite a nauseating odor of boiled cabbage and wet paint, we would eat our meals there.

Throughout the great London Blitz and often during the next three years I would spend the nights under our neighbor's house. My father was rarely with us, as he was often called to be on duty in his warden's post built on a nearby vacant lot and equipped, because we continued to fear gas attacks, with gas masks, gas warning rattles, gas capes, and tin hats. Night after terrifying night, massed German bombers crossed the southern coast and evaded Britain's all too few fighter planes. It was then our home telephone would ring. We had obtained a telephone, as did others, to save our lives. Waiting in bed, unable to sleep, blankets and packaged food at the ready, my father would put an arm out to pick up the receiver. The warden in a command post far away would give him the code word "yellow," meaning the bombers had broken through and were on their way. At this we would get up, gather our things together, and wait in hopes that the enemy would somehow be turned back or that, as we guiltily admitted, they were aiming to bomb somewhere else.

But nearly always the telephone would ring again with the code word "red!" and even as the sirens began their wailing near and far, explosions would light up the sky and boom in the distance. My father would pick up his gas mask and a black steel helmet with a great white "W" on the front, while my mother and I, clutching our civilian masks in their cardboard boxes, would run downstairs, out the front door and across the street. Searchlights would already be weaving and intersecting in the night sky above our heads. The roar of guns would be louder still and in the distance we could hear the telltale droning of the approaching German planes. Then it was quickly through the neighbor's front door and into their front room. Here the carpet had already been rolled back to reveal a dark hole sawn in the floorboards, and we would help each other down into it by a little wooden ladder, hopefully before the bombs began to fall. Only down inside this cavern did we feel at all safe, especially when the local anti-aircraft battery behind the house opened fire with ear-shattering cracks of doom that split the night and tore the heavens above us into several pieces.

In our strange underground space contrived from the foundations of the house, surrounded by sandbags and rough beams nudged up against the brick walls to prevent them caving in, muffled in blankets and eiderdowns, we would munch cookies, drink tea, and try to sleep. Despite a small electric heater, the air was often chilly and stank of concrete, sweat, and damp earth. There were medical supplies at hand and a cache of bottled and canned foods and water in case the house collapsed on top of us. For a treat, one Christmas night, when we had been down below for many hours, we consumed a plum pudding made ten years before and kept for some "rainy occasion."

During the night, my father being a warden and already out in the midst of the lethal maelstrom, my mother would climb up from our hole to gather teapots and urns of hot water that she put in two shopping baskets; then, wearing a tin hat, she too would leave, to wander about the streets carrying tea to those unlucky enough to find themselves in a local street shelter without comforts. My parents were brave. The noise above and around was often terrible, the skies rained shrapnel from antiaircraft shells exploding high above us; the German bombers caught in searchlights would wheel about like moths trapped in their own destruction, while beneath the floorboards I sat and waited, fearing every moment to be blown to pieces or buried alive, or that neither parent would return.

During an air raid it was critical not to show any lights that might indicate to the advancing bombers that they were over a city and its several secret installations and airfields. Down among the foundations of the house we seemed free of such restrictions until wardens patrolling the area noticed lights flashing near the ground and discovered them shining through our ventilating grills above the level of the dirt. We had attached flaps of cardboard to the inside of the grills. These hung loosely over the holes, it being important to maintain our ventilation. But when bombs exploded nearby, their blast would blow these flaps back and forth so that they rattled against the grills, seemingly like signal lights. Accordingly, our ventilation was further restricted.

One morning, about three o'clock, waves of bombers had been arriving for the past eight hours to bomb the city center. Suddenly, to our horror, the ventilating flaps broke loose and a ghastly blue light filled the cave and lit us all up. Two older men who had fought in the First World War cried out "a flare!" which brought new terror, because flares were used by the bombers to light up the terrain beneath them and would betray the presence of the town and the railroad. We sat tight for what seemed an eternity, waiting for disaster. Slowly the blue glare dimmed. Our neighbor tried desperately to fix the ventilators. Then suddenly it burst upon us, lancing through the ventilators, an enormous surge of white light. Instinctively, we shrank away from it and hid our heads in our arms, expecting the end had come at last. The deep-throated roar of an immense explosion, far larger than we had ever heard before, made the walls shake about us. The wood beams shifted, dust fell on us from the wooden floor above. It was, we later learned, an air mine that, following the flare, had floated down by parachute and landed softly in the garden of a house among the branches of a nearby tree. For a brief time, the parachute had floated like an enormous jellyfish, white and ominous in the light of the dying flare, and then the great mine had exploded, wiping out ten blocks of homes. The man in whose garden it had landed had even watched, paralyzed with horror, as the monster slowly descended toward him. His nearness to the bomb saved him, the blast roaring over him as the roof caved in. There were hundreds of casualties, many dying immediately, some from dust particles sucked through their bodies as the blast swept by.

Sometimes, after my father ran off to his post, my mother and I did not make it out of the house in time. In case this ever happened, we had hung seats from hooks inside the cupboard under the stairs. One night, we had been caught by surprise and as the uproar began and the rhythmic droning of aircraft engines grew louder overhead, we ran to crouch inside this cupboard, sitting on our puny seats and clutching each other, shivering with fear. Then came the first whistle of a descending bomb, then another, and another fast upon them. Great explosions rocked the house. We cried out in terror even as more deadly whistles hurtled down toward us. With great presence of mind my mother fled the cupboard and pulled me under the dining room table, where we cowered, I weeping with terror, and my mother with her arms about me, hoping to save me from the horror she had prayed in vain would never come again.

In the morning, exhausted, I would make my way past the rubble of the night's disasters and on to school, where we would spend much of our time in its cavernous crypt, shored up with girders, doing our best to pass exams beneath bare bulbs strung overhead about the roof. I suffered fainting spells, and then a nervous breakdown, unable to work or even think for several weeks without bouts of weeping, nausea, and diarrhea.

The horrors of bombardment—at first by high explosives, later by incendiaries, and finally by robot planes and rockets—taught me about the dangers inherent in human existence. But I also discovered its warmths. My physical excitements aside, my father's role as warden brought into our home a variety of neighbors my parents had not known before. This opened up our perspective on the world around. Meetings of wardens, local teachers, and later all of us as firefighters, enabled us to meet an enormous variety of people in many unfamiliar occupations. There was the First Cello of the Philharmonia Orchestra who lived next door but with whom, in typical British fashion, we had hardly ever spoken. There was a vice president of Watermans, the famous fountain pen company, a tall handsome charmer who could play swing on the piano and who quickly became my hero. Until my parents warned me off lest I embarrass him, I would hang around, gazing at him and following him, wanting nothing better than to be in his easygoing, jovial company. There was the milkman whose horse and cart crunched across the debris and the shrapnel to bring us milk in bottles every morning throughout the blitz; and the cooks in the British Restaurant with whom my mother became firm friends. We ourselves were undoubtedly bourgeois, but we were now thrown together with others whom we would previously have easily dismissed as "workers," and we learned how cruel as well as foolish such distinctions were. Sadly, when the Jewish refugees appeared on our streets, happy at last to be alive and not to have to walk in the gutter, we failed them, not comprehending their agony, and being ourselves long imprinted with hateful religious prejudice. My mother was the first to throw this over when Mr. Greenberg, who came to live across the street, shyly approached her and with subtle European charm praised her legs and her complexion to her face.

Many others became friends for the duration of the war and some remained so always. One couple, a brother and sister, still lived with their ancient, well-educated mother with whom I could talk about anything, including love and what little I knew of sex. The brother was a reader for a famous publishing company, and his sister, an ardent communist, visited Russia and extolled the virtues of the Workers' Paradise. Since both were wardens, my parents enjoyed their conversation and began a close friendship with them also. My mother read the colored magazines imported from Moscow with their extravagant descriptions of collective farm life, and my father, remembering his own father's early difficulties as a union organizer, thought of himself as a Socialist once the war had ended. There was a sense of community in the air, brought about by an adversity in which we all had shared. It enlarged my growing sense of being part of humanity regardless of class, religion, or gender. I was still a snob, but one with a broader perspective.

And as for sex, being sixteen I was in the midst of finding myself a lover, or should have been. The blackout was helpful. The streets of London were like orgy rooms. I would masturbate at night in the street beside the brick shelter and managed to find one friend at school who would do the same with me. (My Campaigner buddy had long since moved on.) The darkness of the great school crypt was another cover in which to slide my hands over the smooth skins of those I would seduce downstairs and hold passionately close to me. One boy, slender and lively, whose sprightly charm quite captivated me, allowed me to put my arms round his ivory waist while he was dressing to play the part of Trinculo in *The Tempest*. He later became a famous television star and was much adored by American teens. I also attempted to make love to another boy upon the football field but was rightly repulsed for overdoing it. Only two other boys I knew were bolder. One would declare his loves quite openly, and the other even published a list of "conquests" for which he was soon, unjustly I thought, dismissed. But I was ambitious, too fearful of similar disgrace, and kept such things to myself.

Perhaps my body provided relief from the brutality that was so apparent in the world around. After all, I was struggling to survive. At the same time, some speculation about the role of God in the universe led me to devise a strict morality according to which every action, every thought, was either good or bad, depending upon its effect within the divine plan. For example, because I perceived (though was never told) that masturbation was condemned, I thought that somehow it caused death directly or indirectly—a kind of domino effect. This self-punishing belief seemed not only correct but demanded something of me, perhaps in payment for offending against gentility. I was attempting to make sense of war and sex and even death, and doing so in an alien, heterosexual world where pious parents of nearly all religions encouraged their sons to pair off with girls, even while forbidding them to make love, no doubt for fear of babies and disease. It was a contradictory world where pleasure and piety cancelled each other out.

My parents' role in this turbulence was curious. Perhaps understandably, my mother remained withdrawn on sexual matters but from time to time would tell a coarse joke I would overhear. My father, on the contrary, remained strictly puritan. He would warn me about his "foul-mouthed" fellow artists editing the documentary film *Night Mail,* whom before the war I had been permitted to watch at work. On another infamous occasion, discovering I had purchased a book of photographs that contained the inevitable nude woman in whom I had no interest, he forced me back to the shop and demanded complete restitution. The shame I felt on that occasion poisoned me against him for many years.

On the other hand, I also felt the cold reticence of Jesus to be inconsistent with what I knew to be "red-blooded," full-hearted life. Did beauty mean nothing to him? To me it seemed an attribute of God. I once found myself adoring another boy with beautiful muscles and what we call a "washboard" stomach, and I discovered that he liked me too. This gave me hope, but the affair was stillborn, for I pounced too soon and lacked the skill to pursue him intelligently. Once again, when I happened to be walking by a street in a poorer section of the city suburbs, I saw another boy, shirt open to the waist, his chest smooth, tanned, and muscular, the body of a working angel; I stood entranced, my heart aching at his perfection. In the presence of such gods I felt the symptoms of love recorded by Sappho. I stopped and stared, my face flushed. I walked back with stealthy glances, my heart beating and my hands clammy with a sudden sweat.

The language I used to describe sexual activity at this time was also fraught with a sense of the forbidden. On hearing the word "fuck," I was both shocked and fascinated at the force of the fricative and the guttural conclusion of the word. I used the word only secretively and in combinations with other swear words I knew like "bloody" and "cunt," which I saw scrawled on walls; even when I did not know their meanings, using them was thrilling because it broke through taboos I was slowly coming to recognize as the enemy of my reality.

The private school where so much of my adolescent sex took place had historic connections. It was a solid, beautifully designed structure of warm red brick and sandstone set in its own grounds. It had three wings, each linked to a central hall by way of glass walkways (from which the incendiary bombs used actually to bounce off); a gymnasium to the left, the science laboratories to the right. Today it has the additional advantages of a fully equipped theater and a computer center sparkling with screens and keyboards, and is even more prestigious than it was.

Following one of the traditions of this splendid place, I was eventually privileged to take dinner with its founder, Jeremy Bentham himself. His mummified corpse still sits in a sedan chair beneath a glass case and he is regularly wheeled out on these occasions to sit at the head of the table. It is a curious ritual. Yet despite the school's utilitarian roots, the students, including the Jewish students, took Christianity seriously and anti-Semitism as a fact of life. Not surprisingly, perhaps, despite actual warnings from teachers and anti-Semitic slurs by fellow students, I found myself most attracted to the Jewish boys. I was entranced by their smouldering eyes, sharp features, strong noses, and burnt sienna skin. The exotic fascinated me and still does. Not that I found fair hair and skin at all repulsive; but for me they were, as I once informed a columnist, more spectacular than erotic.

The headmaster during my time there was a tall, handsome bachelor who had been selected during the "young leader" fashion of the 1930s to bring a new look to fading traditions. The war gave him his opportunity and he won the hearts of boys who, like myself, were spellbound by his style and thought him quite heroic. Under his tutelage I studied the ancient classics in their original languages and ancient history. I led the school crew to Henley's Royal Regatta, played Prospero in *The Tempest,* sang in and was ravished by Handel's *Messiah* and the *German Requiem* of Johannes Brahms, and again became Head of School. Meanwhile, my hero erected new buildings, designed new gardens and sports facilities, and enabled many to reach for fame and fortune. Pupils of his broke the four-minute mile, manned the first nuclear submarine, ran the country's museums, became famous poets and Hollywood stars. And he was homosexual.

He also appeared to believe in God. At school prayers we would sing Christian hymns from a collection he had published. He would read his own translation of selected portions from the original Greek gospels, and required prayers to Someone every morning. Tragically, he was forced by the ironclad morality of the time, and the demands of his profession, to be tightly closeted. Finally, long after I had left, he became increasingly tormented by frustrated emotion and the guilt laid upon him as upon all gay people at that time, and he hanged himself from the banisters in his home. Perhaps he was being blackmailed; we never knew.

When the news of his death reached me years later, I was invited by his closest colleague to select something for myself from his clothes and library. It was then I learned of his long agony and tearful self-recrimination, his vain search for help and his colleagues' bewilderment. His retiring, proud personality had actively discouraged all approaches. He had fended them off with silence and administrative innovations. The other teachers, all males and several of them closeted themselves, nearly all appear to have suspected that some deep disturbance was playing itself out in his life. More and more frequently, they told me, his poise would disappear and his carefully maintained persona would crack. One graduation he refused to permit contingency plans, claiming to know the weather would be fine, just as during the war he had refused to evacuate the school on the grounds that no bombs would fall on it. He was lucky then, but this time a rainstorm swept the outdoor banquet and he retired to his office in rage and shame. Later, one evening, a patrolling teacher discovered him in a lavatory stall "waiting," he claimed, "to catch misbehavior."

Once, during my own time, he had displayed what I now know to be the betrayer-traits of a terrified "closet case," and publicly expelled a student for being gay, while at the same time apparently inviting another student to kiss him in the privacy of his study. I was told he broke down in tears during staff meetings, his imperious front growing the more fragile as it became more defensive. Not surprisingly, he was not popular with boys from more conservative families, nor with former students anxious to maintain the pretended homophobic "traditions" of the place, and certainly not with boys whose own sexuality was insecure. His liking for me was curiously ambivalent. He would take me for long, fast, silent rides in his expensive new Jaguar, but never made a move. He recognized, perhaps, a boy whose sexuality had not yet found open expression. Or maybe he did not desire me and may have advanced me more as a defense than as an advertisement. For I was not a "hearty" boy by any means, yet, as he put it once, I was "stern." That I adored him was as obvious to all as it was no doubt irritating to many. His suicide and the suffering that it represented, multiplied by myriad others, affected the remainder of my life, eventually determining its direction and focusing much of my energy on the need to help the world understand.

Fortunately, I have myself never been suicidal, perhaps because I had never actually been told it was wrong to be homosexual, so that my feelings for what I found was the glorious beauty of those I wanted so desperately to embrace were not tainted by conscious guilt. I had marvelous friendships, and was lonesome for strong, loving arms, but never desperate. However, suicide, and particularly this suicide, raised questions for which I hoped some day to find the answers.

One day, during the war, while fifteen and still at school, I lay in bed, thinking of a handsome fellow student I longed to hold and kiss. The details of the moment are engraved in my memory. I had learned the term "homosexual" from a class discussion of Plato's *Symposium* and understood it to mean those who liked people of the same gender. Thinking about the other boy, I solemnly said to myself, without any sense of fear or self-recrimination, "Well, then, I am a homosexual." Perhaps it was a defense against my unconscious recognition of society's expected rejection, but the revelation did not surprise or shame me. In fact, it was a relief, and a self-acknowledgment I found as congenial as it seemed inevitable. It fit the facts.

Since I was twelve I had loved, and with such devotion that to be ashamed of it would shame me as betrayal of a truth. It was, if anything ever was or is, a sacred, holy feeling about other humans and I resolved never to deny it. I did, of course, from time to time, but I never did so without knowing I had wronged something infinitely precious. Even sexual acts themselves, their physical ecstasy, are drawn from the love which inspires them and are, for me at least, and however passionate, as sacred as anything I know. Heterosexual people no doubt feel the same way about their loves.

I thought then that I was one of very few. I now know that this is not so, and that even at that time millions of us existed hidden behind their acculturated selves. I was only just aware that there also existed homosexual adults and was totally ignorant of lesbians. Girls remained for me fat, squashy things, and, as I could see, getting squashier by the minute, whereas boys were hard, lean, strong, and graceful—physical attributes on which straight boys might pride themselves. During the 1930s Mr. Quentin Crisp had been well known in London for years, but was quite unknown to me. He could have taught me a thing or two about myself, but when once I saw him on a London street, his adoption of what seemed women's ways seemed alien, out of place; the fact that his plumage was intended to attract the same rough, tough males as I was searching for eluded me.

THE COOK

1948–1950

As the war was ending, when I was sixteen, not knowing then that far greater minds had already done the same, I composed my first philosophy of Time and Being. I still took God for granted, and assumed a single act of creation comprehending all time, space, and humanity. God, it seemed to me, was by definition complete; and, if complete, contained all time and space. When existence came about, it came about as a completed history, begun, continued, and accomplished as a single event. And thus, it then seemed to me, all human actions must take place within the compass of that single act of creation wherein alone time and space have meaning. Human actions, though they might have different immediate purposes, were yet undertaken with one common aim: to control otherwise inert and chaotic matter, to bend it to our will and make it conform to the desires of the brain. Everything that I and others did, even the tiniest otherwise insignificant action, seemed to point in this direction. This meant, I thought, that human brains were nothing less than God at work inside time and space, slowly but surely, and with many a mistake, gathering all under divine control. In fact, the whole mighty enterprise was already accomplished; only within that part of the process consisting solely of time and space can the enterprise be said to move forward. Furthermore, if all this is so, the only satisfactory explanation of our existence is that we humans are the working process by which God became God.

At best, I believed that the species should work together for its common goal, either because of Christian principles that seemed to dictate love for one's neighbor, or from sheer kindness springing from a natural love of others. Reinforcing this belief was my discovery of the social contract theory. I took John Locke very seriously. Not only was he a devout Christian, but the principles of social contract that he had identified as an underlying structure of society seemed to free me from the agony of not being an aristocrat. Public service had long been instilled in me as the path to righteousness, and the social contract now appeared to enjoin me to cast aside all pretension and join the fight for the rights of the People. Instinctively, perhaps, I saw myself not as their champion, but as a member of a minority dependent upon their success. But this philosophy is a hard row to hoe, and because my self-esteem was dependent upon its success it was to cause me anguish and nightmares for many years to come.

Immediately on leaving school I was invited by a fundamentalist science teacher—I now believe he was in love with me—to visit the glaciers of Switzerland with him. We drove across bombed-out Europe in an all-metal train, ate our first white bread in five years, and rejoiced to see and climb among the Alps. We returned home without any declaration on either side, but he cared for me as tenderly as a lover would. I admired him, but in school he was made much fun of, and I suppose it was his faith that enabled him to withstand the contempt that straight boys are raised to express for any they instinctively know are different from themselves.

I was then drafted into the army. It had occurred to me, as it did to all of us already sickened by five years of war, to be a pacifist. But my father's argument that we had survived thanks to sacrifices sustained by the merchant marine was reinforced by my knowledge that unlike the American Quakers who permitted themselves to be scalped by Indians, I would have defended myself. Nor could I imagine anyone who was able to resist not forcibly attempting to prevent Nazis from killing their own family. Peace, it was clear, had often to be bought with blood and very likely with one's own, however terrified one might be of shedding it. I believed this then, but could not tell what I would really do when faced with actual death or torture.

Accordingly, the attractions of the common male, my fears of the fate in store for the officer class, and my growing dislike of the social structure they represented, determined me to be a private soldier. It was, of course, a mistake. However, when the draft papers arrived, I set out laden with despair for Aldershot and "boot camp," a term I had not met before and that meant nothing to me yet.

In the eighteenth century, Aldershot was a tiny village set amid rolling moorlands in southern England. The landscape was sparsely dotted with small stands of pine and close ground cover of berried bushes. After the Crimean War, when the British light infantry had been led into the valley of death by the aristocracy, Prince Albert took up a retiring general's hunch that what the British army needed was a home. Aldershot was recognized as a place suitable for just such an honor since the land about it was ideal for military maneuvers.

At the height of the Empire, earlier tents and huts were replaced by a massive camp built of blood-red brick, complete with towers, vast regimental barracks set with verandahs in the style of the Indian Raj, three hospitals, five churches, schools, prisons, water and sewage systems, and overseeing all, even a royal palace. This new home and headquarters of the British army could house as many as forty thousand soldiers. The giant parade ground, cunningly laid out on a slope to enable all ranks to see their officers, was surrounded by solemn administrative buildings reaching in all directions. To the north stretched the "Marlborough Lines"; to the south, the "Stanhope Lines"; at the ceremonial center stood the "Wellington Lines," where barracks and stables were erected for the cavalry. The musketry shooting ground was immense, covering more than sixty square miles of organized countryside. The whole was oriented to face southeast in the direction of the British Channel, as if to fend off any Continental enemy that dared advance on what had become the official battlements of Empire.

This was where the British infantry, the renowned regiments of Guards, the light and heavy cavalry, and all their service units were disciplined and trained to fight. Naturally it also became a patriotic center for all the Empire's forces on sea and in the air as well as on land. Sandhurst, the school for the officer elite where it was expected I would go, was close at hand, its chapel resplendent with the names of locations where victories had been won in blood and which were now carved in stone and illuminated in gold. Over the archway of the pretty apse ran in Latin the direful echo from Homer's bloodstained *Iliad*: *Dulci et Decorum Pro Patria Mori*. It may be, indeed, but I could not find my draft papers either sweet or an honor, however necessary it might be to die for my country.

I arrived at this intimidating home of empire armed with no more than my pyjamas, my wash bag, and a mother-made cake, packed tightly in the tiny recommended-size suitcase, and was immediately led along with other boys to meet the selection board where each of us would be assigned training appropriate to our station. The war was only just over, and now it seemed another was soon to begin, spreading from Korea to the rest of the planet. I had no expectation of sur-

viving and had said farewell to my parents without hope of ever seeing them again. My mother had been distraught. My father was curiously unmoved, saying that it would "make a man" of me. His leg
had itched to join me rather than commiserate.

A sergeant marched us, one by one, into an office on the ground
floor of Wellington Lines. Nearby was "Caesar's Camp," where raw
infantry were being trained. This was the boot camp in which, indeed,
boys turned into men . . . or, no doubt, died. Surrounded by the stark,
unforgiving walls of brick painted unblemished white, and the stern,
unyielding faces of "real" men, I stood paralyzed. This was the world
of the rampant adult male, not the fantasies of bed.

My name was spoken by a balding brigadier behind a desk.

"Officer training. Correct?"

I swallowed. I heard my mother's voice. Officers long since dust
rose up before me from the trenches. I saw them clambering "over the
top" and heard their hoarse cries calling to their men; then the deadly
rattle of machine guns mowing them all down.

"No, sir. I do not want to be an officer."

"Not want to be an officer? Private school, on to Cambridge, so it
says here. What's his IQ, sergeant major?"

"Genius, sir!"

"Genius, eh? Of course you'll be an officer. Put him in 'A' wing."

"Excuse me, sir, I do not want to be an officer."

The brigadier stared.

"Why not?"

I could have said, as indeed I knew, that officers were the first to
die. But in the face of so much "true" manhood this would seem
craven, as indeed it was. And there were other reasons: the glorifica-
tion of carnage, the privileged classes of which Locke wrote . . .

"I disagree with the way the army is run."

I can hear myself even now mouthing this arrogance in the face of
men who had very likely helped to save my life. In my defense, I was
fighting other battles they were not likely to understand.

Dead silence greeted my statement. The sergeant major coughed
and was, one must suspect, sorely exercised by the schoolboys he was
now required by law to train. Finally the brigadier raised a scarlet,
unbelieving face.

"You disagree, do you?" he said, and no doubt wrote "troublemaker" in the file.

"Very well," he went on, "take him away." He might just as well
have cried "Off with his head!" And forever labeled "dangerous—to
be watched," I was led away to a torture chamber known as Sala-

manca Barracks. It was to be an experience as close to the horrors of war as our trainers could make it.

Blind to what was going on around me, clutching my suitcase, I mounted iron steps onto the verandah of the second floor into a long room lined with metal beds on which ugly-looking mattresses were rolled back. Assigned a bed next the door, I was then taken to the quartermaster's stores and given underclothes, two uniforms, a huge pack with arm straps and complete with mess tins, two pairs of heavy black boots, khaki gaiters, and finally a rifle—long, heavy, and the most disheartening responsibility of all. It came complete with a bayonet, glittering sharp, for thrusting through stomachs in hand-to-hand fighting.

We were solemn, our platoon. None like me; all working-class, used to roughing it, familiar with shouted orders and abuse, soldiers of the sort the Duke of Wellington is once said to have described as trash and scum. Even my private-school accents betrayed me now. Yet it was a fate I chose, and the offer of commission, once refused, was never made to me again.

For the moment, even though surrounded by the very kind of male I could have admired, all sexual appetite died within me and I became as nothing, a cipher, cannon fodder, number 22058831, deserving nothing, meaning nothing, fed with noisome food, clothed in loathsome garments, burdened with enormous weights and shod in agonizing boots. Each day, learning obedience without question or complaint, was another day in hell. The sixty minutes of each hour were interminable, composed of infinitely longer seconds, while limbs, muscles, and the mind were being wrenched and re-formed to shape themselves instinctively. Each night was a black abyss of despair, made more horrible by stifled sobs of other boys and their whispered prayers; a bottomless pit of unending travail without hope or future. Each terrible day was followed by another cold grey dawn that opened with, of all things, the recorded voice of some cheerful American singing "Oh What a Beautiful Morning" from *Oklahoma!* blared with a ghastly crackling from the mouths of a hundred hateful black metallic amplifiers screwed to the rafters throughout the lines.

The agony continued unabated: rising; washing in troughs; defecating into holes scrubbed obscenely clean by men on punishment; folding, arranging, measuring packs and blankets to within a quarter of an inch; rifles to be cleaned, oiled and gleaming, not a speck in the barrel; toe caps to be polished with spittle until they shone like glass—a daily ritual seemingly in honor of war and killing made more horrific by the sickly sentimentality of the hateful musical and terminating only with the entry of the adjutant, cadaverous, narrow-eyed, supercilious, merciless, and unutterably cruel. The briefest twist of his iron-bound jaw warned me he had heard of the soldier who told the brigadier he didn't like the way the army was run. Each morning he would nod curtly to the brutal sergeant major, then pick up my spotless rifle, stare through the barrel, and order me to polish the brass screws in the floorboards underfoot, another sacrifice to Mars. I was to abase myself before them all.

Thereafter, though lightened by letters from my former headmaster (he wrote me every month long before he died), and a monthly cake from my loving parents, life continued to deteriorate. Food and tea, sometimes together, were sloshed from pails into mess tins. There was little garbage, all remains seemingly boiled down for soup, even pieces of rotting cabbage which I noticed being picked up from the floor. Outside the mess hall, mountains of tea leaves appeared, bleached white from, it was rumored, anti-sex drugs. As if we had the energy to care! It would never end.

But suddenly it did. Trains appeared. The interminable drills climaxed in a final inspection. Packs were shouldered, the victorious brigadier reviewed us marching past him, and we were carried off by train to a Secret Destination. On the way we caught sight of our replacements, hundreds of frightened schoolboys on their way to hell. Most of us pitied them, but we were already burdened with another fear. Were we now off to war? Some thought and said as much, so that we came to believe our agony could end only in death.

We had been given leave to say our farewells before moving to another camp. Home during those two short days was unreal, a passing dream of loveliness. I caressed books and looked longingly at flowers, played opera and Handel's *Messiah* on our ancient gramophone. The aria "He was despised and rejected" became a favorite piece. My parents must have heard its repetition and wondered much.

Then I donned my hated uniform and embraced my poor mother before my father went with me to Paddington. We had counted up the many months before I was to be demobilized and on the station wall, each time I returned to camp, my father would score another brick to cheer me up.

At the station, I found others just like me. We sat huddled together on the padded seats staring up at framed scenes of seaside resorts, some of which my father had painted in the halcyon days before the war when I was taken on just such a train as this for holidays to Norfolk in sun and happiness. For hours the train puffed and roared its way into the inky darkness of the night while I, at least, thought of home or future agonies in store.

Finally we slowed and stopped. The station's name was blacked out as if still in wartime. Sergeants were waiting to order us up into huge army trucks that carried us onward to what seemed to be a forest, surrounded by a swamp. Nightingale Wood, I heard it named. Caesar would have thought it an ideal encampment, hidden away off the beaten track and protected by marshland. Its trees had been partly cleared and Quonset huts had been built around a central square of black asphalt. We paraded on this square and were sectioned off, twelve men to a hut. We were then almost immediately inspected by courtly officers, threatened with punishments, assigned various duties and ordered to meet our commanding officer in the morning. No one knew why we were there or what we were to do.

Warily we introduced ourselves. The others were all from what were then called Secondary Modern schools designed for students whose results on the infamous "eleven plus" exams prevented them from ever advancing to college or university. Most could hardly read and never wrote except simple notes home to their girlfriends. We were all depressed, battered psychologically and beaten down; none seemed as terrified of punishment as was 22058831, but I think they were.

This small company of youths was to people my nightmares for many years, not as ogres but as fellow sufferers. And yet their presence gave me hope. Though the effects of the daily dose of emasculating tea had long worn off, I dared not look at them with any longing I might have felt, but what I felt for them was mostly not desire. Rather, we seemed bound together by our single fate. We may not have liked each other but we would, I know, have risked our lives for each other had it come to it in war. Had boot camp done that for us? Except as captain of my school rowing crew I had never felt such group loyalty before. Looking back, I think I can detect three or four who were homosexual like me (I use the only word I then knew), but none of us ever openly declared himself. Only one went so far as to get me to caress his naked back.

My first meeting with our commandant was hardly auspicious. My upper-class accent betrayed my background. He raised his eyebrows and sent me to have my intelligence tested. On learning that I had studied Latin and Greek, my cockney interrogators called me "Professor" and again wrote me down as "genius." No doubt the commandant wrote me off as a fool.

The winter months were drawing in and we were ordered on

parade to receive our winter undergarments. Each squad lined up in turn to sign for two undershirts and two underpants. On getting these back to the hut I found they were patched, much stained, and seemingly unwashed. That weekend I was unexpectedly granted my first thirty-six-hour pass, presumably again to say goodbye before being shipped to some fighting front.

There being no adequate cleaning facilities in the camp except the tub in the washhouse, I took the underclothes home. My parents were appalled, and returned me to camp with a complete set of new wooly underwear from the local department store. Unbeknownst to me they also immediately wrapped up my army issue in brown paper, enclosed a letter demanding better treatment for their son, and with disloyal but clever political savvy mailed the entire disagreeable parcel to our much-hated Conservative member of Parliament. Within days, I was later told, the Conservatives, now in opposition, carried my underwear into the House of Commons itself, and holding both pieces high in the air, demanded the resignation of the minister for war. But I knew none of this.

Another station scratch mark later, when I returned to camp, I found the barracks silent and the parade ground empty. My hut mates, sitting on their green metal boxes, were sullen and silent. I was a "lucky sod" who had just enjoyed his leave when suddenly, inexplicably, all leave for the entire battalion had been cancelled for a month.

A sergeant appeared and barked the hated precursor to an inspection: "Stand by your beds!"

But we were not inspected. Instead, my name was shouted and I was marched in quick lockstep, as if under arrest, to the commandant's office. My bones turned to water. Oh God! What had I done now? The dreaded abyss which by endless cleaning, polishing, blancoing, and total obedience at all times I had so far managed to keep closed, yawned waiting at my feet.

Rigidly I stood at attention as the commandant slowly looked up at me from behind his desk. He was, I now believe, a kind and gentle man. Now he seemed sad, almost sorrowful as he spoke.

"Just who are you, Private Mayes?"

"22058831 Private Mayes. Sir!"

The commandant shook his head slowly from side to side, and fingering a bundle of papers in front him, picked them up. His eyes narrowed as he asked if I knew what they were.

"No. Sir!" said I.

He stirred restlessly in his seat. The sergeant who had marched me in looked up at the ceiling, then impassively at the wall.

"I'll tell you what they are, Private Mayes! They are orders confining the whole bloody battalion to camp! And when you don't like the way you're being treated," he went on, his voice rising in anger, "you should see me, not your . . . your relatives."

At which the sergeant barked, "Understood?"

I swallowed. I had no idea what they were talking about, but there was only one permissible answer.

"Yes. Sir!" And back we marched in lockstep to the hut.

Not only was our leave cancelled for a month, but a subsequent government investigation uncovered a widespread black market in army underwear. It was rumored that several high-ranking quartermasters were court-martialed and our poor captain was lucky to escape. Not surprisingly, we suffered inspections every day for a week, and my own rifle barrel, in particular, was so frequently criticized for harboring unseen dust that it must have become the cleanest rifle barrel in the entire British army.

Then, quite suddenly, as if someone feared that such special treatment might again cause repercussions in high places, the pressure eased, and to the envy of my section, I was given extraordinarily light duties. Every officer I encountered henceforward would say significantly, "So *this* is Private Mayes!" I was tempted with offers of advancement to corporal and to sergeant, but feeling that these blandishments might somehow tarnish the curious and unaccountable awe in which I continued to be held, I refused. I did, however, accept the status of marksman, which I seemed to have earned by consistently hitting the bull's-eye not only with my undergarments but also with both rifle and Bren gun. I did not realize that in battle, marksmen are made snipers, a task by which the army can rid itself of meddlesome characters. Snipers do not survive for very long.

Finally, I was put on prowler picket and ordered to guard the huts during the night. This was to provide me with another unforgettable confirmation of what and who I was.

It was a full hour before dawn and I had been assigned the last watch, which included waking the company cook promptly at 0400 hours so he and his minions could prepare our breakfast by the time we fell out from parade. The prowler picket were under orders to move about silently in pairs, checking doors and windows. Although we were armed only with axe handles and flashlights, we were entitled to challenge anyone who looked at all suspicious and run them to the guard house. We worked the huts pincer fashion, one man down one side and the other down the other, meeting at the end of each row of huts. The cook, our sergeant had informed us, could be found at the back of hut E9 and was a deep sleeper.

"Make sure he's awake," he ordered me. "You'll have to poke him. Or it's no breakfast for the battalion and the high jump for you!"

When I reached hut E9, all was silent. The moon, which had been filtering through the clouds and whose light now glittered upon stagnant pools amidst the nearby marsh, was fast setting. There was only the slightest lightening of the sky in the east, and all was still velvet black under the trees. A single nightingale called in the distance. It was 0400 precisely. My mate was on the other side of the line of huts making his way down toward me, as I quietly opened the squeaky door of the hut and stepped inside.

I was greeted by snores as I entered a cocoon of warm, rancid air containing a dozen sleeping men. The beds and the central stove and chimney, still warm, were darker shadows in the surrounding gloom as I cautiously made my way along the coconut matting to the back. I was told I would easily recognize the cook from his grubby white hat hanging beside his bed. And he was, after all, a sergeant and the only one in the hut.

Suddenly I found him, at the far end of the hut under the window, lying on his back, stark naked. He had the most magnificent body I had ever seen in my teenage life. The gentle moonlight reaching through the window caressed his glorious limbs. One muscular arm was slightly bent, flexing hard biceps. The smooth expanse of his pectorals, even the areolas about his mahogany nipples, sparkled invitingly. The other arm was lying loosely by his side, the hand half-open, the fingers slightly extended as if in welcome. The other lay carelessly across his strong, long thigh where his hand was caught up in the dark hair from which arose his erection, sturdy, proud, but all too oblivious of the awestruck private standing in worship at his side. Discovered like this, in the midst of military squalor, he was truly a divinity. And it was nearly 0405 before he was poked awake with a shy prod of my flashlight.

"Wake up, Sergeant," I whispered hoarsely. "It's time."

Breakfast for me that morning was a holy communion.

Mama's boy or not, slowly but surely I was unconsciously building for myself a case for social equality, if not for actual leveling. I envied the seemingly careless abandon with which my working-class hut mates broke rules, suffered punishments, and were able to serve king and country without question, even with enthusiasm. Plutarch recounts many occasions when the men who composed those ancient armies were easily persuaded to endanger themselves and offer their lives for their generals and for the booty their generals could bring them. The generals fought with their men, wept and died for them in their turn, and the unity of such experiences, the mutual embrace in which the participants held each other, seemed to argue some greater and more valuable structure than that which appears to distinguish between moral saints and sinners.

Daily, we were marched out to count and organize guns, tanks, and bombs on their way to join the occupation forces in Europe or the United Nations in Korea where we, perhaps, might soon be fighting. I kept a diary I have since destroyed, listing wrongs I promised later to expose and try to right. Compared with actual war, the real thing, what we were put through was nothing, nothing! During the war, millions upon millions had suffered horribly and died appalling deaths. I had merely sipped a little from that terrible cup. And as for leveling—years later, I trudged the now still and silent sands along the Normandy beaches to pay my homage to the dead. Deep shell holes still pitted the cliffs behind Omaha and I found myself weeping bitterly, not only for those who had died but also because, despite the various crosses on their headstones, few would have welcomed the many, many gay people who lay among them.

As for me, I had discovered that I could easily adore those whom I had been raised to use, manipulate, and despise, and the irony of this, far more than any political or religious argument, concerned me all the time. And since such feelings arose out of the very depths of darkness, destruction, and death, I could not but think that somehow they had to do with basic problems of existence. Many a philosopher has never been to war, lived in fear of death, or wandered among battlefield corpses; many a priest has never been unemployed, walked the streets in fear of starvation, or lived in a slum; most academics, too, working in their bubbles, are personally insulated against such experiences, and easily ignore or dismiss them even while researching them. Yet such experiences are among the stuff of existence, and must be numbered among its pains and be accounted for. And just as leveling was to be a crucial element in my later beliefs, an important clue to what we are and where we fit together, so these earlier experiences were accumulating in the back of my mind like silt, to become the topsoil from which answers to the conundrum of existence might later spring.

And, to cap it all, I was soon to fall in love.

LOVE'S SLAVE

1952-1954

On being demobilized from the army, a day that seemed to take endless aeons to arrive, I saw the world again bathed in sunshine. Shortly before leaving camp for the final time I had been called to an interview at Oxford University but had no clothes other than my humiliating battle dress in which to appear. Consequently, surrounded by the solemn dons of Balliol I was rendered quite silent, unable to answer any questions whatever on the content of the classical texts that the army had driven from my head. Luckily, when interviewed at Cambridge I was able to be more informative, and the welcome I was given when admitted to Downing College was like the entrance into Paradise.

My rooms were in College and I shared them with an older student whom I knew from my school days. Brilliant, he spoke three languages and understood politics, modern art, and opera. I knew him to be an aesthete but with a taste for women and, I suspect, a fear of homosexuality. We would attend the opera, where, when I stood as usual for the national anthem then played at the beginning of all public performances, he would pull me down to my seat with a disgusted shake of his head. Was he a communist, I wondered admiringly? His influence was subtle; I still sign my name in his style, and later came to admire in the arts what he already knew by instinct. He went on to be director of London's Tate Gallery, and despite any socialist leanings accepted ennoblement.

I continued my studies of the ancient world—Latin, Greek and ancient history—to the exclusion of other subjects to which I was far more suited. It was, however, a superior grounding in the history of civilized thought, and I gained the sort of intellectual perspective without which it is difficult for the mind to remain open, to explore and to grow. We were quietly informed by our soft-spoken dons that we were the *crème de la crème;* that our task was to lead the world, partakers in the intellectual feast they occasionally deigned to offer us. At Cambridge during this time, the Leavises were founding a new literary criticism; Adcock and Guthrie were rewriting ancient history; Ord had made music sing as never before; Wittgenstein and Ayer had finally killed off metaphysics; and the esthete Blunt and his mentor Gow, a classicist (and his control, some said), were still smooth and impenetrable. My father had sent me Gow's wartime letters to his former students, and the book with its classical asides had been my constant army companion.

I found much about Cambridge very tempting. It fed my snobbery even while it enlarged my mind. The beauty of its academic buildings is often breathtaking. The honey and pink of its native stone warms one's heart even in the depth of winter. Its spreading lawns and cobbled ways, and the narrow river winding among charming vistas of peaceful courts, spires, and pinnacles, offer a sanctuary of learning like a heaven on earth from which no reasonable person would ever want to depart.

At the same time, I knew it was a heaven reserved for "special" people, young men like myself who had been told they deserved its academic splendor. It was delightful when ordinary people, tourists, ogled us undergraduates as we sauntered proudly in our gowns among glories which belonged to us and not to them—but it also made me feel guilty. The tourists looked like my parents or those Other Ranks with whom I had only recently been living. My aristocratic friends of the officer class seemed to have no conception of such misgivings. The richly carved, sophisticated beauty of ancient buildings set within extensive lawns, the coats of arms, the statuary, were just the kind of things they were used to. They had grown up with them. My uneasiness was born of the very ambitions with which I had been raised and which the upper classes no doubt looked down upon. I wanted to share my luck as well as show it off; the privileges I enjoyed seemed somehow out of place in the vision of the future world I looked forward to. During the war, the "future" had seemed to rest with "all of us," not with those who claimed the land belonged to them.

Had I but known it, I had many allies. Cambridge, despite its royalist pretension, had become a hotbed of not-so-secret socialist thought. Indeed, Blunt and Gow were examples. Moreover, science, in which Cambridge was preeminent, was on the move, challenging the academic values on which privilege had traditionally been based. Marx ruled in this academy, and on confessing my admiration for Americans, I was warned that despite its glitter, America was already in decline. My roommate lectured me, predicting that by the end of the century as many as seventy percent of children in the United States would not continue on to university. He noted that the average academic scores of American children were already below those of European children, a discrepancy no longer attributable to America's testing of a larger percentage of its population than other countries did. Americans, I was told, were more superstitious, more credulous, and less well-informed, largely because they put less store in the advantages of learning.

Sustaining such myths, if myths they were, was a curiously Victorian view of the "Colonies" as backward and second-rate, an attitude toward America that was the result of ignorance amounting almost to dishonesty. For a hundred years British schoolbooks had virtually ignored the capitulation at Yorktown and continued to treat the United States as an upstart and its constitution as of no account. Marxists and aristocrats alike were contemptuous of the commercial success America represented, even though they depended on it.

But the real cause of America's failure, it was said with condescension, was a Downward Spiral: the very leveling that de Tocqueville had predicted would take place had produced a situation in which, as children learned less and less, public esteem for education inevitably diminished. And because ignorant people are reluctant to learn until pushed to it by pain or greed, they become content with fantasies and myths and are easily led by hucksters and demagogues, rather than by the intellectual elite as in Britain.

Fed on such fantasies, and glad to know that Britain was not second-rate after all, I acted in the *Agamemnon* of Aeschylus, performed in ancient Greek, and in several other plays; finished my degree; began postgraduate work; and led our crew in the Royal Regatta at Henley where my obstinacy enabled us to win our first race but lost us our second. Two of my closest friends, who remained so all my life, rowed in the "Gentlemen's boat," which lost races on principle. Nevertheless, gentlemen though they claimed to be, they were obliged at least to stay afloat, and as their coach I was permitted to bully them unmercifully. This cruelty was the product of envy, since I hardly enjoyed my own training, which required daily "courses" on the river in the most appalling weather. We would row for hours, seemingly toward the North Sea, with the snow collecting around our ears, while a hard-hearted coach muttered "poor buggers, poor buggers!" from his bicycle on the bank.

In these ways I was slowly but surely being seduced back into the role of Officer and Gentleman from which I had managed partially to extricate myself. The careful arrangement of College dining facilities, where professors ate at a "board" several steps higher than the seats of their students, and the lack of involvement by professors in any student affairs, established an academic hierarchy I unashamedly embraced in the face of all that I believed. Not being a scientist, my socialism was little better than the condescension my snobbery had prepared for me. Had I married a woman and raised a family at this time, my search for some understanding of the All would have finally foundered.

Instead, an event occurred that like the first domino to fall, or a pebble thrown upon the surface of a pond, had lasting effect. I was in the Classics Library reading up the histories of Herodotus when he sauntered in. He came from the shadows near the door, and I caught the glint of shining blue eyes beneath a tanned, high-cheekboned face and a slender figure. He walked with a careless grace, and unruly dark hair caught the morning light.

Wonder of wonders, as if the Sibyl had foretold it, he approached my table and sat opposite. Again, though far more lastingly than before, I felt Sappho's famous symptoms: dry throat, flushed face, beating heart, and faintness in the limbs. The pen actually dropped from my nerveless hand. I gazed entranced as at a god incarnate and then, utterly abased, down at the now meaningless text before me! With a croak, I introduced myself and he replied and smiled—oh, such a smile! And I was lost.

His name was Anthony. But, as might be expected from the unpromising percentages, this eighteen-year-old student in classics whom I adored was heterosexual to the core. Kind and tolerant of my endless importunity, he put up with me so that, like A. E. Housman, author of the soulful *A Shropshire Lad*, I too lived out my dream without a single hope. After I graduated I followed him around and brought him gifts, made him breakfast, lunch, and dinner. When he was sick, I visited him, fed him, stroked his clammy brow. I became a slave, coached him in his studies, and even cleaned up his vomit when he was drunk. For one whole year, while I was supposed to be training to be a teacher, I could think of no one else and little else. Once I almost pounced, but discovered that beneath his shirt he was hirsute and my passion almost died. He told me I should have been a monk, for he was an ardent Anglo-Catholic and fully intended to be a priest. It seemed he had learned tolerance from both his confessor and his own enlightened mother.

When the summer vacation came he found himself a job in Cornwall as waiter at a hotel beside the sea. Quite foolishly I followed, securing a similar position at another hotel nearby. The rugged coast was beset with cliffs of dark green serpentine and looked out onto the Atlantic. The surf was often magnificent, sending up high spouts of spray as it fell upon the boulders out to sea, engulfing them in a smothering embrace from which they ever rose unscathed and shimmering, the froth streaming from their drowning in the waves. Not far off the shore was a huge rock; ten thousand years ago it had been part of the cliff itself, but had long since divided off and now stood separate, a guardian to the beach. Sand dunes reached the shoreline between cliffs on either side of a stream that ran down to the sea.

Our two hotels stood facing each other across this declivity and after our duties we would meet in some hollow of the dunes, our waiter's uniforms of black and white piled up to the side, while I would take out my writing pad and read him the love poems I had written him:

> Slowly I stood and looked for him
> Blue eyes then turned away . . .

"That doesn't make sense," he'd say. Or, "The scansion's wrong. Just 'blue eyes' would be better. Anyway, is that how you really feel?" he'd ask me, wrinkling his dark tanned brow with its tiny scar. And, shading his eyes from the descending sun, he'd turn quizzically as if to question my muttered affirmative. Then he'd shrug.

"You know, you really ought to be a monk," he'd say again. I wonder now whether he expected me to force myself upon him.

The hotel where I worked was a pleasant place with a blue and white facade and a sunny dining room, but a tyrannical management. I was even taken aside by the co-owners, a husband-and-wife team, and warned against the other help. "Don't be taken in by them!" they'd say. "They're trash." Again that middle-class contempt.

The "trash" had bedrooms built into the cliff where moldy walls gave evidence of water near at hand. At night I would be wakened by a waitress climbing into bed with me, pleading to be fucked, while my roommate, another gay man, was out cruising local bars. We were never fed until after dinner had been served (a management mistake), and since our meals were skimpy, and until "Madame" found out, we hid extra dinners in a filing cabinet for consumption later in the night.

I kept my spirits up with Plato: ideals were to be worshiped, and although unattainable, existed so that we might know in which direction we should aim; a straight and narrow path to wisdom. Seduction was vulgar, and rape abhorrent. Anthony was inviolable, untouchable; yet how I yearned to hold him in my arms!

His curious kindness to me was never flirtatious, and was generous in the extreme. He invited me home to meet his family. His mother disclosed to me that she was herself the subject of similar adoration by another woman who was often present. When we were all together, the impossible relationships with which the two gay people were encumbered caused much "deep talk," and such was the ambience of the household that it inevitably took on a curiously religious flavor. My love, self-serving though it mostly was, was precious, and the beauty that had inspired it took on characteristics of the sacred. "This," I said to myself, "is what love is. There is nothing to compare with it. If God is love, then I have experienced Him." The fact that it was unrequited seemed to guarantee its perfection. Moreover, it seemed to possess intellectual strength derived from ancient classical roots of some authority: Socrates, Plato, the Stoics and even the dog-like Diogenes. It was also as much a part of religion as were glorious cathedrals, stained-glass windows, and Bach's B Minor Mass. I was caught up in an age-old conundrum. Perhaps a monastic life was the answer. And I began to consider it.

My father had long before introduced me to Bernard Shaw's cogent arguments and biting wit. Shaw himself was still alive and in his nineties when first I read his work. I was taken to Ayot Saint Lawrence where he lived in hopes of meeting him in person before he died, but neither his tall spare handsome figure nor his famous Rolls Royce were to be seen. He became another hero whose Life Force, if given the chance, might lead me to a Golden Age. Despite a certain squeamishness about sexuality, he was clearly prepared to accept homosexuality as one of life's variants. He had supported Oscar Wilde in travail and had even hinted that his Professor Higgins, who lived with Colonel Pickering, was "a mother's boy," a code phrase for homosexual in those days. His championing of communism was misguided, even thoughtless, but his sensitive dealings with the Abbess of Stanbrook (for whom he, albeit an unbeliever, gathered pebbles from Nazareth) endeared him to me enormously. His *Black Girl in Search of God* remained in the back of my mind as such a reasonable assessment of Christianity one could not readily dismiss it. The Black Girl tries out each biblical manifestation of evolving divinity in turn, including Jesus, and finding them all wanting ends up with Shaw himself, whom she marries.

It was Shaw's championing of the importance of knowing everything one could about life that encouraged me to become more intimately acquainted with one of its facets other than sexuality. Accordingly, I approached Wilfred, a lifelong gay friend who was already in medical school.

"Do you think you could do me a favor?" I asked nonchalantly one day on the way to lunch in Hall.

"What kind of favor?" he asked (hoping, I now know, for an offer to sleep with him).

"I want to see a corpse."

He looked at me. "I see," he said, taking this setback in his stride. But then, corpses were part of his training. "May I ask why?" he asked finally, adopting a lofty air. The uninitiated were supposed not to know or even want to know the secrets of his intended profession.

"You know," I encouraged him. "The dissecting room. Where you cut them up. I've never seen a body yet, not even in the war. It's time I did, don't you think?"

"It's not very pleasant, you know," he said, continuing to look disgruntled, then suspicious. "What d'you want to see a body *for*?"

"Everyone should see what eventually they're going to be like. It's part of education. Anyway, it's a mystery and I don't like mysteries."

He began to walk away. "No one's allowed in there but us," he went on, dismissing me. "It's where we work. You'd faint or throw up."

"Why should I throw up? Do you throw up?"

"I'm used to it. That's what doctors do." But then, relenting, "All right, you've asked for it! If you feel bad, don't blame me. And throw up outside."

So I was taken to the hospital and then through double white doors into the dissecting room.

The memories of my visit remain distinct: the sickly sweet smell of formaldehyde in which the cadavers were steeped; bins of heads and various limbs neatly stacked; the cupboard in which several corpses hung like carcasses of meat, big hooks through their necks, their heads shaved and hanging as if hopeless and abandoned. Then there was the current "stiff" under examination. His rigor mortis had worn off long ago. He had been a corpulent gentleman, officially anonymous as were all the cadavers, but from the condition of his fingernails, apparently obtained from the indigents' morgue. His stomach was large and round, a distended balloon beneath a flat gray-white chest. Dissection had only just begun and a piece of thick skin containing a nipple had been drawn away from his chest, leaving yellowish fat and tightly bound strands of tissue reminiscent of pork. It was difficult to remember he was not alive, he lay there so calmly, uncaring, while they did these things to him. A scalpel had sliced into a hand to display the various vessels wound round the ligaments and bones. I could see it would take a long time to take him apart organ by organ. The young men around him in long white coats laughed and chatted at some exploit of the day. I remember thinking "one day I'll be like this," and as we left, I asked myself where, in the supposed order of things, do our corpses fit, our limbs sawn off and heads piled up in bins? The answer would perforce include other questions about life and death. What of the brain, which when in working order experiences ideas, hopes, and fears, and can create poetry, paintings, and movies, build cathedrals, and devise philosophies? Years later, when one of my former students, again at my request, opened a woman's head, detached the brain, and, taking it out, gave it to me to hold, such questions arose again. So very much had been contained in that curiously heavy object like a small brown cauliflower; without it "she" could not have been said to exist.

Even while debating such important matters, I took another step toward what I hoped would provide some answers. The seemingly instinctive devout rationalism of my headmaster; the beauty of Christian music and architecture; the religious devotion of my blue-eyed beloved: all these together persuaded me to directly confront the claims of Christianity which, until then, I had considered only in profile.

Christianity laid claim to being the only solution to many of life's problems. At the same time, I did not think we yet knew enough completely to explain pain, death, or the universe. And although I did not, even then, fully accept the idea of redemption and salvation, the elemental teachings of Jesus made more sense to me than did those of any other teacher I had come across. So had they to many others for whom bare reason seemed not to have provided sufficient answers. Not even Shaw was able to offer undying love. And in any case I still believed in the existence of God.

The problem of which devotional structure I would adopt was easily solved. Raised in the established Church of England, I saw no reason not to remain there, other denominations seeming to me but variants of the original source, just as Protestantism was of Roman Catholicism. Until I learned more about the split between Rome and Byzantium, and about other sects such as Mormonism, Quakerism, and the Oriental religions, it seemed wisest to stay put, the mere proliferation of choices showing how unlikely it was for any one of them to claim to be entirely sufficient. So although my renewed faith was thus a compromise as much intellectual as it was emotional, I accepted my Anthony's offer of a spiritual adviser, a quiet-spoken intellectual priest at Little St. Mary's, self-effacing, obviously homo-sexual (or so we thought), even epicene. He took me in hand, mulled over my doubts, sorted them and handed them back neatly labeled. None of them seemed to justify not moving forward, which meant becoming a postulant for the priesthood. After all, I thought, one should always be fully committed or not at all.

For many years I continued to question not only my motives but what I feared might be only a dream, a religion with golden roots but rotten fruit. I was aware that priestly vocation is often subject to hypocrisy, a way of ingratiating oneself into God's favor, or a merce-nary desire for rewards in the hereafter. I also knew that it was my love for another that had prompted my decision to be as near him as I could manage. I sacrificed myself on his altar, knowingly, willingly, and with enormous regret for the life I knew I really wanted to live as a teacher. I reconciled myself to the sacrifice by sheer force of will and what I still believe was an honest intellectual assessment of the nature of religion itself, its claims to deal with the meaning of existence—not merely of everyday life, but of Everything. And if, after much ago-nized thought, I could find no better answer than that offered by Christianity, then Christianity, as an example of religion, became a requirement, and the priesthood an inevitable profession, whether I was sure about it or not.

I have no doubt that religion was for me an exploration of ultimate meaning, rather than an acceptance of some preestablished explana-tion. Like some adventurer preparing to explore unknown territory for which there were few maps, I shouldered the pick and shovel and set off. I did not do so willingly, for I recognized I was leaving much behind that I would miss and I did not like the look of those in whose steps I was following. I thought them soft, mealy-mouthed, self-right-eous, given to pious babbling.

"Yes," said my mentor without a smile. "You will have to learn humility and it will surely be a bitter cup."

Humility in the face of a world made by others, or in one that I had fashioned for myself? To this day I cannot stand pietism of any kind, and the uncritical mouthing of religious devotions frightens me. Mere agnosticism seemed to beg the question and confirmed the correctness of my decision. My task, then, was first to become a teacher, then to work the greatest frontier of all, betwixt life and death.

In the meantime, Anthony, taking no thought for the morrow, abandoned his vocation, leaving me to struggle on alone.

THE BODY

1954

J had obtained credentials to teach and the seminary could not take me for two years. The delay may have been intended to test my vocation; it freed me to join the faculty of a high school for boys in Shrewsbury, Shropshire. They were not unsuccessful years. The new headmaster had introduced bold and innovative methods, among them the teaching of Latin and Greek by the direct oral method (through speaking rather than writing lessons in grammar and vocabulary), at which I was a dismal failure. My emotional life was even less successful and I remained sadly celibate. I was quite unaware of the existence of any homosexual group or even individuals in the area, and coverage in the local press of a teacher dismissed to therapy for merely romping with boys confirmed the wisdom of my inactivity.

My nights were still beset by occasional nightmares, and I contracted debilitating asthma from the fogs that languished round the river near the school. I'm told by those who think they know about such things that asthma is really weeping inside. Maybe; but while at Cambridge I had once consulted Winston Churchill's physician and learned I had what he called an athlete's heart. This needed the daily stimulus of cold baths to dilate the membranes, which in warm, moist climates remain flaccid. Accordingly, reminded of my father's regimen, I plunged myself into baths of ice-cold water every morning. This was not too difficult, because I lodged at a house owned by an apparently incompetent plumber. It boasted a bathtub served by two faucets: one provided a thin spurt of scalding steam, and the other a deluge of cold water under such pressure from the town's main supply that the bath filled in seconds.

Teaching high school made it immediately apparent to me that our

46

species is not uniform in either its abilities or in the ways we approach the problem of survival. Parents would make extravagant claims about the intellectual or physical abilities of their children and only reluctantly acknowledged any weaknesses. All their offspring, to a boy, approximated to some shiny ideal or would do so soon. Yet each child was different, and different again from his parents. The more perceptive parents were those who had several children with whom they could compare the one under discussion. Their additional evidence and experience gave them a perspective difficult to achieve for parents with no other child to observe. The single child suffers from such unrelenting attention, just as, I could now see, I had suffered myself.

Privately, I wrote daily letters to my class to clear my mind and help myself understand what I was supposed to be teaching. Autobiographical, they enabled me to address my charges without the baggage that would have encumbered the subject matter. My former heroic headmaster had once warned me that it was good to be "starry-eyed" about one's students but never about one's subject, meaning that a hard-nosed accuracy was essential to scholarship; students might be forgiven for their failings but should never be deceived into thinking they had done well when they had not, and results alone should dictate grades.

Despite being state owned, the Priory School was an adventurous place. Its pioneering headmaster, C. W. E. Peckett, had devised, besides oral Latin and Greek, an entirely new curriculum called "Humanities." This was a series of classes in history, art, literature, music, and Western thought, each designed to support and inform the others. It was a heady brew that the boys seemed to love. Peckett believed an intellectual dark age would soon engulf civilization and he was "lighting a candle which alone would show the way through it." He was enthusiastic. "We teach them to write, first like Homer, then like Herodotus, Thucydides, Cicero, Caesar, Erasmus, and later even Shakespeare! Of course, there's only time to get exposed to them, but you'll be surprised, the boys never forget. It lives, you see. It lives!"

And so I took my classes through the pyramids of Egypt and they learned to write in cuneiform and hieroglyphics. Then we reenacted the siege of Troy and performed the plays of Aeschylus, Sophocles, and Euripides, and then the tasty bits from Plato's *Symposium* and *Phaedo*. As ancient Britons, they worshiped at huge blowups of Stonehenge, as Greek Athenians at the Parthenon, as Romans in the Colosseum, and beneath the Sistine Chapel ceiling. Thereafter, they conducted mediaeval disputations, argued for and against Saint

Francis and reenacted the siege and capture of Jerusalem; and all this was accompanied by music and art from the time of the early Primitives to the sophistications of Venice. We also pursued the theme of interdependence by showing how our carpets, door handles, toilets, and water pipes, as well as our very letters, numbers, and words, have histories all their own; these benefits of modern civilization were, we stressed, frequently the result of hard-won victories over ignorance and superstition.

However, middle-class morality remained a stumbling block even in this enlightened school. What did I hear coming forth from the tiny chapel that the headmaster had unaccountably put together in a closet under the stairs, but "All Things Bright and Beautiful," and even "Onward Christian Soldiers"? This sanctuary was, I was told, "our catacomb." And it was here that the symbolic candle of intelligence and learning was to be kept burning. At the end of each week we would solemnly close with words from the ancient missal: "Lighten our darkness, O Lord, we beseech thee."

Thus was the notorious body of British dominance and class structure, determined by birth, accent, and education, also being kept alive and made seemingly legitimate by religion. With such theological sophistry was the British monarch and her relatives, together with the managerial and celebrated elite who, to stifle criticism at its source, were now cunningly elevated into the nobility, made to seem occupants of their various thrones by divine right. That an entire nation including the intelligentsia could be cozened into accepting and supporting the dominance of a particular religion, which is then made to support such self-serving ends, is an intellectual tragedy. Some claim this state of affairs has had little effect, but they say this even while also claiming that without it the country could not hold up its head. The pupils of 3M and 4M, as my classes were called, are by now themselves retired or almost so, former captains of industry, no doubt, some maybe ennobled, but although they are probably very patriotic, I hope they remember by what paths humans have come to where they are.

On sunny days, the Yorkshire moors, with their long reaches of scrub, heather, bracken, and an occasional stand of gorse, are a broad and generous upland. But when the grey mists creep down across them from the northern hills, they make a lonely and forbidding scene. The heather weeps with moisture and the short, tough grass grows spongy and boglike underfoot. Where the rocky soil is not too scant, dry walls of flat grey stones, picked up and laid down by peasant farmers generations since, divide the land. Narrow, winding roads offer no more than stony tracks reaching from them to lonely cottages or, here and there, a farm. Here Sherlock Holmes pursued the hound of the Baskervilles. Here the repentant Cathy broke her heart and cried in vain for handsome, chthonic Heathcliff to return to her. Here lived the Brontë family in their austere vicarage with its hard stone stairway inside the house, its cushion covers woven with human hair, and its windows staring across a sea of graves. And not far away, upon a hill, gathered about a honey-colored church is a monastic community founded in 1892 by six Puseyites dedicated to Anglo-Catholic ritual, public service, and the Body of the Christian God.

It was not inappropriate to build a monastery of sorts upon these moors. The nearby town is solemn, self-contained, and constructed almost entirely of the local ironstone that turns black as it oxidizes in the mist and rain. Its steep, sable streets lead up to the collection of buildings designed by and for the Community of the Resurrection, along with the church they constructed and the college or seminary they founded. Since Pusey's day, when the Oxford Movement in the English church rediscovered Roman ways, the brothers have observed all existing Catholic practices and others that had been forgotten, balking only at obedience to Rome's Holy See. One of their founders, Charles Gore, had at his death in 1932 left behind a regimen that emulated his distaste for autocracy and regulations, and his belief in the efficacy of the individual conscience. His admiration of ritual was based on its claim to represent reality, a principle I found noble and inspiring.

It was among these "monks" that I went to study, following the advice of my blue-eyed god and his confessor. For me, in 1954, the monastic community was another world, one where the love of men for men was supposedly anathema but nonetheless proved to be quite common.

My appointed confessor was Trevor Huddleston, the celebrated South African reformist and author of *Naught for Your Comfort*, the tragic story of apartheid in South Africa, where he long had worked. "There'll be a bloodbath there soon," he'd predict. "You should see my hate mail!" The principal of the college, Hugh Bishop, a bald, angular priest, was also highly placed, being confessor to British royals. We would take walks together and discuss the state of the world, after which he'd say, as if to subdue my pride, "Things are just the same as when we started out, for all our talk." I thought (quite incorrectly) that this was perhaps how he justified the life he led somewhat cut off from the world.

The Mother House itself, with its enormous church, had been constructed in a style reminiscent of William Morris, whose enthusiastic and pious medievalism had influenced much religious architecture around the turn of the century. The Community wore black-belted cassocks and, over them, when at work, full-length grey scapulars that hung from their necks back and front almost to the floor, and when inside they wore black sandals: a stylish outfit suiting the austerity of their close. Their hair was cut normally, and their pink, often jovial faces, their careful gait, and solemn deportment marked their movements round the place as well as to and from their church to say the Hours. The Community preferred to be described as Brothers. The several priests among them were content with this, regarding their paternal identification as a sacred responsibility and the fraternity as their earthly home.

Some of us students suspected, however improbably, that all the brothers might be gay, but who could tell? Among them, besides eminent theologians, a confessor to the royal family, and the outspoken critic of apartheid, was a sailor who once worked minesweepers in the war when minesweepers had no more than a three months' average survival rate. There were also several sober alcoholics long rescued from addiction, and others whose secret triumphs and tragedies we students learned only in whispers after Compline. It seemed one brother had once been a celebrated chef but was permitted only to serve his regular turn as cook, as he did at cleaning, gardening, and washing up. For all brothers took their turns regardless of ability, and if the meals seemed inedible, the brothers did not flinch but ate them up, remembering the poor or themselves when they had been poor, and loved that day's cook the more. In such ways did they humble pride and raise the lowly incompetent to equality.

We students, of course all male at that time, were housed in a separate building and ate together in our own refectory. Each had his narrow cell furnished with a table, a single narrow bed, and one hard wooden chair. Our lectures were held in classrooms among the buildings and in the library. Every day we attended Mattins, sometimes Low Mass, Evensong, and Compline. On holy days we would be permitted to join the brothers for the Hours and learned to serve and celebrate High Mass, which at Easter was a splendid climax to the long dank weeks of Lent, ending in a dramatic ritualized reconstruction of Christ's last days on earth.

We were taught theology and divinity; learned Hebrew or Aramaic and brushed up our New Testament in Greek and Vulgate versions. We were coached in the elements of theology and divinity; we were trained to sing plainchant and to read the bible aloud with what was considered proper devotion, while various visiting lecturers from the university to which we were officially attached told us how the body can be made to serve the soul and so fulfill a "proper Christian purpose." For these theologians, we were all members of Christ's body and Christianity was a whole fabric, each tiny detail of its long history and doctrines woven together to form an indissoluble and everlasting structure, infinitely self-consistent, and prefigured from the beginning of the world. Like the unity of the Christian year, this whole devotional cloth provided security for those unsure of where they stood with their Maker. And the supposed permanence of the structure gave endless reassurance and consolation.

Our coaching in bible reading confirmed a suspicion I had that the unctuous tones adopted by clergy when reading the lessons in church were as intentional as they were nauseating. My attempts to make the bible sound lifelike were severely chastised. "These were holy men," I was told, "be more reverent"—reminding me of the angry letters received by Dorothy L. Sayers for putting curses in the mouths of Roman soldiers who nailed Jesus to the cross.

Our lessons in pastoralia, however, were woefully inadequate, those who taught them cleverly skirting important issues like homosexuality which, clearly an embarrassment if not an actual sin, was more than an anomaly, and seemingly widespread in the College. The pad, pad, pad of feet and the rustle of cassocks down the ever-creaking corridors during the night was not always, as I initially thought it to be, evidence of devoted meditations in the church. They marked love trysts of fellow students with each other or sometimes, I was told in awestruck tones, with an occasional Brother who was bold or skillful enough to leave his cell without discovery.

I had carried a lamp for my blue-eyed boy for three long years and only slowly succumbed to another Michael, the *homme fatal* of this place, to whom, I quickly learned, several others were also in thrall. At first I had dismissed him as possessing looks too obvious to mean much to me; then, while sitting next to him in his room, learning Hebrew grammar, I found myself leaning over to kiss his beautiful neck, and he, with another trophy on his belt, could not resist playing me along.

Now in love a second time, both less and more in control of myself than I had been before, I kept an austere front, but in the privacy of my cell next door to his, broke down in agonies of jealousy and despair as he bestowed his favors elsewhere, even upon women he knew. Heroic in stature, well educated and well informed, with the physical grace of an Olympic medalist, he would caress me with his green eyes and long, strong fingers, yet could not give me the physical love for which I yearned in vain. Listening to exegesis of Old Testament prophecy, or serving mass, I could see only his long golden hair, glowing in the sunlight, the strong line of his jaw, and the peaches and cream of his immaculate complexion. My heart turned over at his laugh; I trembled at the sight of his handwriting; and when I passed my examinations, I did so hoping that following ordination we might serve the same parish.

Only once did he agree to walk with me in the nearby woods, and wearing only shorts, shirts, and shoes, we made off. We lay together on the leaves. I held his hand which, lifeless, was so clearly a measure of what he himself felt for me that I could only turn away. I have kept the memories of all my loves, each one so different and irreplaceable, but Michael shines among them resplendent.

My inability to woo without encouragement is not untypical of those raised too protected from rejection. My sex life had been arid, desperately obedient; perhaps not unlike that of any supposedly well-bred middle-class heterosexual. One did not push oneself forward, make a scene, demand more than what is permitted. One always respected the other person's wishes and so never seemed permitted to respect one's own.

During one summer vacation from the College seminary, I attempted to exorcise my passion for my newly beloved by working in a steelworks. This, I thought, would be a manly task! The British Labor government had threatened to nationalize steel but the gaffers, being middle management, nonunion, and conservative, had almost universally worked to rule—a go-slow tactic that had so reduced production that nationalization of the industry had been abandoned.

The steelworks I selected was a Victorian monster that had been only partially modernized. It was set within a new "model" town that had been constructed around it to provide employment for those who had been moved there from the slums. A town replete with libraries, swimming pools, and parks, it had the look of Shaw's ideal company town in *Major Barbara*. But the steelworks itself was a mostly unreformed maze of pipes, smelting ovens, blast furnaces, and molten steel belching showers of sparks along with vast sheds from which huge engines clashed and clanged—a veritable battlefield of smoke and noise. My task was to assist an electrician, a thin man not much older than me, with a fiery tongue, an unrepentant Communist. He served the sheds with their soaking pits where great ingot "pots" full to the brim with white-hot molten steel matured in searing thousand-degree heat. Every so often, immense cone-shaped covers built of firebrick upon a grid would move aside from off the pits. Open-construction steel cranes in the roof moved to and fro with clanking hesitation like spiders, fifty feet above. They thrust massive, clawlike grabs down into the pit, took hold of the pots by their lugs and shook them up, releasing gases that had accumulated within the molten steel. Occasionally a pot, caught unevenly within the grab, would tilt, and the gas inside the steel would explode up, spurting molten globules high into the air. More than once such great sparks had shot into the crane's cab and through the body of the driver, killing him. Yet only one of the three antique cranes had been made safe and its cab equipped with air-conditioning.

I was set to clean ancient electrical circuit breakers at the ground level and would meet other workers, incarnate Vulcans, with faces dark and worn by a daily life of wrestling with iron bars and steel girders, the secret riches of the planet. Sweat pouring from our limbs, we'd drink bottles of ice-cold Coca-Cola from scarlet dispensing machines, the only evidence of a benevolent management. Our gratitude to America for this nectar was enormous. After drinking many bottles of the stuff, I'd search for lavatories and was warned, not entirely in jest, that those on the top floor were labeled "Gentlemen"; on the gaffers' floor, "Men"; and on the workers' floor beside the soaking pits, "Males." Mortified, I scuttled back to my master with more respect.

So old were the circuit breakers in the roof that it was not unusual for a crane's engine to stall. Once this happened while I was on duty. The crane had just moved aside the cover of a pit, revealing a supply of ingots full of bubbling steel. The grab was only partially extended into the shimmering furnace, which was now directly beneath the cab. My master called me to him, thrust a bag of tools in my hand, and ordered me to follow him. We had not a moment to lose. The incandescent heat was overpowering. An ancient iron ladder with thin metal rungs reached up the side of the stalled crane to the top of its cab. Grease and oil from the crane's mechanism were already melting and running down the ladder's handrail in a slippery sludge. A long electric cable encased in rubber served to carry power to the crane, and this was now dangling below the cab directly over the pit, melting fast, great drops of rubber peeling off and bursting into flame as they dropped sizzling into the furnace.

As quickly as I could manage I followed my boss upward into the roof and toward the cab. My hands slipped on the rails, and I could feel the hot iron rungs through the soles of my special steel-toed boots. The shimmering oven was below me, its heat reaching up through my pants as if to claw me down into its maw. Slipping, sliding, increasingly terrified, I reached the top, jumped onto a narrow metal platform and then made my way across a series of flat iron struts in the roof to where the electrician stood waiting for his bag of tools. He seemed somehow far away, and with sickening dismay I realized that to reach him I had to walk across a single oil-slick beam no more than two feet wide and ten feet long which stretched over the abyss, with only a single handrail on one side for support.

I hesitated. He shouted. It was, indeed, an extremely dangerous time not just for me but for the crane driver, stuck in his cab and perhaps already asphyxiated, if not dead.

Abuse hurled through the air. "Come on, you cunt!"—a common insult aimed at those whom he-men despised.

The expletive shocked me forward, as it was intended to do. This was no place for prudery. Lives were at risk. At that moment I, too, would have voted for whatever party would bring an end to the inhumanity of the conditions that I suffered along with the rest of the steelworkers.

Before I returned to my seminary, I went searching for my new beloved, whom I eventually found in a tent with another lover I had been unable to oust. I was not bad looking and attempted in vain to develop a tan to look more robust. But I was twenty-four, older than the rest, no longer quite so clean-cut, and once again, numbed and miserable, I took myself to London to work on an experiment which from sheer despair I had devised in the loneliness of my cell. In some strange way, perhaps, I wanted to make amends; to prove myself.

It was not only in the steel mill that church talk had always seemed to me somehow out of touch with reality. Accordingly, I had devised a questionnaire to test what common people, like my army mates, my electrician, and his fellow workers, thought of church language. My hypothesis was that to many people at their daily work the church was an alien institution, not because it taught what they did not believe, but because it taught what they could not understand.

My method was to make up cards on which were printed key words occurring in what was then the current *Book of Common Prayer*. It is still widely used today, a beautiful seventeenth-century English compilation largely drawn and translated from the Latin of the Catholic missal, parts of which date back to the early church. Its vocabulary was used only in church, and, I knew, was often misunderstood even by the priest and certainly by many in the congregation, let alone those who never went to church. It was a standing joke among us supercilious students that even the Lord's Prayer repeated so frequently by almost everyone in Christendom might actually be incomprehensible except to the educated, the rest merely mumbling the sounds like a spell.

Attempting an unscientific cross section of the London public, I toured the metropolis exposing my cards to as many as I was able to persuade to give me an answer. I asked laborers, washerwomen, business people, housewives: what did these words mean to them? The replies were all too often as significant as they were hilarious. And though devoid of their context the words that I had selected were an unfair test, they certainly indicated that a modern translation would be more easily understood. Among the answers I received, I remember: *wast,* "something to do with rubbish"; *magnified,* "made bigger than it really is"; *erred,* "something to do with an errand boy"; *lowly,* "what a cow does"; *art,* "a man's name"; *hallowed,* "when you call someone Harold"; *spake,* "a cross between a spade and a spike"; *trespass,* "a law"; *saith,* "name of a place"; *wroth,* "something rotting"; *oblation,* "wearing down"; *vouchsafe,* "like in a bank."

I wrote up the results and sent them off to the Society for the Propagation of Christian Knowledge, and they were quickly published in the form of a booklet entitled *Getting It Across.* Surprisingly, this led to visits from agents who wanted more of the same and I at once began a study of church hymns. As I was soon to learn, these were among the first shots fired in what was later to become a movement for prayer book reform.

It was usual to invite professional visitors to the College to talk to the students. Sometimes a celebrated Christian psychiatrist would discuss the soul, or a Christian social worker would describe how to save the poor. I was dismayed by the biased piety of these church-appointed visitors. However, on one occasion the Archbishop of Canterbury himself stopped by to greet us. He had no doubt been examining the Community to see whether, as an Anglo-Catholic order, they had not strayed beyond the confines of the English church.

As usual, we sat around in easy chairs, our black-bound prayer books folded in our cassocks, honored at such condescension. His talk was avuncular, traditional, punctuated by loud guffaws from amongst a double chin. Plump hands, soft and be-ringed, patted the large belly behind the purple stock. Then suddenly a chilly tone set in. His Grace began to frown.

"Hasn't one of you written something?" He stared around accusingly. "About language, it was, I think."

I colored up, for it must be me. My pamphlet had been widely distributed. I nodded and an icy stare froze me to my seat.

"Can't have it, you know. The English Book of Common Prayer is a sacred thing. A thing of beauty, a national heritage, a treasure chest! Beautiful seventeenth-century language. Sheer poetry!"

A plump forefinger was now raised reprovingly. Dare I beard this lion?

"B-b-but . . ." I stuttered. "Supposing no one understands the language? What if—" I dared to continue, but he interrupted me. "What? A jewel? You'd tamper with a miracle?" His stinging scorn of my arrogance made it sound like sacrilege, or worse, blasphemy!

The giant face was suddenly rosy red with fury and then, as if remembering himself, he turned away and talked of other things.

That only a well-educated person could understand the church seemed to be of little concern to him. I, however, was torn between emotion and reason. I could see that my fellow students had long ago taken the side of tradition and I had already determined that beauty was a way to know and love God. But now I was accused of abandoning beauty and was being required to uphold it at the price of ignorance. But flesh and blood meant too much for me to abandon them in favor of intellectual perfection.

In fact, as I soon learned, I was not alone in my misgivings. There were then many far more outspoken critics of the Christian church than I, and especially of the Church of England. Books with provocative titles such as *What Is Wrong with the Church?* had begun to appear, but I discovered that all were essentially apologias. Usually their authors thought the church should return to its original message, or restore what had somehow been deleted from former doctrine or practice. Such criticism was to recur over the next forty years with increasing depth and often quite revolutionary suggestions. Even the Incarnation itself was to be subjected to telling scrutiny by a group of eminent theologians, but, as with former seemingly revolutionary movements, such criticism eventually faded away in a plethora of accommodations and second thoughts. A bishop, John Robinson, a former friend of my old headmaster, had already published a provocative but not entirely new assessment of the metaphysical and proposed that God was dead. This led me to visit him in his episcopal residence where, after we agreed that the church had somehow to be made relevant to the general public, I was invited to say mass together in his private chapel, his reforming zeal quite forgotten.

I survived the intensity of my second love and the deadening sense that I had been rejected by the most wonderful man in the world. The academic status of our prospective ordination was finally confirmed by examiners from the nearby University of Leeds where, ironically for me, as it turned out, Joseph Priestley, the clerical scientist, had once preached. Priestley had gone on to discover what he described as "dephlogisticated air," or oxygen, and so was the father of modern chemistry. Being nearly burned alive for his republican sympathies, he left in disgust for America. Unlike Priestly, however, I reluctantly signed the oaths of allegiance to the British Crown as divinely appointed head of the English Church and prepared to kneel and receive the burdens and responsibilities of the Apostolic Succession that the Church of Rome in vain denies was ever granted to the Church of England.

A venerable archdeacon came toward me and, trembling with outrage, pointed to my lack of a clerical collar, a Victorian relic that I had refused to wear as being a public declaration of self-righteousness.

"What's this? What's this?" he gasped, the silver buckles on his mediaeval pumps glittering in sympathy with his icy wrath.

I told him it was a tie and explained what I meant by it. I left him dismayed, for he was responsible for how we comported ourselves. I then knelt before the waiting bishop and was made first a deacon, then, the following year, a priest by the sacramental Imposition, or Laying On of Hands. I became a "father."

Not surprisingly, I was at once shipped off to what was then considered a revolutionary parish, in hopes, as I was later told, that it would either kill me or cure me of my arrogant enthusiasms. It was to be a trial, perhaps a sacrifice. I was not expected to survive it—not because it was too devotional a cure, but because it was not thought to be devotional enough. It would so offend what were assumed to be my Anglo-Catholic sensibilities that I would see the error of my ways and learn the value of traditional theology.

MASS MAGIC

1956–1958

$\mathcal{I}$f Christianity's compassion for the ordinary world has sometimes been obscured, intellectual interpretations of its message are largely to blame. Reforming movements have attempted to correct this tendency. Saint Francis, Martin Luther, and John Wesley each derived inspiration from the common people. Anglo-Catholics also have often sought work among the poor, as evangelicals have done.

Near the great industrial city of Leeds in northern England is a mediaeval palace set upon a hill. Once fortified, it belonged to the Knights Templar, and is now a monument and private home. The village gathered about it once housed the castle servants and their families. Round this, still further from the House, the suburb of Halton grew up, self-contained, its middle-class inhabitants mostly Methodists or Congregationalists. Below this community of well-appointed homes the county council had built a model suburb, a tract development, to house the families whose city slums had been demolished during and after the war, working-class people, artisans, sometimes very poor. The streets linking these new homes had been laid out in such a way as to meet and continue the streets within the middle-class development, but the citizens of the latter, being of the professional classes, had erected concrete barriers and chains across the roads to prevent access. They did not want lower-class traffic such as motorcycles and city garbage trucks trespassing upon their tree-lined sanctuary. However, the government, with the help of the established church, had erected a well-designed modern church building of considerable charm to serve the new model community, and it was here I was invited to be a priest.

The parish was already being run upon experimental lines. And the success it was reputed to enjoy seemed to its vicar, Ernest Southcott, to provide solid evidence that the church as a whole was distancing herself from the very people she claimed to serve. My own suspicion was that the long-lasting edifice of traditional Christianity had managed to maintain a consistent front against ever-improving knowledge of the facts of life only at the cost of its honesty. Unless there was something really solid at its base and not imaginary, and which, moreover, served humanity rather than faith for its own sake, its days of significance were numbered.

The experiment, being hailed in America but largely ignored in Britain, was known as the "House Church movement." Ernie had devised it and he still led it. He was a commanding presence, a charismatic Canadian priest, six foot five inches tall, with long black curly hair and a broad forehead. He was forever to be seen striding around his parish in a voluminous and much-stained cassock complete with yoke.

The House Church, as Ernie had named it, matched a movement in France that I was already interested in. This French movement had been inspired by a persuasive study of the French working class called *La France, pays de mission?*, written by two French priests, Yvan Daniel and Henri Godin, chaplains who served within Jeunesse Ouvrière Chrétienne, a Catholic organization dedicated to working-class youth. The study had appeared in 1943, before the end of the war, and challenged the church to face up to the existence of a "wall . . . between the church and the French working class." The wall was composed of class, language, and even buildings. Godin's own experience of industrial city life caused him to describe priests as bourgeois who don't care about the working classes, and with official blessing he had gathered around himself young priests who were similarly devoted to serving factory workers. These eventually became the celebrated "worker-priests" of the Mission de Paris. They worked on the factory floor, joined unions, and supported the causes of the laboring classes. Inevitably, they lived double lives and were alternately misunderstood and idolized.

The fact that priests had donned workers' overalls and said mass on the factory floor provided a domestic model for the House Church movement, which took the mass out of the traditional church building and into the homes of the people. If the people would not come to the church, explained Ernie, the church must go to the people, just as did the worker-priests and Jesus himself. I was already much taken with the French history lesson, and our discussions explained the House Church plan in a way that made a sort of sense to me. Ernie argued that the only way to change people's way of thinking was to "take them from where they are to where they are not." No other way would work. It was practical advice based on experience I myself had confirmed and which, as a teacher, I believed in.

But the Mission de Paris had run into difficulties; it had become, as academics would now describe it, "problematic." The factory floors were unionized and the workers, no doubt knowing what they were about, required the worker-priests to join their unions, which at that time were strongly communist. Total identification with the working class thus posed a threat to the Holy See, and the experiment was closed in a welter of bitterness and acrimonious debate. Godin, thinking his work was over, appeared to have taken his own life some years before, and many other worker-priests either abandoned their commissions or withdrew into the laity, often in disgust. It had been, they believed, the church's last chance to reach the people. Ernie's House Church, however, not subject to such vows of obedience, survived. It was, after all, a practical solution, one of those compromises for which the Anglican communion is celebrated. If, as in Britain, few were attending church, then something drastic had to be done. As Ernie told us, to take people where they are not, you must always start where they are.

The House Church system, however, was extremely demanding, not only of its clergy (there were two of us and the vicar) but also of the parish. Ernie was a High Church Anglican who prayed for his parish, street by street. Each week, he would call upon parishioners known to be loyal to him and cajole them into allowing an early-morning mass to be celebrated in their home. Each morning there were three or four such early masses in the hopes that together they would give the entire parish an opportunity to partake in the course of each week. Ernie organized an ideal schedule: every month was divided into weeks of "house meetings" with "house celebrations" each morning, and special meetings for women, the young, and the old.

Parishioners who accepted the invitation to hold a mass in their homes were expected to provide a small table, a clean white tablecloth (as the prayer book enjoined), and some bread that had previously been cut up into small pieces. If they wished they could also provide the wine, a plate in place of the paten, and, as was the practice in the catacombs, a glass or even a small bowl to stand for the chalice. The clergy, vested in albs and stoles, brought candlesticks, prayer books, and whatever remaining "furniture" might be necessary.

Because it was a congregation of working people, these celebrations were usually set for six, six-thirty, or seven o'clock, generally depending on the time when the father of the family had to get to the factory or other place of work. We clergy, ready robed and in beat-up cars or on bicycle, would make our way around the road barriers by a back route so as to avoid the "nonconformist" enclave, and arrive clutching our *sacculum* or bag of communion vessels. Sometimes the previous month's arrangements had been forgotten, for not all the faithful were in favor of this early-morning invasion of their homes by loudly singing and praying clergy. Some, indeed, thought the whole idea sacrilegious, and it was not unknown for the women attending a service to be grouped around some little table in the kitchen while the husband, his working clothes only half pulled on and in the midst of shaving, watched the morning news on television with the volume turned up high enough to drown both the devotions and, we dared presume, the guilt he was expected to feel.

The count of twelve to twenty morning masses per week was maintained regardless of weather. The vicar was as insistent as he was indefatigable. Neither snow, hail, nor the heaviest downpours of rain could keep us out of those homes. As had been promised me, it was an endurance test. Many a time, some housewife or nursing mother would vainly attempt to escape our ministrations. Some would plead with me to be excused, often on the reasonable grounds that people took part only from loyalty since, as they complained, the volume of communion bread and wine being consumed each week was surely sufficient for salvation!

Occasionally I would hear from former seminarian friends. They had nearly all been assigned to traditional parishes where the ritual was still authentically Anglo-Catholic. The conservatism of these parishes was illustrated by a story about a subdeacon carrying a chalice full of consecrated wine who, unused to the thick carpet around the altar, had tripped and spilled the contents across the chancel steps. The sight of the Sacred Blood splashed about had so shocked the clergy that the celebration had been abandoned, the people sent home, and the church censed and officially cleansed in accordance with mediaeval rites of exorcism. The tale was recounted with great seriousness and sense of catastrophe, and I was glad I had not been subject to such foolishness. However, my belief that my own ministry was not liable to these embarrassments was to be undermined in due course.

I was greatly taken with the practical measures that the House Church experiment had adopted. It was a realistic solution that seemed to respect people over tradition. It also established in no uncertain way the pastoral role of the clergy as servants, just what Jesus was thought to have called us to be. Moreover, it seemed to divest the mass of the ponderous solemnities that overpower the essential simplicity of its meaning. In people's homes, in their kitchens and round their own tables, we were able to escape centuries of devotional baggage, with its burden of decorative verbiage and ritual so earnestly imposed that in the seminary it had given me the willies. Celebrated in several parts, the mass first memorializes the written authorities upon which the ceremony and its meaning are based; then refers to the human need—personal, local, and widespread—that the ceremony is to satisfy; and finally reenacts in ceremonial form the Last Supper itself, climaxing in the consecration of the bread and wine, which are "elevated" or exhibited to the congregation then finally invited to partake.

According to Roman and some Anglo-Catholic teaching, the bread and wine are actually changed into the body and blood of Jesus even though they appear unchanged. The theological explanation of this miracle is the subject of whole libraries. Even the Protestant *Book of Common Prayer* avoids directly contradicting it, holding to a sophistry known as "the Real Presence" that neatly avoids "popery" by taking refuge in rhetoric. (Indeed, a papal nuncio once reported back to his Pope that the official doctrine of the English church, albeit not ambitious of Catholic interpretation, was nonetheless capable of it.) Staunch Anglo-Catholics like our leader believed the elements were miraculously changed, though not the "accidents" or the "forms" of bread and wine.

To our unsophisticated British congregations, as time wore on, our daily domestic celebrations, designed to serve as reminders of Christ's vicarious sacrifice on our behalf to expunge the sins of the world, suggested by their quantity that the effect of this sacrifice was not quite as reliable as we claimed it to be. "Do we have to take so much communion?" was a complaint heard many times. "It's an insult," others said. "Have we sinned all that much? I'm sick of saying I'm a lost sheep." Doctrinally, such complaints were frivolous and missed the point—unless, of course, the doctrine itself was unbalanced. For there was certainly an obsessive element in the constant repetition; a daily sense of only temporary fulfillment that was difficult to deny. I was reminded more than once of spinning prayer wheels and even of my childhood head-beating addiction. To our leader, however, the situation was quite otherwise: the daily reminders of the Last Supper provided him with evidence of Christ's sacrificial bounty, not of its inadequacy. And, as I was to discover, there were also other forces at work.

One Sunday, I was the priest and celebrant of the Sunday High Mass, which we continued to celebrate in the church building. It was not a concelebration and Ernie was serving as my deacon. I had reached the section in the ritual devoted to the consecration of the bread and wine. We had a "modern" altar pulled back from the rear of the apse so that the priests could stand facing the people across it, making it more of a Protestant "table"—our single concession to the Reformation. With hands clasped and pointed, I bowed and prayed, crossed myself, and knelt, first when consecrating the wafers—one large one for myself and my other ministers, and the small ones to be distributed to the congregation—then again, when consecrating the wine, both before and after. This was followed by loud ringing of the altar bell from its three separate hammers, and the Invitation to the congregation to partake.

I had remembered all the details in the correct order. The local butcher who was our narrow-eyed Master of Ceremonies had watched my every genuflection and the position of my hands. He knew by heart the exact wording of all the prayers and had nodded approvingly at my well-trained performance. The congregation lined up obedient to the call and we priests moved solemnly toward them away from the altar, I with the decorated silver ciborium piled with consecrated hosts that were now Christ's Body, and the other two ministers with chalices heavy with the dark red communion wine that was now the Precious Blood. Visions of tripping over our albs and showering the congregation with the sacred fluid floated at the back of my nervous mind, but all was well; the communion was slowly completed and we returned to the altar to commence the Ablutions and my Lavabo.

The Ablutions consist of ritual cleansing of the sacred vessels, first by consuming the remainder of the hosts and the Precious Blood, and then carefully wiping the paten clean of crumbs with a "fair cotton cloth." In the Roman rite, this is followed by the celebrant's pouring a little unconsecrated wine into the chalice, consuming it, then placing his forefingers and thumbs together over the chalice so that a second small amount of unconsecrated wine and then water can be poured over them from special cruets into the chalice, which is then also wiped clean with the same or another cloth. The fact that molecules of wine or Blood are still present is essentially ignored as an irrelevant scientific fact, although just in case, each act is accompanied by special exculpatory prayers and sentences selected from the bible. The celebrant then returns to the altar to begin the Thanksgiving, the final part of the ritual.

I had carefully completed these tasks and bowed to my fellow priests and to the server, when, on preparing for the Blessing and the Recessional, I heard a hoarse and urgent whisper in my left ear.

"You forgot the hosts!"

I froze. It was our leader. Were there, indeed, hosts I had forgotten? I looked around the altar, which seemed to stretch far on both sides of me. The front rows of the congregation, matching the eagle eye of the Master of Ceremonies, were waiting impatiently for me to continue.

I stared straight ahead and without moving my lips whispered back, "What hosts?"

"In the box!" he hissed, also staring straight ahead.

"What box?" I hissed back, well aware that the silence from the altar would soon cause unrest in the congregation, who wanted to get home. Our whispered conversation was unseemly, to say the least.

"Over there!" His hands and head jerked to the right. I swiveled my eyes to the right. And, indeed, there was the box of wafers from which I had taken the appropriate number for the consecration. It now sat smugly hidden behind the missal stool. Surely—

"You consecrated them!" There was no mistaking a new steely quality to his whisper.

"No I didn't. Only what was on the paten." Of this I was quite sure. Of what use would two thousand wafers be in a congregation of a hundred?

"They were on the cloth!" This said still without moving either hand or eye. "You must consume them!"

I stared down sightlessly at the altar cloth. What did he mean? The ablutions had been completed. I glanced at the Master of Ceremonies. He slowly inclined his head. This was serious! I heaved a big breath and began the Blessing while I cudgeled my memory. They were not consecrated. How could they have been consecrated? Ernie was mistaken.

I finished the Blessing and then half turned to leave for the Recessional back down from the altar and along the nave. But our leader stood obstinately facing forward across the altar, hands still flattened together in proper style, thumbs crossed. He was clearly not about to budge. I turned back. The organ began for the final hymn as if to remind us to get going. Now he could speak louder. He again waved his locked fingers to my right.

"The box was on the Cloth. You consecrated it. They must all be consumed."

I thought quickly.

"But my hands didn't go near it."

"It was on the Cloth. That's sufficient." He spoke furiously if to an errant student. His voice conjured up ghastly terrors while learning correct "altar etiquette." I was suddenly impatient.

"Surely God can tell what he wants to consecrate and what he doesn't?" This enraged him. A dark red glow suffused his face.

I picked up the box and opened it. Row upon row of tightly packed wafers stared up at me, layer upon layer still in their wrappings. To consume them would be a orgy of devotion. Heaving a sigh at my obtuseness, Ernie stretched out a hand as if to begin the feast, then suddenly, shaking his head, pulled back and consented to move.

"We'll consume them in the Lady Chapel and repeat the ablutions there. Genuflect to show we have the consecrated hosts with us. The Censer precedes." But by now he was anguished, ashen. It was the Spilt Blood problem.

So, picking up the box of wafers, I laid it on the pall atop the paten and covered the whole with its corporal, and we moved off to complete the Recessional, terminating in the Lady Chapel with the acolytes, the crucifer standing about while the thurifer, a handsome lad, continued to make enough smoke to smother everyone.

In the Lady Chapel, Ernie genuflected, took the box, opened it and took out a bundle of wafers and handed them to me, then another bundle and handed them around. The Acolytes could not swallow many. Being unleavened and highly absorbent, the wafers immediately adhered together, forming lumps which stuck to the roof of the mouth. The difficulty this caused being almost immediately apparent, even to Ernie, he stopped. Raised in an unforgiving evangelical as well as Anglo-Catholic tradition, he could not bring himself to consider simple disposal with other common wastes. Despite its apparent benevolence, the theology he inherited is aristocratic and patronizing, not generous enough to encompass the ordinary world, for all its talk of divine condescension. It had no conception of a holistic synthesis honoring the sanctity of all material things as divinely created, even though it also claimed they were so created. Trash, in such a belief system, is trash until the end of time, and toilet bowls are only for the disposal of matter that is ineluctably profane, far beyond any Redemption. I suggested burning or burying as possible alternatives to the toilet and as smacking of sufficient ritualistic history to satisfy the jealous God he apparently believed in. But such methods were deemed too violent. The wafers were undeniably and irrevocably the Body of Our Lord, and he ruled "they must be eaten."

"I'll intincture them tomorrow at mass in the morning. It won't fit in the tabernacle. We'll put them in the aumbry"—a cupboard—"and use them for sick visiting."

Intincturing is a simple procedure requiring great care. It involves the placing of a spot of wine on each separate wafer. We used intinctured hosts in visiting the sick because some patients are not permitted wine, and wine, even from the usual miniature chalice, may be difficult for recumbent patients to drink. At this point an irreverent thought occurred to me: to justify the use of so many wafers for the sick we would need an instant plague! Perhaps we should pray for one, so as to satisfy this God who couldn't distinguish boxes from patens. After all, we often prayed for rain, for peace, and for health.

We placed the offending box in the humble aumbry, completed the Recessional and unvested. However, Ernie's brow remained clouded and he looked sad. I had let him down. Early the following morning, we collected the box and took it with us to our first House Church celebration. Monday morning masses were always difficult—the parishioners not understanding why, since they had all attended High Mass on Sunday, they had now to attend mass again on Monday—but we persevered. Two or three women had pulled themselves out of bed at 6 A.M. and were now waiting in the parlor of the duly designated home. We lit our candles and said mass using four of the wafers from the box rather than the carefully cut up Wonder Bread that our parishioners preferred. After mass we completed the intincturing of the many hundreds of remaining wafers in the box with some Precious Blood we had held back.

Our regular visitation of the sick had been arranged with hospitals and families so as to take place as close as was practical to Sunday High Mass, which some of our parishioners did not like to miss. But on Friday it was raining. Dressed for traveling on bicycles we gathered about the aumbry to collect our intinctured hosts. The aumbry was unlocked and the box within it opened. I gasped. Nearly all the hosts were infested with dark green mold. It had congealed about the spots of wine with which they had been treated. Ernie paled. (I could hear my High Church mentors groaning that this is what comes of using aumbries to reserve the sacrament instead of the proper tabernacles.) Scientific facts had triumphed.

None of us had ever experienced moldy hosts. Not surprisingly, they upset our leader almost to the point of tears.

"They must be consumed," he whispered brokenly, and gathering a handful reverently in his cupped hands, strode solemnly from the Lady Chapel into the vestry, where we found him attempting to eat them by stuffing them into his mouth. We stood by, unbelieving, as he gagged, rushed to the sink and threw up. Later, I picked up the remains, wrapped them in a "fair white corporal" and buried them in the church garden. If only we had assumed the concomitance of the

Body and Blood as the Council of Trent had permitted Catholics to do! In that way, intincturing would not have been necessary: the Body would have taken upon itself all the virtues of the Blood.

Like the rejection of gay people, such grotesque piety aroused in me questions that I had long thought permanently laid to rest. Were such oddities no more than anomalies which, like language, hymns, and denominational differences, would eventually be corrected, or were they evidence of flaws in the foundational belief? My conviction that, despite the undoubted eccentricities of the more devout Christian life, there was an as yet eternal and sacred "context" in which human existence fitted and could be judged, was shaken. The Christian Other seemed to be suspiciously like the ancient gods of old.

It was just such a doubt that seems to have surfaced long ago in the mind of Plutarch when he related that the gods of Nicias, a most pious general, turned out to be as capricious as was chance. Nor could I forget that Jesus, too, was reported to have been surprised that at his execution, his God also had forsaken him. Such things were not supposed to happen to those whom God loved—were scandals, in fact, that took centuries of much clever rhetoric to explain. Could they still be ignored or discounted?

I longed to talk the problem over with the vicar—to find out what sort of God he actually believed in, or whether, as might be the case, the priesthood had endowed me with mystical power such that unless I used the correct spells and arranged the objects to be miraculously changed in the correct order, it might fly from my control, regardless of the intentions of the original Source. The priesthood itself, for instance, once bestowed, is considered to be indelible regardless of the recipient's record. However, the vicar could not discuss the matter. The problems that the doctrine of transubstantiation had ever caused still remained after centuries of agonized recrimination and bloodshed, and we dared not resurrect them. For Ernie, as for many calling themselves Christians, it was as if the new world of science and reason were like popular opinion and had no real meaning; forces beyond the understanding of the human mind were to be regarded as the sole authorities. It is this simplicity that lies at the heart of Catholic intransigence even today.

But for me, once such doubts had returned, they provoked a search. Was the doctrine flawed? Something was not right, and too much was at stake to ignore such questions again demanding answers. I went back to my books. The fathers of the church, the schoolmen as they were called, had taught that after consecration of the host, through miraculous divine intervention, the "accidents" of quantity, shape, size, and even ingredients continued to exist without inhering in the true "substance" of Christ's body. By the end of the fourteenth century this had been widely accepted, though reformers such as Wycliffe, Huss, and Luther would dissent. The Council of Trent, however, officially substituted the term "species" for "accidents," but (and this was the point) neither this nor the "accidents" themselves and their effects have ever been explained.

I was now very troubled. I began to review my beliefs yet again. Questions about ritual and ceremony that I had put aside once more assumed importance. I began listening to the Lessons with a more careful ear. I read Compline with suspicion. I was now looking for more clues as to what might be wrong. If there were flaws, they might betray themselves anywhere, even in superficialities. I turned back to my promise to my agent to write something about hymns and as I looked at them I was increasingly exercised by what they taught and how they taught it.

Much of churchpeople's time is still taken up with singing hymns. Yet even devout churchgoers cannot sing the great majority of hymns without making many reservations, a situation which eventually, one would expect, alienates intelligent people while also befuddling the innocent. Many such hymns were originally poems in their own right and later set to music, sometimes disastrously; but the majority range from the sublimely mystical to the dabblings of devout bishops pumping party lines.

Vocabulary of some antiquity and therefore appropriate for religious ritual might be expected to be odd, but hymns also include words that have aural meanings far different from those intended by the authors: *carbuncles* for instance, or *foul,* which would be satisfactory were it not for its context: "Foul, I to the fountain fly!" Then there are inversions, often so numerous as to trip each other up, as in "There is a book who runs may read. . . ." Or sometimes the hymn writer weaves in transliterated Hebrew words such as *Sabaoth* or Latin and Greek like *Miserere Domine* and *Paschal.* There may also be references of great subtlety which imply theological training for their authority but which read more like crossword clues: "Bosrah's Way," "sultry glebe," "Protomartyr," "Great Original," and "Trisagion."

Singing this stuff day after day, year in year out, especially around factory workers' breakfast tables, I was determined to examine, even expose it, if not to bring hymn books up to date, at least to get some of the more inappropriate material eliminated. What, for example, could it mean to those not educated in doctrinal metaphor to sing "Hither the poor may repair, winning a Solomon's wealth!"; and what of the reference to Revelation 19:7, "The Bride of the Lamb joy-fully weddeth her Spouse"? Far more objectionable were exaggerations that are actually orgiastic: "There is a fountain filled with blood drawn from Emmanuel's veins, and sinners plunged beneath that flood. . . ." Children's hymns were just as bad, being little better than mock-feudal rhyming pruderies. God, they are reminded, "marks thine every deed and word" to see if they "kept their bodies pure." They were promised a heaven stuffed with harps, bright raiment, pas-tures, banners, golden pinions, diadems, and the supposedly pleasing spectacle of sinners looking their worst beside rapturous saints.

Maybe it was that churchpeople had never been very careful of the songs they sang in honor of their God. It was certainly preposterous to celebrate their adoration with lines that turned salvation into, of all things, a toilet bowl that "poured upon the night, drove away the shadows and *flushed* the world with light!" Accordingly, I took the bull by the horns and did some research. The result was accepted by the much respected Manchester *Guardian,* which made it the leading article of the day under the heading "More Ancient Than Modern," a play upon the title of a popular hymn book. And subsequent letters to the editor suggested I was not alone in thinking that it was time hymns were improved.

Of course, our leader was incensed. His evangelical sensibilities were offended, and after the affair of the moldy hosts he found my implied criticism of his choice of hymns difficult to bear. However, the newspaper article provoked much discussion among the country's establishment. I was appointed to a special committee of the Oxford University Press to make recommendations for an entirely new hymn book which they hoped would bring more life and vigor to congrega-tional singing. But to the consternation of the committee, I was unable to support more than half a dozen existing compositions, mostly of simple rationalist origin. When I was taxed with being an Anglo-Catholic, an intellectual, who didn't know how ordinary people felt about such things, I was able to tell them not only about my prayer book experiment but also about our Church youth club, of which the vicar had put me in charge. It was a responsibility which, for the time being at least, took my mind off what I hoped were not unusual and probably unfounded doubts about Christianity. In the event, it served to reinforce them.

The Youth Club met, as most such clubs do, in the Church Hall, once every week. The youths that had been coming to this club did so, one must suppose, because of its distance from the town and the freedom it offered from parents. They were all teenage girls and boys who rarely set foot inside a church. The girls at that time wore their skirts very short and their hair long. The boys were Teddy boys, their hair greased back and up, falling forward in carefully managed disarray over their foreheads, with long sideburns but otherwise clean-shaven. Their bodies were clothed in long, usually black, half-frock coats with padded shoulders, which flapped about their narrow waists. Their pants were drainpipes: skin tight, reaching down to triumphant "winkle pickers," shoes or booties the toes of which came to long slender points. If they had lived in a previous century, their pointed toes might have curled up and back upon themselves in an ecstasy of sartorial elegance. It was a fashion that inevitably exaggerated differences in gender: the boys with strong, hard-muscled legs, bulging genitalia, and long aggressive feet balanced by heads made arrogant by sideburns emphasizing their jaws and cheekbones above broad, padded shoulders; and the girls, their "birds," flouncing about, showing off luxuriant hair, their short skirts exposing the folds of plump buttocks and thighs leading the heterosexual eye, and no doubt the lesbian eye also, up to obvious panties.

The wild, untamed lawlessness of these youngsters was fascinating and sometimes terrifying. To me, trapped by my upbringing, education, and professional training, they seemed gloriously free. (Later, drag queens in furtive downtown bars would strike me the same way.) Although I was an outsider—cultivated, unnatural, and oddest of all a priest—I was drawn to explore our Youth Club as if it were another world with different values. Unable and unwilling to hide my sexual preference, inert though it was, I would openly admire the boys (something I discovered heterosexual adults rarely did, seeing in them only competitors), and compliment the girls on their choice of boyfriends. Thus I was often approached by boys who to the delight of their friends would openly flirt with me. Though they could see I was "queer," the most contemptuous adjective in their vocabulary, they would try to set me up with mates among themselves, and when I told them it was useless to make fun of me, they ceased trying. My long black cassock, when I wore it, was considered by both girls and boys to be attractive. Like their own Edwardian garb, it was fancy dress from another age. But when dancing began none offered to dance with me. Their dancing was their religion and perhaps did as much for them as did communion for their elders. However, they seemed to recognize it was the church that had offered them sanctuary and appeared grateful for it. Their home life was all too often punctuated by shouted abuse from exhausted mothers and drunken fathers.

Hidden inside their black Edwardians, the boys carried weapons. Knives were common, but knuckledusters guaranteed prestige, as did the modified bicycle chains some carried rolled up in their wide pockets. Each link of these chains had been filed to razor sharpness and when wielded horizontally so that the chain became immediately rigid, they could slice through clothes and into necks and limbs with comparative ease. This arsenal was an insurance in time of "rumbles."

Sometimes we would learn from parents who had overheard their sons' conversation that a rumble was underway. As this term implies, it was evidence of gang warfare fast maturing in the area and we would close the youth club for the next month lest the ensuing battles break out on church premises. The girls, too, would warn us when their boyfriends had determined to fight and would always seem saddened when they did, as if they were already women preparing to mourn the loss of their menfolk on real battlefields of the future. As priests, we were angered by the readiness to maim and even kill, and our leader, true to his belief in a God of compassionate intervention, would offer up prayers in hopes of preventing the inevitable.

Immensely attractive as I, and their girlfriends, found our Teddy boys, they did not often take advantage of me. I was their "father." They were reverent in their own way, dutifully mumbling the Lord's Prayer whenever I blessed them at the end of each weekly dance. Some would come for Confirmation lessons, and when they "stepped out" or finally wanted marriage, we would marry them and Ernie, ever generous, would baptize their babies regardless of the date of birth, at a specially devised solemn High Mass.

One of the girls, growing up, left the club and sang soprano in the church choir. It was she who one day sought my advice. She had been married for several years and had a daughter, but told me she was now in love again. Anxiously she asked if she could trust me. "I know how you are," she said. "That's why I want to talk to you, because I think I must be too."

She had fallen desperately in love, she told me, with the teenage daughter of one of the Church sidesmen. She wanted to declare her love. We spent anxious hours trying to resolve a situation for which the church, still ignorant of sexual orientation and its complexities, had nothing to offer except excommunication. Was her love evil, she wanted to know. Was she a sinner? Should she excommunicate herself and stay away from mass? These and other almost mediaeval questions, spawned by the intransigent and ignorant teaching that the church had long fostered, were tearing her apart.

Counseling and therapy in those days had no more answers than the church. Only Roman Catholics, secure in age-old formulas, brooking no compromise with scientific fact, would have ready answers, however tough to bear. My own defiance of church doctrine on the subject was the only evidence this young woman had ever found that love was love regardless of gender and, I told her, as acceptable to God as any other love; but even this defied official teaching, as I knew. How could love be evil, or such tears as she was shedding be sin? Yet there were important practical considerations that she needed to take into account. I urged her to love at a distance, as I did myself, and to continue caring for her earlier responsibilities, the family now dependent upon her. Who could tell, I offered, what the future might hold in store? Even the most passionate feelings may change or be replaced by others. She could, perhaps, seek counseling—even marriage counseling, since it was unlikely that her husband had no inkling of her state. Revealing her feelings to her beloved was ill advised: both the girl and her parents would be troubled by the disclosure, and, in those days, without effect. My advice was similar, I hoped, to that which our leader had given only the previous month to a married young woman who had fallen in love with me and left a passionate note to that effect beneath a bar of soap in my bathroom.

Because the subject was not openly discussed until quite recently, it has sometimes been supposed that people did not fall in love with those of the same gender until the 1970s and that consequently the homosexual (a late Victorian term) is a modern invention. But centuries of records show this to be false. Passionate physical as well as so-called Platonic loves regardless of gender seem always to have occurred as a fact of life. Lord Alfred Douglas's allusion to the "love that dare not speak its name" rang true because those who experienced it did not have a satisfactory name to call it by. And research has now shown that there were couples and groups of what we now call gay people even in the early Christian world, as why should there not have been?

Our daily house celebrations continued, their prayers and oblations piling up week by week at the feet of our seemingly indifferent God. My instinctive distress at such devotional junketing was exacerbated by the eventual discovery that much of the parishioners' supposed willingness to have mass said in their homes on such a regular basis and at such early hours was only skin deep. The women were entranced by the vicar's persuasive ways, his tall, imposing figure with its mane of dark hair, his searching eyes and earnest sermons. Some of the men were openly contemptuous of our daily parade and some stopped coming to church altogether, thus undermining what the House Church was designed to achieve.

Concerned lest this lack of enthusiasm for spiritual progress might spread despite our mass production of communions, we priests accordingly took part in group training sessions organized by the local diocese. Some of these sessions were led by a psychologist celebrated for his ability to give Christian meaning to what was then modern therapeutic theory. I hoped briefly that he would provide objective explanations for what was troubling me about Christianity in general.

Seated in a circle, overlooking the psychologist's garden, we were each conjured to present a problem that had come up in the course of our parish ministries. Being still a virgin who had only kissed those I adored, I was about to offer a question about homosexuality in church life, when the psychologist made it quite plain that in his view men might like other men only when reminded of women. Buttocks, he claimed, reminded homosexual men of breasts, and the young male's skin of women's skin.

I was dismayed. He might be plumbing the depths of Freudian psychology but he was also merely transferring his own heterosexual desires onto us. The seed is not the tree, and there are good reasons for left-handedness, lopsided faces, and small stature. There are also reasons why we have only two hands. Who knows whether, despite the need of the species to procreate, everyone's sexual energy may not one day, absent cultural pressure to do otherwise, also be directed at everyone regardless of gender? To listen to this man, it seemed that not only the heterosexual church but also heterosexual science had become out of touch with reality.

As a priest, I was to be faced with many personal problems with difficult twists and turns, some of which, I know, my mentor purposely and wisely set before me. Such were the usual ingredients of the priestly life, and it was good that I should learn them. However, some were more telling than others and caused me to wonder not only about the Christian message but more generally about humanity and our place in the universe. Such questions were eventually to converge in a single question with a single answer, but for the time being they jostled uneasily within me.

There was research, for instance, that I undertook for the sociologist Peter Townsend on behalf of the Nuffield Institute to determine why London's working-class poor refused to leave their slums to live in newly built model towns outside the capital. The poor assigned to me lived in Katherine Buildings, Stepney, overlooking the eternally busy Royal Mint. It was a dark, Dickensian brick building ten floors high. Its inhabitants lived out their lives listening to the rumble of machinery producing instant wealth next door. It had been designed with the help and advice of Sydney and Beatrice Webb, who, with George Bernard Shaw and H. G. Wells, had formed the famous league of socialists known as the Fabians who believed in infiltrating conservative thinking rather than direct attack. (Significantly the Webbs, limousine liberals, later joined the nobility.) Iron balconies ran round each floor of Katherine Buildings and were reached by two black iron staircases, one at each end, serving a total of some hundred apartments. Three metal chutes were attached to the balcony at each level, and carried garbage down to bins at the ground floor.

Though the apartments sometimes housed two families, they were tiny. Each one contained a fireplace whose chimney joined the nest of chimneys on the roof; apartments had no bathtub or shower, only a small lavatory bowl; and outside, on the balcony, a single faucet served only cold water to the entire floor. Water was collected in buckets and heated individually by each family on their tiny gas stove as needed. Each apartment also contained a large cupboard, ceiling high. This cupboard had been specially designed by Beatrice Webb and contained several divisions for crockery at the top, clothing below the crockery, food below the clothing, and coal in the box at the bottom. Many of the apartments I visited stank because the ancient sewer pipe that ran brokenly along each floor enabled rats, attracted by the scent of food, to eat through to the cabinet. The coal in the bottom of the cabinet would then fall into the rat holes and often blocked the sewer.

Although none of the inhabitants went to church or had much respect for it, many families talked to me, but some individuals were recalcitrant. An elderly retired marine who had fought in the war lived by himself and permitted me into his tiny room only after much cajoling and reassurance that I was not a police officer in disguise. He was an obsessive collector. His tiny room, the odor of which nearly caused me to vomit on the doorstep, was crowded with statues of the Virgin Mary standing in glass domes, many of them broken. He had also collected his urine in bowls and buckets which he stored around the walls, because his toilet was stopped up and he didn't know what do with it all. He had been assigned a modest home in the model town, but, like the others, had refused to leave. He had no relatives and the only people he knew or who knew him were his neighbors. Indeed, it also seemed as if all the families had intermarried and the building now housed aunts, uncles, and cousins, none of whom wished to leave their relatives. In the stress of poverty, family relations are critical to survival. Blood lines and alliances are also important to those in power, but only wealthier people can afford to live apart and independently. The poor need all the help they can get, and these people knew it. They weren't about to be shifted by politicians eager for votes to keep them in office, however condescending their policies. The solution to this particular problem seemed to be to move all one hundred families at the same time and blow the place up, a plan quite beyond the powers or the imagination of government officials.

Ernie once arranged for me to meet a special parishioner who was also a hospital patient. He suffered from lupus, a disease that can have terrible effects. His face, as such, hardly existed; only raw flesh still attached to the living skull, with rimless eyeballs and two holes for a nose above teeth still in position but protruding from gums from which the lips were distorted and pulled back, mere pieces of dark red skin. A nauseating odor exuded from what flesh was left upon the bones and he wore a pink plastic mask that hid the more unsightly parts but made him seem somehow impersonal, robotlike. Despite the severe and terminal nature of his disfigurement, a nurse had married him, but he now believed it had been for his money rather than out of hoped-for compassion, and he despised her for it. I could find little to offer by way of consolation. The promise of a happier life hereafter seemed a blandishment that argued in favor of suicide, just as Job's story raised questions that have been answered only by blind faith.

One day, I visited him and sat by his bed. Suddenly, he whipped away the mask to display the horror that lay underneath.

"How d'you like it, eh?" he whispered.

He tested all his visitors this way to remind them, so he said, that sympathy and prayers meant little in the actual face of such a loss. I grasped his hand and, leaning over, kissed what remained of his forehead. Was I not faceless too? Great tears oozed from the raw skin around the eyeballs. And then I blessed him as I knew I should, but he had made me think again, more troubled than ever.

Whatever the true explanation of existence, divine as well as human, it had to comprehend such conditions of life and make sense of them. Besides the victims of disease, I knew also of hospitals and homes for veterans with no limbs at all, their faces quite burned away, no mouths with which to speak. Christianity claimed to offer hope to all humanity, but in the conditional nature of its hope, did it not fail as a panacea? Yet, I thought, a *pan*acea is surely what we need! Whatever the answer is, it must include us all.

As if to confirm how far Christians still were from all-inclusiveness,

I was one day called upon to visit the family of the senior church warden who had two teenage sons, one of whom was an acolyte. When I arrived at the house, this time within the "professional" part of the parish, the elder of the two teenagers, aged eighteen and apparently returned from a tour of duty in the Guards, was polishing his army boots on the front doorstep. I had not seen him before, as he was always away guarding Buckingham Palace. He looked up as I arrived and a pair of startling blue eyes met mine. It was a face of steel, bronzed, beautiful, and unsmiling. We talked briefly. His parents were out. Yes, he was on leave. No, he didn't come home much. What did he do in London? He spat on a boot and then, looking up at me, said, "I beat up queers." Instead of arguing, I fled. Could I have made a difference? I knew only that the Nazis and the SS also used to say and do such things.

THE BOX

1958

The House Church, like the worker-priest movement, was never so successful or widespread as our leader's enthusiasm would have had us believe. Wesley, long ago, had managed to siphon off the evangelical enthusiasms that more than two hundred years ago resulted in Methodism. Indeed, the Methodists of the parish, well ensconced within the professional classes and rarely seen in working-class homes, looked askance at our efforts. Eventually, however, we managed to attract considerable publicity in both Britain and the United States, among Protestants in general.

Ernie having consequently become something of a celebrity in his own right, we were visited by various journalists, among them Peter Hamilton, a producer for the British Broadcasting Corporation who had also heard of my attempts to reform religious language. At a dinner party we learned that the BBC had commissioned Hamilton for an "OB" or remote broadcast outside the studio, on live national television, of the anniversary of the founding of the famous Guisborough Priory in the twelfth century. The broadcast was to take place in two weeks' time.

During dessert the producer turned to me. "Would you care to have a hand at the commentary?" he asked.

"I've never written a script," I told him.

"But you seem to understand how ordinary people think and speak. I'll show you how, if you're game to have a go."

Some visual sequences had already been shot or decided upon; the commentator would have to refer to these while covering the entire proceedings from beginning to end. I researched the history of the Priory buildings and the land and the occupations of the people round

about and wrote an hour-long script in such a way that the commentator would give meaning to the pictures on the screen without
describing them—a basic rule, the producer told me, and too often
broken.

I wrote the script in a couple of days and it so pleased the producer
that he followed it up with a voice test, and I was hired to be both
scriptwriter and commentator. I was not to be seen on camera but
would wear a "lip mike" and be installed behind a pillar in an aisle of
the mediaeval building where the ceremony was to take place.

Rehearsals went according to plan. A remote truck was parked
some distance away, stuffed with engineers, monitors, and the production crew, who would watch and produce the broadcast by remote
control. Heavy cables stretched from the truck, winding around
tombstones dating from the twelfth century, and through great carved
doors, finally to snake about to four mobile cameras stationed inside.
These were each strategically placed, one on a trolley to cover various
aspects of the ceremony, the others to catch reactions from the audience. Immense lights were placed behind pillars, pointing upward
from under pews, to show off the carved stone ceiling, while microphones were placed among the roof beams and beside the various
podia to be used for speeches.

The main events of the ceremony included several processions, and
speeches to be given by local dignitaries, a royal personage, and an
archbishop standing in a floodlit pulpit. We had the texts of the
speeches, and I had carefully contrived my script to include not-too-
subtle references and echoes of their meanings in the course of a historical commentary. The speeches referred to such subjects as "the
press," "the mediaeval craftsmen whose families are still among us,"
"the elderly and the little children," and so on. Such phrases were to
be illustrated by cleverly orchestrated camera work, with close-ups
and pans that would relieve the usual tedium of the focus on speakers'
faces.

Both cameras and crews had been rehearsed according to the script
and were positioned so that as the words were spoken they could tilt
up or down and in panning, as if it were by chance, could get good
shots of the very items or people being referred to. To enable this to
work smoothly we had affixed a newspaper to a chair and ordered an
old-age pensioner and a small child to occupy particular seats, while
an entire ancient family of craftspeople, discovered after much trouble, were to gather in a special corner near one of the statues. So that
the historical references in the script would also be properly timed I
was given a small television monitor which I was to watch—and

watch nothing else, since it would show what was actually being broadcast to the nation.

"All you have to do is sit glued to the screen," Peter Hamilton told me. "Don't look about or you'll be distracted and miss what the cameras are doing. And listen to me. I'll be coming in on your right ear. You'll hear the program in your left."

I looked at the earphones and then at the lip mike. It seemed more like a mask than a microphone.

"It fits tight round your mouth so that it doesn't pick up any other sound but your voice. Now remember," he continued seriously. "It's no use referring to things if the audience can't see them. And you mustn't speak to anyone at all under any circumstances, because whatever you say will be heard by the audience around the world."

On the day of the broadcast, the ancient building with its towers and windows was made even more spectacular by floodlights even though it was daytime. However, the local public must have awaited the event for months and were no orderly, easily accommodated group. Instead we were faced with a mob of citizens who began pouring through the doors very early, crowding inside in ever greater numbers. They tripped over the cables, filled all the seats, and quickly overflowed the place, finally sitting on the floor or the backs of chairs and standing three or four deep along whatever steps could be found. I had been stationed, with a cushion beneath me, on the stone floor beside my column and quickly felt my back being attacked by the shoes of those pushing hard to get a view of the proceedings. My monitor had been strapped to the column before me and was several times nearly demolished.

Eventually, in my right ear, I heard someone from the calm of the remote truck announce "ten minutes to go." At this, the picture on the screen before me, which had been carrying our own camera shots, suddenly changed as I had been warned it would to the program that preceded ours. I could hear its music in my left ear while the producer's calm instructions to cameras and their replies came through in my right.

The people around me continued to make themselves felt but the noise was muffled by the earphones. My lip mike was in position. Then the producer's voice rose in frustration. The crowding in the place was causing confusion.

"Where is Mrs. Timmins? Find her, find her!"

Then a cameraman's voice: "Lost the newspaper, Peter. Someone's sat on it."

Then the producer again: "Can you find anyone, anyone with a child? Any child will do" and the reply: "Found a child but it went off. I can't find anything but heads now. How about matching them with gargoyles? No, forget that . . ."

This anxious, disembodied conversation, my introduction to the perils of live broadcasting, was sounding more and more urgent as the minutes passed. Soon the previous program I was watching gave signs of drawing to its close. In seconds I would be on the air!

I tried to forget the millions who, in my pride, I supposed would be listening to my every word. I concentrated on the tiny screen before me.

The producer's voice spoke in my right ear.

"Coming up to you, Bernard." And in the background the assistant director began counting me down.

"Ten, nine, eight, seven, six, five . . ." In my left ear another voice, this time broadcasting from London, announced my name, even as the screen in front of me suddenly changed to the preplanned view of the countryside round about taken from our mobile camera. I could hear muffled crowd noises in my left ear as the microphones picked them up, even as, in my right, I could hear the producer's voice.

". . . three, two, one . . . You're on! "

As I began speaking the view in my monitor panned and then dissolved into the inside of the very building where I was sitting on the stone floor, a shot taken from a camera immediately behind my head. I began by telling the history of the place and immediately there appeared on the screen a memorial tablet with an ancient date as another camera picked up the story exactly as I had planned it.

I was breathing normally now, though the lip mike was biting into my cheeks. The directions to cameras continued in my right ear all the time. I struggled not to listen to them.

Suddenly trumpets began blaring. Someone important had arrived in the midst of my introduction!

"Sorry about that, Bernard. Speak normally. Well done. It's going well. Coming to you, Camera Two. . . . Close-up, Camera One, when Bernard says "Children." Great . . . lovely. . . . Get that old man out of the way, someone. . . . Get round him. Move down from the roof, John, that's right . . . nice and slow."

Then, as we came to the mayor's speech: "Wait for it, Bernard, wait for him to appear. . . . Right . . . go!"

It was timed to the second, but as was usual with live broadcasts, anything might happen and it did. I was describing how the building had been founded, trying to sound spontaneous while also matching each shot with my voice: "The stone from which these magnificent gargoyles were sculpted came from ancient quarries first dug by the Romans. . . . The medieval craftsmen were the first masons organized into the guilds which—"

Suddenly, my monitor, my lifeline to what I was referring to, turned to snow. I stared at it and must have paused in shock.

"Don't stop, Bernard. Help him, Camera Two," came in my ear from the producer who, of course, did not know I was inexplicably "blind" and couldn't see what Camera Two was showing me. Nor could I tell anyone because whatever I said would be broadcast to the world! Another part of my brain, already addled by being fed two messages at once, began contriving ways to disclose the fact that I couldn't see: coded messages such as "If I could only see the roof beams" or "From my position I cannot see the Norman columns . . ." Instead, I had sufficient presence of mind only to chatter on aimlessly, hoping that the cameras could follow me, instead of I them. Eventually the pictures returned, but not before I had been reduced to a jellied wreck.

Apparently it was the perspective of my script that had made it appealing. My voice had also found favor far away in London and I was thereafter invited to give occasional reports on programs organized by the BBC's Religious Department. The errant official who had tugged at a bothersome cable had almost concluded a promising career before it began, but I was never to look back. The modern media had me in their grasp.

In 1958 our parish remained on the tourist route. We were visited by spiritual leaders of a variety of denominations interested in the revival of Wesleyan methods. There were also economic reasons for the interest. The slow decline of practicing Christianity in Britain since the end of the Second World War was causing anxiety among those whose responsibility it was to keep open the doors of our ancient heritage. Despite the establishment of the church in Britain, the income that clergy might expect from their parishes to pay for the heating and upkeep of church fabric as well as to pay their salaries had diminished considerably. The number of parishioners at Evensong, for example, had dropped to no more than a handful. Indeed, I would sometimes find myself saying this office to a congregation of one, usually a woman. Many clergy had been forced by such lack of enthusiasm to abandon all services except Eucharist or Holy Communion and to say the other obligatory offices in the privacy of their vestries.

Across the Atlantic, whence many of our visitors came, scientific discoveries had long been largely ignored or dismissed by the widespread religious fundamentalism that increasing social turmoil had only reinforced. Yet even there the churchification of society was beginning to diminish. There was a church on every corner and churchgoing was allied with the patriotism of the so-called American Way, but disillusionment with traditional organized religion had been slowly but surely reducing the size of mainstream church congregations. Sects were congealing around charismatic leaders intent upon feathering their own nests. It was also the time of Norman Vincent Peale's *The Power of Positive Thinking* and of the Niebuhr brothers, Reinhold and H. Richard, who by then had taken up political activism. Paul Tillich had been offering the world a new approach to relationships between God and creation. The influential psychologist Rollo May was causing a stir with his marriage of theological and psychological theory, while Bishop Fulton Sheen was holding a strong Roman Catholic front on television. Among American attempts to stop the spread of doubt, one ambitious plan called for a specially designed Garden of Meditation where all faiths (usually meaning Christian churches) might meet and find evidence of their unity in New Harmony, Indiana.

The House Church appeared to be another such experiment to these hopeful Americans, and eventually it attracted a film crew to document our work. "They're coming with some kind of bishop," Ernie told us. "I think he's Congregational." He couldn't hide the disdain in his voice. "They're going to film us as we go about the parish. I'll explain the House Church, and then they're taking us all to Scotland. The film's meant to contrast two ways of renewal for the church. Ours, and the new monasticism on Iona."

"But isn't that community Presbyterian?" one of us asked.

"Presbyterian, Congregationalist, it's all the same in America." And with this we had to be content.

Our visitors were a senior minister of the United Church of Christ and Robert Newman, the documentary film director. Our faithful were interviewed and their daily lives exposed to view. We said our masses just as we had been doing, in kitchens, dining rooms, even garages. We were then carried off to the rocks and winds of the island of Iona where Duncan, of my family's clan, one time king of Scotland, and perhaps Macbeth, his murderer, were said to be buried.

Robert Newman took pictures of everything: the cliffs, the sea, the gulls screaming overhead; we priests wandering about, our black cassocks blowing in the wind; the brothers of the Iona Community at their meals, saying their prayers, and making bread. I remember admiring a slender Scottish brother, freckled, wearing shorts showing strong young thighs, tanned from the salt wind, his grey eyes quite at peace in all the wildness about us. Ernie and his friend Macleod of Macleod, both tall, imposing prophets, kept talking of the "holiness" of the place. Yet there was a strange coolness between this High Anglican and the Presbyterian Laird. Both were intent upon convert-ing the world, and history had made them wary of each other. Their denominations had spilt much blood between them, and this isle remembered it. It would give an unexpected edge to the documentary being made, as would the contrast between our working-class congre-gation with its rough, tough Youth Club and the quiet piety of this island sanctuary: two faces of the many-faceted enthusiasm called Christianity.

On our arrival back in Yorkshire, our American guests took me aside. "This country's no place for you," they said. "You should be in the States."

Such an idea had never occurred to me. "America" was not a coun-try, it was a dream—a wondrous world peopled with heroes and hero-ines, tall white towers, a place throbbing with enormous, unap-proachable power, a land of saviors whom you called upon when in need and who came bursting in from far away; a nation of whom the entire world was envious, admiring, and increasingly afraid.

"If we sent you a ticket," they went on, "would you consider it?"

"A ticket?" I replied. "That'll be the day!" And went back to our daily masses and my Teddy boys.

But within a month, a paper typed on delicate white onionskin let-terhead arrived, offering me the directorship of the Judson student house in Washington Square at the heart of Greenwich Village, Man-hattan. Enclosed with it was a round-trip air ticket to New York. If I accepted I would be an assistant pastor with Howard Moody, a cele-brated former marine who was also attempting to convert the world. I was still in my twenties and could not bring myself to refuse such gen-erosity, though my acceptance would certainly change life as I had known it.

Before leaving Britain, I decided to set down my beliefs as I had once done ten years before. They ended up nearly twenty thousand words long, written in a tight spidery hand. They examined God from the point of view of creation, the place of Jesus and humans in the universe, and our duties in relation to all this. It concluded with ideal-istic abandon that a human must consciously decide that every part of him and all he owns is available for other people should they want them. He must keep himself and his possessions free and available until he dies. The overall strategic purpose behind creation was to "control" matter and put it to good use, ignorance and pain being thought of simply as matter out of control. Stern Puritan fears were still strong within me.

At the end of my last Youth Club dance, the Teddy boys and their birds crowded out to their motorcycles. Among them was an unattractive boy, the toughest looking Teddy of them all, idly swinging his bicycle chain, his knuckleduster glittering across his fingers, threatening the world around.

"I wanna tork to you, Father," he snapped and nodded me to one side of the crowd, which went on, leaving us together.

"Come 'ere," he said.

All unsuspecting, I followed him to the side of the hall where it was dark. Was I to be cut up?

Instead, he rolled up his chain, pulled me on to himself, clumsily thrust his face onto mine and began kissing me. Passionately he forced his tongue into my mouth and clutched me to himself with both arms.

"Goodbye, Bernard. I'll miss yer," he whispered hoarsely; and releasing me, he walked slowly off to his bike and joined his mates.

I had carried my heart in tatters for so long now that this simple violence quite undid me. Unsure what it meant, I hoped the use of my name signified real affection and not some insult or pretended thing. Perhaps he was already telling the others what he had managed to do to the pansy priest? I tried to write it off, but never have. In a culture where love and sexual affections are so damnably suppressed, denied, and hidden, how many millions must continue to stifle and cripple their true selves for nonsensical reasons and, above all, to please intellectual tyrants claiming to speak for God? The moral theologians indeed considered every aspect of sexuality known to them as fairly as they could, but because they feared to undermine existing doctrine and imperil their immortal souls their conclusions were mistaken; that I know, if I know anything.

I visited my theological college. It had meant a lot to me, one way and another. As I slowly climbed the stone-black streets toward the Community, I wondered how many centuries more the Christian Church had to survive. In the New World of which I knew nothing but myths, would Christianity be the same? How would I fare? I caught up with a favorite brother on his way to Terce. He looked as usual ebullient, untroubled by the fate of anything.

"Say hello for me to the Bowery Bums!" was his response to my news.

Who were they, I asked him. "You'll find out," he laughed, and left me for his devotions.

The College corridors were quiet. The rooms where I had loved so hopelessly now had other occupants. Preparing for what?

Then it was time to say farewell to Ernie and his family and to the many friends I'd made. Leaving the vicarage, I picked up the latest parish magazine on its way to being mailed around the world. Glancing inside, I saw the vicar's "Parish Letter." It began: "Dear Parishioners: Bernard Mayes is queer." A final Parthian shot? I looked again. No, he had not written "a queer," but only "queer," and went on to include everyone as being somehow odd. I had long been "out," as we say now; nonetheless it was a warning. Had I been living in a fool's paradise?

THE VILLAGE

1958-1959

I arrived in New York on what I quickly learned from the lack of work being done was Labor Day, 1958. My first American paradox. I was greeted by a handsome young woman and her husband in their car.

"I'm to be your secretary," said she.

And they took me on a tour of lower Manhattan with its phallic skyscrapers standing serene and proud amidst empty, silent streets on holiday. It was love at first sight.

From the canyons of Wall Street I was taken to the Village. Greenwich Village, I was informed, was like nowhere else on earth, and I quickly found this to be exactly so. Once no more than fields and cow pastures two miles north of the original Battery that was once New Amsterdam on the tip of Manhattan island, the village of Greenwich had been laid out in 1811. Crisscrossed by Indian trails leading to the island's coast, the hamlet had accumulated shacks and small dwellings, then more substantial houses, first along the trails and footpaths and then officially by blocks. Several times it had been a sanctuary from the yellow fever epidemics that beset the residential area of the Battery behind its "Wall" and thereafter had slowly grown until it reached from the gallows in the potter's field (now Washington Square) across to the piers on the waterfront and down to the Wall itself, becoming a haven for original New Yorkers. The later waves of European immigrants usually went elsewhere, leaving the Village to itself. Its narrow winding streets embodied histories all their own: Waverly Place, Minetta Lane, Gay Street, Christopher Street, and Bleeker, where the stalls sold everything from clothes to mussels and an American invention called "meat loaf."

It became the home of artists of all kinds, poets, and philosophers.

Isadora Duncan danced in its parlors, the anarchist Emma Goldman, offered political seminars, and Mrs. Gertrude Vanderbilt Whitney sculpted statues of beautiful nude young men. Eugene O'Neill wrote plays for the Provincetown Theater on MacDougal Street, and Edna St. Vincent Millay wrote poems while young men fell in love with her sisters. James Joyce's revolutionary *Ulysses* was first published here in installments by the *Little Review* of Margaret Anderson and jane heap (who insisted that her name be printed in lower case). It was also here, in 1918, that the first *Playboy* magazine had been founded by Egmont Arens, working over the Washington Square Bookshop on the corner of West 8th Street. It was advertised as being "free from puritanic suppressions," and was "daringly modern . . . the magazine of today!"

Judson Student Center lay behind the campanile of the Judson Memorial Church on the corner of Washington Square at the foot of Fifth Avenue. Designed, as was Washington Square Arch, by Stanford White in stripes of yellow brick, the church was built in 1890 to honor the memory of the Baptist missionary Adoniram Judson, who compiled the first Burmese dictionary. Attached to a set of rooms on Thompson street was one where Edgar Allen Poe is reputed to have written "The Imp of the Perverse." My lodgings were in what was thought to have been his bedroom. The walls, painted a bright orange, bulged ominously in the shape of hidden corpses.

Overhead lay other rooms and cubicles granted to undergraduates from nearby New York University, the "halls" of which were across the street on the site of the old city university. There it was that Samuel Morse had experimented with telegraphy and designed his famous code, and Samuel Colt had perfected his revolver. So, almost immediately, I found myself engulfed in histories which until then I knew nothing of. Tom Paine, author of the deistic *Age of Reason,* had died in the Village, an unrepentant "infidel" who still believed in God. Raison Street had even been named for him.

Washington Square, now a park, had been the site of stonecutters' riots in 1855; it was still lined on the side opposite to Judson by pretty Georgian row houses where once the wealthy of lower Manhattan had taken up residence to be safe from the fever. It was now notorious for its pot-smoking teenagers, its avid chess players, its gay hustlers, and its folksingers. When, finally, I managed to shed my prudery, and got to know the inhabitants, I became enamored of Village ways, its crowded coffee shops, the new "pizza parlors," the complicated pattern of Old World streets with their taverns filled with talk, smoke, and handsome men.

*   *   *

My job was to look after some two dozen students of all religions and backgrounds, and also to help with Judson's Sunday services. That I had been trained a high Anglo-Catholic did not worry them or me. Real Christianity, I now thought, was too big, too generous a thing to insist upon such petty distinctions. Moreover, I was invited by my BBC producers to file regular recorded reports on life in New York and elsewhere, and the more varied the life, the more my location suited such a task. I had entered a world different from anything I, or most of my British friends and colleagues, had ever experienced, and Britain, the Church of England, even the Queen of England, seemed suddenly alien. Indeed, I had to take care lest I became too enthusiastic and turned "native," losing that essential journalistic "cool."

For a time I was lionized. Learning that I had arrived, the editors of the *Village Voice* quickly fastened on me as likely to provide objective criticism of America in general. I filed a piece they refused to print as being far too positive. They had expected British Marxist contempt for capitalism, whereas I told them I found New York exciting and America a land of promise where change actually happened and where the people could take life into their own hands. A BBC friend from Oxford who emigrated shortly after me described this feeling as "knowing that the land belongs to us, whereas in Britain we knew it all belonged to them," meaning the elites and the aristocracy. This feeling was almost immediately and violently confirmed by a riot that took place in Washington Square itself. Just as the *Village Voice* had predicted, local landlords eager to increase their profits had allegedly conspired with the governor of New York to close the square and turn it into a private enclave for the wealthy. The Village erupted. Everyone joined the demonstration on behalf of the People's right to sing wherever they wanted. Urged on by my students, I joined the fray, all too visible in my new striped pullover, and was nearly deported then and there. It was my first experience of what is meant by civil rights.

I had not been more than a few days in Manhattan when I lost my virginity. A dinner party hosted by Robert Newman, at whose invitation I had come to New York, included several couples and a young man who found my hand under the table, took me back home, and made love to me. Or tried to—I was still inexperienced—but the feel of another man's hands upon me at long last, of muscles as firm and as powerful as my own, enlarged my awareness of the world and seemed to strengthen as nothing had ever done before the truth of my existence. Genteel culture and its pruderies were suddenly eclipsed by this man's affection, his strong need of me. It was a revelation of God's own creation, of its beauty and loving-kindness; a rapture. The world did not fall apart; instead it was renewed. It was a revelation of humanity breaking in upon a world that had hitherto been peopled by dreams and shadows. Most of us did not yet describe ourselves as "gay," but we knew well enough our existence was authentic, not imagined. As my sudden lover whispered to me, I had "left the past behind."

Quite soon afterwards, when some visiting Baptist students reported to Howard Moody, our senior pastor, that they had discovered I was a homosexual, he told them that he knew it, called me in, and informed me that he had, of course, been told what he supposed had been my secret long before. "I discussed it with my wife," he explained. "And we decided that if there was nothing wrong with us making love in a consecrated building, there was nothing wrong with you doing so either. Anyway, it's not you I mind," he went on, "it's pansies I don't like." Unwilling to test this highly suspect, new-made alliance too soon, I left its challenge for another day. I was not to leave it for long. A whole new world had opened up, and almost at once I embraced my rediscovered nature, fully, wholeheartedly. And sitting in my new, truly romantic home, I tried to think things through.

I saw that the state of being homosexual, operating within an environment predetermined over the centuries by a tyrannical heterosexual majority, forced us who were this way to hide from ourselves and from others and sometimes quite unconsciously to associate our most precious feelings and affections with darkness, guilt, fear, and punishment. But as if in compensation, this also granted us a view of human existence that the heterosexual majority, inhibited in other ways, could experience only with difficulty.

At the same time, too many of us, struggling in vain to cross over into the heterosexual world, became obsessed with pleasing others rather than ourselves, and lived, as I did, virginal, puritanical lives, seemingly content to accept the judgement of the world around them and to conform their appetites to the common rule. Very many of these not only managed to pass as heterosexual but were proud to have done so, even while they hid their real selves by being what they described as discreet, often to the point of denying or betraying their own.

Still others, wallowing in excess, gorged themselves on the forbidden fruits. Some even claimed that since our judges did not grant us the right to an existence, what we did must not exist either, so why worry?

But however we managed our situation, we also sought to push back the loneliness we were likely to feel by ignoring the contempt and even by embracing the pain of rejection. Such substitutions can become a way of life, a pretense that all is well when, in fact, we have merely become hard, callous, and dismissive of sensibilities in which otherwise we might have rejoiced.

Finally, as it was then doing with me, our orientation may adjust our intellectual view of the whole of existence, of religion, and of whatever we call our God. During my Greenwich Village days I had only begun to sense this change, but exposure to new discoveries and intellectual adventures had already begun to encroach upon beliefs that until shortly before I had thought were impermeable. My new life was encouraging, perhaps even demanding, a fresh look at the nature of things.

Something like this seems also to have happened to Lucretius, born a hundred years before Jesus, and seventeen hundred years later to the Dutch Jewish thinker Baruch Spinoza, whose family had fled the Spanish Inquisition and whose thought helped prepare the way for new freedoms in what is now liberal Amsterdam. Lucretius it was who, on embracing the atomic teaching of Democritus and Epicurus's findings on happiness, concluded that all existence is of one kind and that the soul and the body are one entity. Spinoza appears to have thought something similar: that all existence is based in one substance which might properly be called "God." Those who feared abandoning the traditional way of thinking managed to silence both of them; only one manuscript of Lucretius has survived.

For years I too had found myself treading delicately, Ahab-like, lest the solid ground of orthodoxy might break and plunge me into the frigid waters of apostasy, the fate of those who like Hans Küng and Father Edward Schillebeeckx questioned overmuch. Those were hard thinkers indeed, battling even within themselves. The crust upon which I had been sojourning for so long was lavalike. A mental misstep could thrust me through into the seething pit of atheism that awaited all materialists. Moreover, being gay I walked a minefield doubly sown.

Yet even in the 1950s, at the heart of such struggles with reality, we gay people knew we were right, knew that we stood for a principle that could never be denied us. Some might become financially successful; some might be professionals; some might find contentment in the service sectors; some might become politicians; others might end in prison; many might die; but the truth of our existence would survive. We had suffered a myriad agonies of despair and deprivation; we clawed our way forward, sideways, upwards. We hid, became our own worst enemies, married, lied and pretended into safety. We were, as a popular national magazine once described us on its front cover, "the most despised minority in the world."

But although blacks might spit at us, whites turn on their heel, browns cut us dead, we each had our secret knowledge that we existed in our own right—that we were not artifacts, mistakes, or even heterosexuals who were merely misbehaving; we were authentic. We rarely took to violence; we did our bit for society, served in its hospitals, helped its poor, taught in its schools, fought in its wars, designed its palaces, prepared its food, made its movies, and even helped run the country. This is why we are subversive. We have done so much for society and yet to have accepted us would have undermined what heterosexual Christians had taken centuries to establish: the subservience of women, the rights of machismo, sex as sin, the body as temptation, materialism as ungodly, religious dogma as incontestable.

It's a wonder we survived. Once discovered, we were doomed. This was why for centuries we appeared to be so few, hidden among the general population. And this was also why we each thought ourselves the only one in the world. Yet we went on loving even though the percentages were (and still are) appalling. Even if Kinsey's large 10 percent was correct, among every ten people only one might be gay. Out of this restricted pool of potential romantic partners, few might like you; and of that tiny number who might like you, you might be attracted to no more than one or two. Those one or two have also to be available; then, if available, compatible as well as aesthetically and intellectually acceptable.

If Kinsey's figures were exaggerated, then the situation was even worse. So we grabbed what we could, on the slightest chance of success. In doing so, we skimmed the surface, too often unable to commit, and the search continued. This is what supported the heterosexual myth that gay people are highly sexed and will go for anyone, but in fact it meant only that we were prepared to cross social lines. Thus we were forever looking for compatible needles in the human haystacks, whereas heterosexuals had virtually half the entire species to choose from, ready and waiting to be wooed.

I could now see that such a situation makes it especially tough on gay children and on parents, too, since parents are nearly always heterosexual. They raise their children with every expectation (and, indeed, hope) that they will be like themselves, with the result that gay children suffer terribly. They need caressing from the same-gender parent in the same way other children do from the opposite-gender parent. They need identification and models opposite from the identification and the models welcomed by other children; and they need spoken reinforcement when they choose models different from those other children choose. As their sexuality develops, they long to touch, hold, and caress not children of the opposite sex, but children of the same sex; to take them out, make dates, enjoy physical excitements with them. To be forced to do otherwise warps and twists their personality into hiding, pretending, withdrawing with shame and guilt. Gay people in an aggressively heterosexual culture like ours grow up to be extremely needy of physical affection and are likely to remain that way until they die. The relief that gay children exhibit when finally, often too late, they come out of the closet is a moving experience. One mother I met reported that her daughter was miserable, moody, obviously unhappy until the day she fell in love with another girl who responded, and then, the mother said, "it was like the sun had risen."

The Village, with its wide-ranging way of life, its bohemian values, and its exciting experiments, became my home. How dried up I had become! How shriveled in spirit and mind! Inhibition, rather than modesty, and the need for physical love so long suppressed for fear of retribution had taken their toll on me. I had never been permitted to enjoy dates, or necking with those I really liked. My physical need was, in fact, both chronic and insatiable—a condition I had to live with as best I could, and perhaps for the remainder of my days. Discredited theories of arrested development, parental imbalance, or even poor diet had assumed heterosexual development to be natural, inevitable, and universal, but certainly it was not.

Consequently, prickly though I still was, new flowers and shoots were budding within me. I met and was made love to by a poet, a painter, a playwright, and an actor. And also by gay teenagers yearning for a man to hold them in his arms and who begged to make love to me. Although the mutual sharing of unleashed affection and physical desire that these affairs called forth was relatively short-lived, they were far from being sordid or manipulative. Duration is no guarantee of worth. We would lie in each other's arms with such relief that sometimes even the ecstasies of orgasm were beyond us. When one of my younger lovers put his head on my shoulder and whispered, "If only we could live together for ever!" we knew it could be true only in dreams. To write off such relationships as "lust" ignores the importance of the body in love's expression, an importance long denied and vilified by Manichaean heterosexuals fearing both hellfire and babies.

Luckily, babies are an achievement gay sexuality finds impossible, so
that for us, the physical components of love, from kiss to caress and
ecstatic orgasm, need include no guilt.

On Sundays, still warmed from my new birth, I managed to deliver
a few faltering sermons about love and gratitude. I also assisted at
what I had been taught was a Nonconformist "memorial" rather than
a mass, handing out tiny glass cups of sweet wine to a variety of com-
municants.

Judson was a special place. Everyone seemed welcome: drag
queens, bums, intellectuals, and especially Jews, whose very ritual we
had reclaimed for our own. For my first despatch back to London I
quoted the famous lines of Emma Lazarus inscribed on the Statue of
Liberty, "Give me your tired, your poor, your huddled masses yearning to breathe free"—corny for native-born Americans, but when,
standing on the bow platform of the then five-cent Staten Island Ferry,
I turned to face New York, I too saw the spires and palaces of a
Promised Land and choked up at the sight. England was my home-
land, where my loving parents were, but like a cradle in the attic of
my brain, or an old tree stump where flowers now grew, it had
become and was to remain a place in the past.

One component of religion that continues to cause much heart-
searching, even anxiety, although the entire edifice of religion might
be said to depend on it, is our so-called soul. Ghosts, spirits, and the
importance of rescuing or saving one's immortal soul had been part of
my upbringing. During the first part of the century, psychic phenomena had become quite an industry, but since the war, the deaths of so
many millions had caused seances to seem profane. The celebrated
experiments of J. B. Rhine in what he described as "parapsychology,"
conducted at Duke University in the 1940s, had provoked further discussion, but they had mainly to do with telekinesis. Spirits themselves
seemed somehow out of bounds. Back in Britain, I myself had been
fascinated by the story of Borley Rectory, which, like Bailey Piers, had
supposedly been haunted by ghosts and poltergeists for years. The
BBC had even persuaded itself to permit a commentator to spend the
night in the rectory equipped with microphones, cameras, and an
emergency telephone in case of "accidents." The resulting programs
and books had apparently been inconclusive.

Accordingly, I was surprised that one day, over lunch with a producer of broadcast religious programs in Britain, in a quiet, intimate
basement restaurant just off Fifth Avenue, he recounted an unsettling
experience which, he said, had to do with spirits and still caused him
much worry.

Like many others in religious broadcasting, he was himself a member of the Christian clergy, apparently devoted to the cause of converting the world to his faith, but in the modern British way, which meant as discreetly as possible. The religious broadcasting department of which he was a part even sported a "choir" of some dozen adult voices who, although they rarely sang quite in tune, might embellish such programs as *Thought for Today* or *The Epilogue* with some tasteful hymn or unassuming psalm. The department also gathered in their offices each morning for prayers conducted by the director, who would plead for inspiration and guidance in their daily productions.

The Church of England, of course, was well represented by such programs, but so were various Nonconformist denominations, despite their continuing underclass status. Judaism was hardly heard of, the audience still being too anti-Semitic to tolerate much emphasis in that direction, and since the Church of England was established by law, the use of public money for the broadcasting of programs with a Christian flavor was hardly questioned by the general British public, who over the bloody centuries had learned, like the Vicar of Bray, to take what they were given.

The producer told me he had found himself criticized for not acknowledging beliefs other than those that the State had officially recognized or that were otherwise familiar. Accordingly, he determined to plan a series of programs presenting the variety of religious experience. This Jamesian responsibility was to be fulfilled by inviting representatives of all denominations together with various religious sects to describe their practices and explain them to the general audience. It was to be an eclectic series, necessarily; many small sects could not be accommodated, but the associated scripts would refer to as many as could be identified. In this way, it was hoped, the department might escape the occasional charge of narrow-mindedness.

In due course, a Catholic priest had celebrated mass, a Quaker had described the Society of Friends, and a rabbi, an Islamic ayatollah, a Buddhist, and a Shinto priest had each had their time on the air. It was then the turn of other less well-known congregations, including the Spiritualist Church. The latter organization, however, proved unwilling to permit intrusion into their private rituals. Spiritualism, so popular in the States during the first part of the nineteenth century, and in Britain in the first half of the twentieth, had fallen afoul of charlatans who had given the movement a bad name. Accordingly, a substitute was sought and found by way of the Society for Psychical Research, whose energetic secretary was able to arrange for a genuine medium to talk about her life and experiences.

When the medium was brought in, it was discovered that she was a cockney, and largely inarticulate. Apparently these flaws were betrayed by her dress, her accent, and her constant nervous sniffing as well as by her lack of conversation. But she was also plump and friendly, and although she seemed unable to describe her life as a medium, she offered to provide an example of her work. This, it was found, meant a seance. When asked if this could be accomplished in a studio, and whether she needed dim lights and "atmosphere," she laughed at the suggestion as so much "folderol."

Accordingly, a studio recording date was arranged. A chair was set beside the studio table, which held a microphone and beside it a two-way intercom for the producer. The engineers and the producer himself sat watching behind their glass screen, their instruments and machines ready to record whatever might happen.

The medium refused to take off her hat and instead poked in some hair.

"You can ask to talk to anyone you want," she told them, "provided they're on the other side, of course. Nothing may 'appen, yer know," she continued. "I can't promise nothin'."

And settling herself more comfortably in her chair, she closed her eyes. The producer and the engineers looked at each other and shook their heads. They were clearly being had. As the machines slowly turned, faithfully picking up the slightest sound in the studio, those listening first heard the woman's steady breathing. It was a rough, rasping sound as from congested lungs. Then her body began to twitch occasionally as if in a spasm of irritation.

The producer had determined to test the medium by asking to talk to his former tutor at Oxford, whom he had known well and who was long since dead. He had also prepared some difficult questions designed to detect fraud by including references to theological and philosophical problems that only an expert would understand. He turned to his intercom microphone and said he would like to speak to his tutor, whom he named.

The woman's lips began moving. She twitched violently, and then suddenly a voice could be heard. It was the educated voice of an elderly man.

My companion leaned over his lunch plate towards me.

"I was astounded. It was he, my old tutor!"

I looked bleak. The story reminded me too much of Madame Blavatsky.

"So you asked your questions? Your theological questions about heresy and God . . . ?"

"I asked them. And he answered. He—'the voice'—was correct in every particular."

"And you were recording this?"

"We recorded every word." He looked as nonplussed as perhaps he had been at the time.

"But there was something else," he went on, his fingers working at his napkin in curious agitation. He paused, looking down at his half-consumed lunch.

I urged him on. "Something else?"

"You understand our purpose was a serious one. We had researched the field and found many questionable mediums—or media, I suppose you classicists would say. Ha!" He sat back in his chair and stared upwards at the restaurant ceiling.

"You were saying there was something else."

"Yes, well . . . My questions were designed to ferret out a fraud. If this . . . this spirit . . . had told us that everything was fine 'on the other side' and asked us to give his love to Aunt Julie, we would have written the whole thing off. But he . . . it . . . didn't. The voice gave answers politely and correctly to all my questions. He even referred to our tutorials together. So that it was as if he was actually down there in the studio. In fact, I began to ask him questions that I had not pre-pared, technical questions about theology and which, forgive me, you, as a priest yourself, might also have asked."

"You mean . . . ?" I hesitated, not quite understanding him.

"I suppose you'd call them blasphemous. Whether God actually existed." He looked across at me, troubled, suddenly defensive. "Wouldn't you have done so, in my position?"

We were clearly exploring difficult and important territory. If this "spirit" was as real as the producer seemed to think it might be, there was no end to the questions he might have asked. I waited. It was clear I would hear the whole story however it had turned out.

"You know what he said? He said, 'We don't know any more than you do. It's a question which we, on this side, frequently debate.' That threw me, you understand. I didn't know what to say. But then he warned me off. He actually told me not to dabble in the spirit world because it had no answers for us of any moment. Finally he talked about the medium! He said she was tired and that I wasn't to attempt to contact him again. And the woman gave a sort of snort and woke up."

I stared at him.

"Did she say anything? In her own voice, I mean? If she knew what had been going on, then surely . . ."

"She asked us if anything had happened. She seemed not to know a thing."

I looked across the room to where other New Yorkers were energetically talking business deals in the "real" world.

"And you have it all on tape? It's powerful stuff."

"Too powerful. We couldn't broadcast something like that. It's
dynamite. We'd have the world about our ears claiming we'd faked
the whole thing. So we put it in the archives. By now it's probably
erased."

"Did you pay her anything?"

"Not a penny. She wouldn't even take the usual fee. In fact, she said
her gift, as she described it, was an embarrassment to her. She had a
regular job and would never think of taking money."

We finished our lunch in virtual silence. My friend seemed upset by
his memories, and they also caused me some concern. If, indeed, the
seance had not been rigged by the SPR itself, for example, some kind
of communication appeared to have taken place either between the
woman and the producer alone, or among the woman, the producer,
and the spirit together. If the latter, then either the spirit was that of
whom it claimed to be—a former Oxford professor of theology—or it
was a re-creation drawn in some way from the producer's mind and
reproduced in the physical organs of the medium. For the voice was
clearly not imagined; it was heard by everyone in the control room
and even recorded.

Alternatively, as was more likely, I myself had been "had" in a test
of my gullibility, and the story, well told though it had been, was no
more than a luncheon extravagance. Yet its very subject raised questions, as had my childhood experiences at Bailey Piers. And there have
been other phenomena reported that are seemingly evidential of
another world existing alongside our own, whether a divinely
ordained world called heaven or a pagan purgatory peopled with
souls of the dead awaiting rewards or punishment. Or such things
might be evidence of electromagnetic communications which our
brains, except for those of mediums, are not yet equipped to receive.
Christian mythology is certainly replete with "miracles" suggesting
that the immediate senses may be insufficient to account for everything that happens, and, moreover, that the human mind is far more
powerful and complex than we know. So that, although I was increasingly unwilling to believe in such reports exactly as related in the
bible, it bothered me that the impulse to think about them again
should have come from a tall tale.

But there it was. My friend had raised questions for which neither I
nor my religious training had answers unless they were to be taken on
faith as ineffable mysteries. And the more ineffable such mysteries

were said to be, the more suspicious I thought them. Augustine, I remembered, felt forced to attribute such phenomena to devils. But the existence of the soul, which my priestly examiners had never doubted for one moment, deserved to be reconsidered.

Many and various are the constructions that faith has offered to answer the question. The soul is usually thought to be attached in some way to the body, within the head perhaps, inside the brain. It is certainly within the brain that ideas and values originate, which in turn are believed by the faithful to affect the future of the soul in the after life. It is this relationship that becomes the basis of religious morality. Ghosts, poltergeists, the manifestations produced by psychic mediums, and a general belief in "spiritual" forces outside human control are also invoked, at least by those who believe in them, as further evidence that the soul exists. If such phenomena are the product of spirits, perhaps these are souls which like Hamlet's father have been somehow condemned to wander the earth.

The strongest evidence for a soul would seem to be our consciousness of self. But what if this self-consciousness is the result not of some mysterious entity inhabiting the brain but of the activity of the brain itself? Its two hemispheres, as has been shown experimentally, interact endlessly upon each other and in so doing produce the effect of a third entity with a life of its own, apparently autonomous and independent. Paint, for example, on a canvas can produce the effect of a scene, and even a scene identifiable as the work of a particular artist, but the scene is nonetheless utterly dependent upon the existence of the paint from which the scene is composed. In the same way, our sense of self is demonstrably dependent upon the continued functioning of our brain and, we observe, ceases when the brain ceases to function. Our "personhood" is dependent. All we have available to deny such an obvious conclusion is hope, or, if you like, faith—certainly not reason.

In the same way, ideas, values, what we call thoughts and memories, all within the brain, depend also upon the continued existence of the brain, and the patterns of its subatomic, atomic, or molecular parts, since without the brain the patterns do not and cannot exist. I, for example, do not exist. You, my reader, are hearing or reading only codes made up from combinations of letters expressing patterns (ideas, thoughts) which, albeit complex and culturally conditioned, were formed in my brain and which are now being formed in your own. Yet to you I seem to exist, just as, in a vaguer way, as I write, so do you seem to exist to me. The words—mere congregations of sounds or shapes—are totally dependent for their meanings upon the sum of their parts.

Such epiphenomena are possible because, based on recent discoveries, the brain's structures themselves process, send, and receive myriad messages and responses all *within* themselves, and without ceasing. Our sense of Self is thus the most consummate artifact of the brain, which is capable of employing the body and itself in great feats of creativity that can survive its own separate existence, just as a painting, a poem, or a building survive their creators. In the same way, everything could be said to be an epiphenomenon of its own essential energy.

But if soul, understood as a separate immortal entity in addition to the brain, is a figment of the religious imagination, what of the afterlife that it is said to inhabit? And my curious luncheon conversation led to still more questions. The soul, in the traditional meaning of the word, may not exist, but why could there not be other states of existence beyond those we presently know or understand?

I had already raised such matters with clergy assembled to watch the premier of *Alf Goes to Work,* Robert Newman's documentary about the House Church. I was then preparing to cover the training of the first astronauts and so asked my fellow ministers whether the God we believed in also existed in other galaxies. Did Jesus mean the same to Martians as he does to us? How would the Christian churches explain salvation to green creatures living somewhere in the midst of Alpha Centauri, presumably far away from the Garden of Eden? It was an old question, perhaps first raised in the seventeenth century by John Wilkins, the scientific bishop of Chichester who thought the moon might also be inhabited.

They had looked blankly at me. They wanted such questions to remain part of some transcendent mystery, because, I suspected, to do otherwise would have endangered faith, however intellectually dishonest such refusal might appear to be. In my upstart way I had chided them, but they had laughed. "We leave such things to God," was all they offered, and were outrageously content.

I was worried. Millions believe things without a shred of evidence apart from hearsay or imagination and misname them "revelation." The Assumption of the Virgin Mary, even the Resurrection, are both usually matched in religious rhetoric with conviction that the world is round or that unvisited places exist, which are considered good arguments in support of faith. Yet upon the existence of the soul depends the theory of Salvation, which has caused so much agony for outcasts and faithful alike.

It was after my attempt to disentangle the soul that I was assigned to interview the first astronauts, newly selected. I was to ask them, somewhat incongruously, about their belief in God. It was grist for my own mill, and with this rather presumptuous task in hand, I set off for Langley Field in Virginia. My New York congregation were fascinated by such an assignment, though some shook their heads. "You preach a social gospel," complained one woman, "not Jesus Christ and Him crucified." Having the previous week discovered that "Bowery Bums" were homeless alcoholics, I was forced to agree with her.

"You must also stop by and report back on Koinonia Farm for us," ordered Howard Moody. "Tell us how they're getting on." Then added, sadly, "If they're still alive, that is."

I knew only that Koinonia Farm was another religious experiment in Georgia, and wondered what he meant. He shook his head.

"You'll find out soon enough."

So, with questions still jangling in my head about the soul, salvation, and the afterlife, I set off for the future and the stars.

HE-MEN

1959

The term "astronauts" was a fanciful and romantic exaggeration of their task, which, although it did not include touring the stars, was certainly hazardous in the extreme. Moreover, during this time of cold war, there was great fear among Western governments of Russian experiments in space, where the entire planet could come under surveillance and threat. So, inevitably, the romance of space travel took second place to military need. As I knew well, rockets carrying lethal explosives had breached the stratosphere in the Second World War and the Russian sputnik launched only one year before my arrival in the States showed how far behind the Western powers still were.

The new National Aeronautic and Space Administration had been developing the American manned space flight program at Langley Field in Virginia. NASA had taken over from an Advisory Committee for Aeronautics and was now engaged in a program that would make use of the rocket research being conducted at the Jet Propulsion Laboratory of the California Institute of Technology, backed by experimental programs long underway at the Ames Research Center in Mountain View, California. The British Interplanetary Society had already come up with a design for a machine that could land on the Moon, but the math required to send up a human, keep him safe (no one imagined it might one day be a woman), and bring him back alive were still being worked out.

Langley Field was the air force base where the first seven astronauts were in training. They had been selected from as many as 508 pilots whom the Defense Department's computer had initially determined might fit the bill: John H. Glenn, Walter M. Schirra, Alan B. Shepard, L. Gordon Cooper Jr., M. Scott Carpenter, Donald K. Slayton, and

Virgil I. (Gus) Grissom. Their names have long been history, but then they were largely unknown because the pace of the Cold War had been accelerating and secrecy was essential. If the Redstone rockets on which they would ride had exploded, no one except their families (and maybe not even they) would have been told what had occurred.

The astronauts' task was to be clothed in a shining silvery space suit designed to withstand both appalling cold and terrible heat, and stuff themselves inside a cone-shaped metal capsule not much bigger than a broom closet. It had been decided to fill this capsule with pure oxygen instead of air (a mixture of gases), because a single gas would be more predictable and easier to control, and would also reduce the pressure inside the suit and the amount of equipment required to monitor it. Should a spark inside the capsule ignite a fire, the pure oxygen would cause it to be virtually uncontrollable, but this was considered unlikely and, under the tight deadline NASA had set itself, a risk worth taking.

The capsule, with the astronaut sitting inside facing a panel of instruments, was to be hoisted eight storeys up to the very top of the rocket, a converted intercontinental ballistic missile. The rocket would blast off with a sound like thunder, and at a predetermined speed and distance calculated to within split seconds the capsule would be released and sent to circle the earth. After a few revolutions, and again at a crucial point in his journey, the astronaut would fire tiny nozzles of gas which would turn the capsule so that its saucer-shaped bottom would back into the friction of the earth's atmosphere through which it would have to descend. Specially invented plastic coating on the skin of the capsule's base would begin to glow. White-hot and finally incandescent, this coating would burn off in molten globules as the craft hurtled down into the earth's atmosphere. Should this heat shield fail, the capsule together with the astronaut inside would burn to a cinder, becoming no more than a momentary flash in the sky. Chimpanzees strapped inside the capsule had already arrived back safely, and the daredevils I was to interview hoped to do no less. Yet it might certainly be expected that even astronauts had thought seriously about death, if not about God.

Space was clearly a world of "he-men" (we believed in such species) who were engaged in a scientific and mathematical effort of great significance. To nearly all humans on earth, the rest of our universe was still the enigma it had been since we first looked up at the sky. Cosmogonies had peopled the heavens with gods and crystal spheres, and Christians, ancient and modern, had located there the glories of heaven itself. Jesus was supposed to have been taken up beyond the clouds, soon followed, Catholics were now required to believe, by his mother. After a thousand centuries even our neighboring moon remained a thing made of we knew not what. Down at us she stared, once a goddess whose mysteries and influence could still be detected everywhere. What could Christianity offer to explain such immensities?

I had left Washington behind and was approaching the very coast where the United States as we know it had begun: past Jamestown on the James River, where the very first settlement had been founded years before the *Mayflower*'s arrival in the north; and then Yorktown where the British, trapped by the French fleet, finally capitulated to Washington. In those days, Virginia had stretched far and wide and was the pride of America. From its agricultural wealth and its vaunted patriarchal heritage sprang presidents, fathers of their country, among whom was, of course, Thomas Jefferson, who freed his Commonwealth from religious intolerance. And now Virginia had become the headquarters of another historic effort, this time to lift humanity to the stars.

As I was permitted through the gates of the base, beneath a bright blue sky, my BBC credentials ever at the ready, I marveled how open this secret place seemed to be, and how quiet it was. Stretches of empty green lawn were lined with neat white buildings overlooked by tall pylon towers carrying electric cables from far away across the orderly Virginian forest. Around a corner there even appeared a short row of what looked like Elizabethan cottages, half-timbered in black and white. This, I had been told, was where the Big Seven and their families lived. The anachronistic style contrasted oddly with the pastel colored flat-roofed administrative structures around.

I was met in one of the buildings by an officer in civilian clothes who was to be my guide. He explained that the majority of my potential interviewees were either at Cape Canaveral, on leave, or doing their homework to be ready for tests and experiments on the morrow. The tests involved being hurled around in a massive centrifuge built like an enormous horizontal wheel at the edge of which was a chair within a box containing cameras and recording devices. As the giant wheel with its electronic seat spun faster and faster, it produced pressures many times that of gravity, which would eventually take their toll on the hardiest constitutions. To just such pressures would the rocket's rise from the earth and then the capsule's reentry subject bones and vital organs, and they had to be experienced and endured.

My guide was a tall, thin, cadaverous man with a winning smile who introduced me to space flight in what I took to be a typical

American manner, as if it was merely a stunt. He had all the buoyancy and eagerness of the GIs who helped rescue Europe. Outside, we were met by a messenger. A meeting had been arranged with Gus Grissom, boldest of the seven and the man who had been selected to lead them to the Moon. I marveled. I was at the frontier of history! Only a month before I had been traipsing the dreary streets of England beneath grey skies worrying about what hymns to sing! I thought of the look a Teddy boy had given me when I told him I was off to America. It was beyond his imagining, as it had been beyond mine. And now Major Grissom, it seemed, was currently in the centrifuge but was willing to be interviewed by me, inside the hour.

In order to write and broadcast my despatches, I obviously needed to learn as much as I could about NASA and about outer space, just as, in later years, I had to do for hundreds of subjects. This was to be another baptism of fire, for if the mathematics of space travel were daunting, the physics were overwhelming. No humans, only chimpanzees, had yet experienced space flight, and although the instruments that had measured the chimps' reactions had provided evidence that the human skeleton might also be able to withstand such stresses, the figures extrapolated for human flesh and blood, including the human brain, were far from certain. I asked to see the clothes that the men would wear, and was taken to the dressing room where there stood rows of metal lockers painted army grey. Opening one of them, my guide took out the various sections of a silver suit made of plasticized rubber coated in silver aluminum to ward off heat. He explained the tubes and wires that carried air and coolant, and the instrumentation upon which the life of the man inside would be totally dependent. "Outside the capsule," he went on nonchalantly, "the cold will be deadly. Nothing living would survive; in seconds, a man would freeze solid. On the other hand," he continued with a smile, "the heat engendered by the increasing friction of the earth's atmosphere during reentry would roast him alive!"

All that separated the human flesh from these extreme temperatures was the thin metal skin of the capsule and this silver suit. I asked to put it on, not believing that such a wish would be granted. But this was America!

The suit was designed to be entered section by section. My guide, an expert dresser, motioned me to lift up my feet, pulled up silver greaves and locked them onto my legs. Then came the cables and tubes dangling about my waist. The boots were of one piece with the leggings, and somewhat roomier than they were supposed to be, presumably because they had been tailored for the man who would be wearing them.

I had not counted on the fact that one cannot enter a space suit on one's own. The victim is totally dependent upon the dresser. I was slowly being encased inside an impermeable shell from which there would be no escape. The body of the suit and its arms were constructed so that a circular metal flange gripped me around the midriff, and the legs locked on from behind. A zipper running diagonally across the front then pulled the suit tightly together, forcing me to bend forward, hunched over like an ape. "So this is how the species could end," I thought. "Just as it began—but flying through the stars instead of trees!" The arms terminated in gloves for the hands and were again attached to the body by the dresser. I was now almost totally locked inside the space suit up to the neck. There was no way I could possibly escape from its tight embrace.

Suddenly my heart began pounding furiously. I did not need to be told that great beads of sweat were standing out on my forehead. From my extremities, my hands and feet, I felt a panic desperation begin to rise. I was not only constrained and caught, I was trapped! I could not escape, even if I had wanted to! But it seemed this was not an unusual condition, even among astronauts.

"Shall I take you out?" asked my guide, smiling, and holding the helmet. "It sometimes happens. I was expecting it sooner."

"Not on your life!" I gasped. "I have to know what it feels like. Is that the helmet?"

He was holding a bubble of what looked like white enameled metal with a visor of dark glareproof glass. It seemed very large.

"I'll be feeding you oxygen. Breathe deeply if you can." I tried in vain to slow my pulse before the helmet came down, passing over my head to be clamped on to the rigid neckband of the suit's body. I was not merely wearing a suit, I was now totally *inside*. Had I been an actual astronaut, I would already have had thrust into my rectum a bulbous probe which, according to the military manual, "takes cognizance of the anatomy of the rectal sphincter and whose rigidity is sufficient to permit easy introduction." This was to relay internal temperature and pressure. Electrodes to measure temperature and heart rate would also have been attached to my skin at previously identified places on the second cervical vertebra and on the sternum by means of special cups containing a newly invented paste sensitive to changes in electrical potential. The changes would also be fed to a transmitter sending the measurements back to doctors, psychologists, and scientists watching what would now be considered primitive computer screens in Mission Control on earth.

Inside the helmet, I could feel the slender bar of a narrow black microphone lying against my lips. Built inside this mike was a tiny open funnel that caught the carbon dioxide I was expelling from my nose, and compared it with the amount of oxygen taken in through the mouth. During flight, this figure too would be fed to biologists watching oscilloscopes on earth. Plastic tubes for carrying much of this information now wound round my body inside the suit, and cables and wires for transmitting the measurements of my continued existence were all in place. I gulped. So this is what they went through! The dresser's voice came faintly through earphones built into the helmet.

"Just remember that the suit is a lifesaver."

I was rescued from the need to prove this point, however, by movements I detected around me. A flash bulb went off nearby. Because the helmet's visor was polarized to prevent dazzle from the brilliant sunlight out in space, I could see only what looked like a completely naked man standing in front of me holding a camera. Was oxygen that powerful, I wondered? But it was astronaut Grissom himself! He had burst in through the changing room door on his way to the shower and was, indeed, totally naked. I saw him laughing as he made a dash to escape. The dresser unlocked the helmet and began taking me out of the suit.

"Thought you'd like a picture," he said. Nodding to the changing room door he added, "That's your man. He'll be out soon."

Grissom was stocky, round-faced, almost boyish, and, they told me later, more genial than the other men; ebullient but very careful—the "astronauts' astronaut" and the ideal professional already selected to lead a team to the Moon. When he finally appeared before me, a towel wrapped round his middle, he was drying himself off. I made slow waving movements of welcome with my cumbersome arms, which had not yet been released from their silver sheaths. "My masters want to know whether you think of God while you train to leave earth."

He guffawed at this and toweled his marine-short hair.

"God?" he cried. "Didn't you know God's everywhere?"

"So you're not frightened of dying in this great undertaking?"

He looked serious. "Other people ask me that. And you don't become a test pilot without thinking about it. I always put it behind me. You couldn't do the job unless you did." Again the guffaw.

We soon were talking technical matters and I was then shown the capsule, named *Mercury,* in which the astronauts were to leave the planet. It was just as my guide had described it: a grey metal cone containing an armchair. I was invited to "step inside" and did so. To crawl through the hatch and sit, or rather lie, on the specially contoured couch, custom-built to match the bones and shape of each astronaut, made me feel as if I was being scrunched into a tin can. Through the thick tiny window I could see only shadows. I was faced with panels of switches, special handles to operate tiny rockets to maneuver with, and numerous warning lamps and dials to indicate the vessel's "attitude," alignment, fuel levels, and much else.

With the interview done, on my way out from Langley Field I slowed my hired car to take a second look at the Elizabethan cottages where the Big Seven lived. The complex seemed so orderly. No difficult theological problems, no anxiety about offending against divine laws or challenging the gods. Simply a bundle of mathematical equations. It was as if centuries, even millennia, of superstition and ignorance had suddenly been tossed into the trash, leaving the sky clear and inviting. Religious theories, their churches and temples, seemed far, far away, quite out of touch with reality. Back in London, my interview was given screamer headlines in the BBC's house journal with a picture claiming me as their "Man in Outer Space."

Gus Grissom's responses had not been unpredictable, and now that my memory of that unusual confrontation is overshadowed by the knowledge of his terrible death in the 1967 Apollo I accident, they are somewhat consoling. He was trapped with his two copilots, Roger Chaffee and Ed White, inside the pure oxygen fire of a burning capsule on the launchpad, and no one could save them. He had been very critical of the way cables were hastily crowded into the capsule, increasing the slim chance of a spark, but it was a risk they had taken. They had died as do many pioneers, casualties of our yearning for the truth as well as of our ignorance and fear of each other.

It was impossible not to recognize that the task of reaching out beyond our own planet called for a discipline as great as any demanded by religion. It represented a new phase of human understanding about the constituents of matter, even about existence itself, far beyond the vague mists of Bergson's *élan vital* or Shaw's Life Force. It was a phase prefigured by rational thinking centuries ago, its roots in ideas that had been recorded more than two millennia earlier and had been awaiting tools with which to explore their meaning. The meticulous care with which each detail of these scientific experiments was being undertaken; the lives risked on their behalf; the sense of an enormous undertaking previously impossible or, to traditional religious thinking, impermissible: taken together, it was majestic. Could it be that as Shaw had once hoped, America and Russia were forcing their intellectuals to use their genius for the general good? Not surprisingly, some members of the Space Science Board had gone on record as believing that the exploration of outer space was perhaps the "greatest inspirational venture of this century" and that "inherent" in it were "great and fundamental philosophical and spiritual values which find a response in man's questing spirit and his intellectual self-realization." Although science had found a champion in the military and such rhetoric might be "ballyhoo," I found it at least partly true.

Thereafter, scientific enterprise took on an increasingly important role in my thinking. I could now understand why religious leaders had feared exploration and experiment so intensely. In leaving our planet, just as in delving deeper and deeper into the constituents of matter, it would be remiss of those claiming to have the answer to the enigma of existence not to look to where these discoveries might be leading. And in doing so, we could leave behind ancient ideas of "heaven" and "hell."

Tools with which we could now establish and prove important theories had previously been lacking, but great cyclotrons, powerful radio telescopes and electron microscopes, and computerized systems capable of prodigious feats of computation and memory were increasingly available. Media of communication sufficiently sensitive, powerful, and ubiquitous were already linking scientific findings together and enabling them to build and explore further in theory as well as in practice. Hitherto, we had unearthed bones and pots but could not date them; we had seen anomalous phenomena in rocks, stars, and animal behaviors but could not track them; psychology, like sociology, anthropology, and much of medicine had been largely theoretical.

Age-old ideas had begun to fail us. The idea of national hegemony had been exploded in the First World War; the idea of ethnic supremacy had brought about the second; the battle between free choice and social engineering had long been underway; and religious people, whose gods would once have ruled over such movements, were confused and rapidly losing intellectual ground. It was increasingly obvious that infinitesimal calculations, cosmic rays, neutrinos, quantum theory, and the rest of the newly discovered phenomena and all that they implied had to be built into the philosophy of existence.

My new world of astronauts evoked memories of being rescued from war, of warmhearted unity in the face of overwhelming odds, and of strong men with broad smiles and hard muscles being tender with each other in the face of danger. At the same time I sensed a ruthlessness about the space enterprise that frightened as much as it appealed. And as I drove away, I was saddened by wondering whether, had Gus Grissom known that he was talking to a "pervert"—the official description of homosexuals—he would have turned away from me in contempt. But as I told myself, we were also facts of life and our existence was just as critical to the success of any new ontological theory that might now emerge as were cosmic rays, atomic particles, and outer space.

I had tasted American freedom, and glad at the success of my research, I looked forward to my next encounter with American experimentation and generosity of spirit. I left Virginia behind me and moved deeper into the southern states, through both the Carolinas, then inland toward Koinonia Farm, the experimental farming community near Americus, Georgia. I remembered I was to report on how they were faring. The air grew warmer and then hot and dry. The land stretched around, offering a welcome of peach trees and flowering shrubs. It was an expansive, embracing climate I had imagined but never before experienced.

The orchards around Americus grow peanuts and pecans. Koinonia Farm had been founded before the war's end in 1942 by Clarence Jordan, the independent-minded son of a southern bank manager, and Martin England, a Baptist missionary. Jordan had become an evangelical Christian minister and with his wife and family had been living and working with a racially mixed company of like-minded Christians ever since. It had not been easy. Jordan had been enraged by the hypocrisy of those who attended Christian revival meetings yet continued to inflict brutal cruelty on African Americans almost uniformly insulted as "niggers," whom they segregated from all protection of the law and even murdered at whim. One of the goals of Jordan's communitarian experiment was to serve as a witness to the possibility that whites and blacks could live and work together harmoniously.

The farm buildings were some distance from the hard, dry town of Americus itself. A highway passed beside the farm compound, beyond which lay the pecan orchards where every morning blacks and whites together picked boxes and barrels of the pinky brown nuts of a kind I had never seen before: their interior flesh like that of walnuts in size, but their outer shell smooth, unwrinkled, and so delicate one hand alone might crush it—another American improvement.

Jordan himself was away, so the Reverend's wife, Florence, introduced me to their family, their friends, and the laborers with their handsome children, and showed me around the farm. There were sixty members, fifteen of them black. Everyone lived on the farm and ate together. It had been, they told me, an unexpectedly fruitful, if difficult, experience.

To learn the trade, I too went into the orchard, and was immediately befriended by both blacks and whites. Together we picked and boxed pecans, adjourning in the heat of the day for lunch together in the shade beneath the trees. How happy they were, they told me, that new hope had come at last to their difficult lives: the blacks, that here, at least, they could eat and talk and pray with white friends and neighbors without fear of the law; the whites, that here too they did not have to feel superior when they weren't. We laughed and chatted hour by hour, then picked and packed some more. Did I detect the danger of their situation? I did not.

Dinner was a celebration too. Broad tables set with platters of corn bread and cheese, chilled soup, fresh vegetables galore, and everyone, black and white, sitting together at the common feast. Will Wittkamper, one of the community, said grace and a short hymn was sung. Then, as the evening cooled and the lamps were lit, we told our tales. Koinonia was a success, it seemed.

Then, behind the talking, I could hear what sounded like a distant train hooting in the night. I saw Wittkamper turn to listen as the rest too fell silent, watching him and listening as the noise grew nearer. Florence turned to me.

"We should have warned you. If it's what I think it is, do what I do."

And I could see the rest were slowly moving, some away from the table, some toward the walls. A child began to cry and was quickly pulled in and comforted. But it was only a train hauling cotton and tobacco to the North.

The previous week, it seemed, the noise had been no train. Suddenly, in the midst of dinner, it had hit them like a storm: squealing tires, loud blaring horns, screaming shouts, and scattered rifle and machine gun fire as two open trucks roared into the farm, around the farm house, firing through the windows, anywhere. Bullets shattered the glass, smashed into the walls. People pulled each other down and under the table. Hoarse shouts of "nigger lovers!" were hurled at them through the night. Then, just as suddenly, with more squealing tires, the trucks had roared away into the darkness and everyone had slowly climbed off the floor and continued with their dinner. No one had been hit.

As I was being told this, others shook their heads and muttered. I was horrified. Florence shrugged.

"We once had a plan to turn out all the lights, but then we thought that might suggest no one was here. Then they'd burn the place. So now we don't, and take our chances."

She, of course, assumed I understood. I looked around. Everyone was talking, eating as before. I was astounded that they all seem to have taken what had happened so composedly.

"What was it, then? Who were they? Are they coming back?"

Wittkamper sighed. "Oh, they'll be back. They do it when they're drunk. Last week they blew up our roadside store with dynamite. They're the Klan."

The Ku Klux Klan! I had heard of them, watched their antics on the movie news, as of some harmless, distant tribe that dressed themselves in long white hooded robes, not as an actual murderous crew intent on war.

Jordan's kindly wife, bearing more food, served it round. Then, speaking of her husband, she said, "They want to string him up, of course. Last month they burned a cross in one of the fields."

"Burned a cross? String him up? You don't mean . . . ?" I still looked mystified.

"Put up a cross of wood, douse it in gasoline and set it afire." She served me corn, then went on. "They do it all the time. Childish stuff. We're told the number of lynchings is down, but if they catch him . . ." She left the awful vision undescribed.

I was reminded of SS raids on Jews in Nazi Germany and my enthusiasm for things American suddenly began to drain away. The country now seemed as naive and brutal as the editors of the *Village Voice* had said it was. I felt even closer to Emily and Lucy, my black coworkers on the farm. Their "offences" could not be hidden as could mine. But I had to find out more.

I asked why the police didn't stop the raids.

"The police?" They were surprised at my ignorance. "Why, some nights the sheriff's among them! You'll find them all over. That's why the locals stopped dealing with us. Clarence tried to reason with them, tell them it's not Christian, but they're frightened. They want us out."

I had clearly landed in the midst of social chaos, a sort of Wild West of the South, or worse, a new Nazified world. I asked who organized them. Did they gather at some bar and get drunk? Could I meet them? If I could land a naked astronaut, I could certainly catch a Klansman. But this raised eyebrows. They were not only farmhands, these thugs; some were powerful community leaders, members of the local White Citizens' Council and the national guard, and even . . . an embarrassed pause . . . attended the local Baptist church on Sundays. It was mighty dangerous to mess with organized brutality. Again I was reminded of the SS. However, if these thugs attended the local Baptist church they were certainly grist for my broadcasting mill. It had never occurred to me that there would be a second religious connection to the story. The Baptists, I seemed to remember, had originally fled to the peace and security of America to avoid persecution by the Catholics, not to engage in murder and mayhem.

"Ah," said the Wittkampers, "Prejudice breeds hatred. Long ago, many immigrants arrived already infected. That's why it's so difficult to cure."

I could not but agree. The Koinonia Community was, in fact, an island, a sanctuary and, as it turned out, perhaps the only one in all the southern states. Even though Sumter County was 65 percent black, Emily and her friends had often thought of retreat to some other district where the Klan weren't so active, but work elsewhere meant a return to virtual slavery. Among the Koinonia pecan trees they felt not only safe but free. Like the Hebrew people of the hymns they liked to sing while working, they sojourned in a foreign land.

Later, when I was able to work up background material on the history of the American South, I discovered that many white landowners still traced their ancestry back almost exclusively to Virginia and even to Jamestown, where the white British aristocrats had eventually reestablished a class structure that the South had never gotten over. The plantations had eventually impoverished the soil; the landowners were tempted to their own destruction by introducing slavery; and the land became home to white "lower" classes, long weakened by lack of education and easy prey to religious fears as insidious as was the rage they inspired among those they oppressed in their turn.

These social differences were so deeply ingrained that even though it had all started more than three hundred years ago and had been fought over in the bloodiest civil war, when I was there the slow crawl toward civil rights had hardly started. Martin Luther King Jr. and other black clergy had only just begun preaching, and in vain had determined black lawyers been standing up for justice since the 1920s. It was now nearly 1960, but while the hot sun beat down upon the pecan trees, the South was still barely changed.

Next Sunday morning, against everyone's advice and dire warnings from Emily, I drove up the highway to the Rehobeth Baptist church. I carried my heavy recording equipment slung over my shoulders and tried to look as much like a professional reporter as I could. The church building was small and pretty with a white painted steeple, a typical poor southern conventicle sitting in a field of about half an acre. A white wooden fence with a little white gate surrounded it. Outside its stubby white painted tower hung an old bell the rope of which was being pulled intermittently by a stalwart fellow with his back to the incoming congregation of white folk arriving in the long cars of the period.

The bell's jangling summons stopped almost as soon as I arrived and I climbed the half dozen worn wooden steps leading to the porch. The doors were open. Men in dark suits and women in pretty organdy dresses topped with summery hats were already seated in the twenty or so rows of stained pine pews. "Rock of Ages" was being played soulfully on a harmonium and the antique hymn moaned out into the already stifling air.

There was no pulpit, merely a speaking stand on a platform across the same wall where the entryway was. A tall, thin middle-aged man in a white suit sat facing his expectant flock as I made my way into a pew and pushed my equipment into one corner. By his side sat six other men all in white suits, three on each side of him. These were presumably his deacons. The air inside the church was close and smelled of new-mown hay. Both men and women were fanning themselves with stiff round or rectangular paper fans, some of which one could see from the printing on both sides had been provided by a local mortuary.

The pastor, for it was he, rose slowly to his feet and the organ wheezed to a stop. The fans continued to waft their welcome breezes throughout the service, during the hymns and even during the hellfire sermon in which we were all conjured to "welcome the Lord Jeeesus into our hearts" or face "the fahz of torment in hayall."

The deacons, resplendent in white suits, passed a plate for the collection and polite reference was made by the pastor to the "stranger" in their midst, at which the ladies turned to smile at me and I was handed an extra hymn sheet for my edification. Then the prayers began, even as once they used to do at the same moment in the Sarum rite of the early Christian celebration: the pleading for guidance, for forgiveness, for salvation, but this time extempore and endless, seemingly for half an hour. Could this really be the headquarters of the dreaded Ku Klux Klan who firebombed innocent families?

The orgy of prayers and bible reading finally ended with a blessing. For an Anglican priest, it had suggested what the early church might have been like. For we had sung many hymns that I already knew by heart and this, I could see, quite charmed my neighbors in the pew beside me.

Eventually the more formal hymns concluded with a rousing repetitive chorus and people made as if to leave. A plump woman in a large, gaily decorated summer hat turned to me with an expansive smile and asked me who I was. Other women and a few men quickly gathered around. I told them I was reporting for the BBC.

"Is that so?" she replied. And where was I residing?

"At Koinonia Farm," I told her.

Her face, and the faces of all those peering into our conversation, suddenly went hard and blank. Without another word to me, she turned and bustled out. The others, too, moved quickly away and I soon found myself alone. The little chapel was suddenly empty.

Through the windows I could see the blue sky. The sun, not quite overhead, glanced down onto the now-vacant pews. A few fans and hymn papers had been left behind. I picked up a fan and put it in my briefcase. I had secretly recorded some of the hymn singing and was glad to see the batteries were still at their peak. The pastor had stopped greeting people by the doors, which were still wide open, giving a view of grass and the road where some of the women seemed to be standing. The noonday heat poured toward me as I made my way to the door over the smooth bare wooden floor boards, feeling somehow bereft and vulnerable.

Passing through the outer door, I found myself on the porch but no longer alone. The six tall deacons who had sat on the stage were now lined up close and stared me down. They stood along the bannisters of the porch, coats off, sleeves rolled up and what looked like staves or axe handles in their hands. It was the Klan!

A face is burnt in my memory: that of a youngish woman with wisps of blond hair and a hatchet look. Her right hand was hooked into the left of the nearest deacon, whether attempting to restrain him or urging him on, I could not tell. A urgent voice from behind was screeching, "Go on, Elmer! You show him!" The largest of the men, more than six feet of armed muscle, stepped forward, his face bent down against my own.

"Yew a nigger lover?" he rasped.

It was the question I had been warned about. Say no, and you betray your friends, abandon your principles, and never forgive yourself. Say yes, and you lose your story and possibly your life.

I had often considered similar test questions ever since the vicar of the fundamentalist church where I was a choirboy had challenged his congregation with a situation drawn from Roman times. "A pinch of incense," he used to cry, "was all the Pagan wanted! But would you spit in the face of Jesus?" Whether from cowardice or because the need to martyr oneself must somehow be flawed, I had long ago come to the conclusion that demands by tyrants were valueless. True, novels had been written and church fathers had also sermonized about the example that martyrdom holds up to us. In the Nazi death camps some Jews had become accessories merely to save their own lives.

Faced with such a horror who could blame them? All died anyway, and martyrdom, of itself, proves nothing.

My knees were shaking. I was, indeed, a "nigger lover." I would certainly not deny it. But I also wanted a story. To have arrived back beaten up or maimed might have made a better story, perhaps with international repercussions by bringing down the FBI upon their heads. Perhaps that, indeed, is what I should have done. However, with trembling fingers I switched on my heavy recorder and held out the microphone.

"What does that mean?" I asked, this always being a useful question to ask in difficult, life-threatening situations because it makes the other talk.

Another deacon joined in. "He's from a Commie country!" My accent had given me away. They all shuffled a step forward, grasping their truncheons more firmly, ready for the kill. One man began to raise his arm.

But instead of retreating, I advanced, pushing into them. After all, this was what both Clausewitz and Patton recommended. I poked with my puny microphone.

"I'm from Britain. I want to know what you mean."

As they closed around me I could see their pastor. He was sitting on the gate beside the road, swinging one leg; a bystander looking on. I spoke again, "I want to talk to your pastor . . . over there!"

Reluctantly, they pulled apart, letting me walk down the steps and out toward the gate where the pastor was sitting. Still shaking with fear, I hoped I was moving in a dignified manner. The pastor who had called us so fervently to the love of Jeeesus was tight-lipped, unwilling.

I played the ignoramus and half an hour later, in the Pastor's house nearby, with the deacons seated round us and still looking as if they could finish me off, I had my interview. I wanted to hear their beliefs; to learn what these beliefs were based upon; and why they continued to hold them. But they took their directions from their boss, who quoted and used the bible to justify his hatred. He denied all knowledge of violence or threatening behavior and the deacons looked blankly at me. They were just "good ole boys" larking about for a bit of fun with the nigger-lovers.

"After all," said one of them, "niggers are animals, as the bible says."

They were quite unable to explain their fear of integration except in such terms. Their ignorance had been reinforced, perhaps even encouraged, by religious teaching conjoined with long-standing eco-

nomic and social structures from the past, and now produced only
mindless gut reactions which to them seemed natural and divinely
authorized. At least, much later, that's what I fed to London, for at the
time I was as lost for words as they.

As I gathered my things together to drive back to the farm, still
wondering at my escape, a brilliant white police car emerged from
behind the pastor's home and slid across my bows. It was the local
sheriff himself. He got out, a short, lumbering fellow, hatless, the butt
of a revolver poking from his belt, his hand hanging beside it, fingers
fluttering, aching to get round the trigger. (It now occurs to me from
what he said that perhaps he too was afraid.)

"You from around hyer?"

I explained again.

"We heard bout yew. Yew're an agent from a Commie country."

I explained again. But it had no effect. The South at this time was
still paranoid about Communists and this was the local gestapo.

"Yew come off a submarine." Unbelievably, this appeared to be a
statement.

No, I replied, I came from New York. To mention Koinonia Farm
again would have been asking for it, but I had forgotten the American
Civil War!

At this, he pushed down his face at mine and hissed, "Yew a guest
hyer, mistah! You bee hayve, or Ah'll run yew outta town."

Had the pastor called in the sheriff in case I had been beaten to a
pulp, or to stop the beating he himself expected?

After the exhilaration of outer space, it seemed this country was as
"decadent" as Ernie had warned, its apparent generosity hiding arrogant self-righteousness. I was reminded of my German uncle, whose
experience of police was only of bullies trained to kill. But was Britain
any better, with its racism and anti-Semitic class system? I reminded
myself that these southerners were all Americans too, men capable of
great heroism, men whose urgent strength had helped to save my life
in war. One southern town had lost its entire male population in Normandy. Nevertheless, what a sadness came upon me!

My journalistic assignments, as well as my sex life and my meetings
with believers, took me into situations all the more interesting for the
light they shed not only upon history but upon the state of Christianity. Accretions to the original words of Jesus and theories as to what
he was, accumulating over the centuries, had so layered the core of the
faith that all manner of irrational behavior appeared justified. Christianity still presented itself as exclusive, its benefits confined to the

chosen, or the saved, whose life (and maybe their genes) must not be contaminated—an attitude not unusual among religions. Had I been visiting a Catholic farm in Puritan England, I would have been greeted with similar, perhaps worse, threats. Had I earlier been an Albigensian or a Muslim I would have been burnt by the Catholics. And, inevitably, I could never forget that to be homosexual seemed to call for ostracism from all religions, sects, and denominations.

On my way back to New York, I continued to think of my plight and that of others. Religious people seemed to believe either that gay people were heterosexuals who were sinning or that we chose to be homosexual, that our existence was somehow a matter of willed belief so that we could potentially be converted just as Protestants and Catholics, Muslims and Jews, could be. Many humans, like Jane Austen's Mr. Woodhouse, believe everyone should be the same as they are and cannot conceive why they are not. There is generosity, perhaps even kindness, in such a disposition; but in the American South, where traditional dependence upon class and family relationships dating back to the distant past are reinforced by religion, such blindness with regard to differences becomes a liability, inhibiting change and improvement. Even Thomas Jefferson, a freethinker in favor of a "natural" aristocracy, nonetheless still thought in terms of class, whether natural or artificial. From a deeply held conviction about the value of "purity" that he assumed everyone shared, he could not forebear to examine the bloodlines of his slaves and family in meticulous detail.

I now attempted reconciling my experiences in the States with living again in London. But I found the capital still a dismal place. I quickly found I had reentered the class system. People did not talk to each other as they did in New York. Comparing this city with London showed how the constitutional structure of the United States had truly affected the daily lives of those who live there, just as the British class structure affects the lives of the British. Most Americans had few inhibitions in public discourse and I could see that they had learned to be this way at their parents' knees. They liked to answer back, even if they had nothing much to say, and, except in military families, were unpunished for what was taken to be the exercise of a proper right. In their schools, I had discovered, American students questioned their teachers and might even be rewarded for doing so. In fact, as my college students in Greenwich Village had quickly taught me, discipline, like standards and even authority, were neither admired in America nor considered self-justified. Alistair Cooke, my famous Anglo-American colleague for whom I later acted as producer, once recounted how in a crowded San Francisco bus he found himself crushed against a large African American mother. Being aristocratic by nature he felt obliged to protest such an intimate encounter, and after several times being thrust unwillingly against the woman's broad bosom, he muttered somewhat scornfully, "Democracy!" Being a liberated San Franciscan, the woman responded immediately. "You betcha!" she said, and expanded herself even further.

In Greenwich Village I had also found matching sexual intimacies even in difficult places. The warm hard thigh pressing against mine in darkened movie theaters; the intense relief to discover other living bodies of men who wanted my own; the triumphant outwitting of cultural tyrannies to caress each other in a blessing of unexpected joy, making us one, restoring us to each other. There might even follow a quietly whispered "thank you," sometimes even a surreptitious kiss. As if it was a pejorative, such occasions are given the derisive label "anonymous" by those whose values depend upon language. But we did not need to know each other's names or where we lived. Nor did we care about economic class, ages, or occupations. We had selected each other by the subtlest clues and shadows, looking for an identity more deeply rooted than were cultural artifacts. In the heterosexual tyranny in which we lived, other information was irrelevant, often dangerous. We had learned that talk might easily undermine the simple affection we sought, for it was the product of another dispensation. A grotesque way of making love? As grotesque as the very denial of our existence that forced us to secrete ourselves away.

Such experiences were also to be had in London. One cinema was patronized almost entirely by gay men of all ages, teenagers to ancients. The movies being shown were irrelevant. We moved about the aisles seeking congenial sexual companions, giving the place the air of a busy ant heap, pulsating with desire. The religious tradition and its talk of "lust" (a word whose original Germanic meaning is happiness or delight) orders us to seek "spiritual" rather than physical love. The body, and its needs and works, was a snare. Yet there it surges, unsuppressible, yet unappeased, thrusting itself into our lives, forcing itself into our consciousness, straight or gay, old or young. We ignore it to our cost and to the cost of whatever perception of reality we might have.

In New York, I had found friends who were less inhibited or psychologically repressed than those I had in England. We lived in coffee bars or like beatniks wandered the streets. There, too, little old ladies could be seen speeding down lower Fifth Avenue on roller skates eating ice cream cones! I had missed the history of Europe with its triumphs and tragedies, its architecture, and its offers to join the elite class, but I discovered I missed more what America and nowhere else could offer: not only New York but also the plains, the mountains, the great deserts; and, above all, the sun.

Life elsewhere seemed grey, by comparison, hedged about by conditions, caveats, and hypocrisies and, despite memories of the Klan and McCarthyism, I found I could stomach the stifling British air no longer. Working briefly in my father's studio, I felt the past indignities reaching over me again. The academic and religious life, despite its deprivations or even because of them, had invoked other things than trade, had raised issues and introduced me to ideas that I found I could not talk about as I had talked about them in the Village for all its brashness.

I called on the Bishop of London, sitting resplendent in the Athenaeum surrounded by other members of the elite class. This Bishop was still technically responsible for the me and the Episcopal Church in America. We discussed my prospects.

"You don't like it here?" He was urbane, considerate.

"I find I am stimulated by the environment over there."

He nodded and said, "Yes. I understand." No doubt he had seen Ernie's parish letter. He went on.

"What will you do? Where will you go?"

I had only recently read about James Pike, the Episcopal Bishop of San Francisco, and his bold assertion that the Holy Trinity was a mediaeval concept best dispensed with. He was being charged with heresy by his fellow priests. It was a frontier situation after my own heart. I longed to meet this man.

"Pike? Yes, a problem." Boney hands went up across the purple stock in what seemed to be some agitation. He fingered his sparkling pectoral cross. Yet he smiled.

"Why not? You never know what you'll find out."

"I might do something for suicidal people."

"Yes, indeed. Do you have a reentry permit? Good. Well, goodbye. Let me know how you get on." Again a benign smile, and I was dismissed. Was he pleased to get rid of me, or was it, as I preferred to hope, a blessing in disguise? The Athenaeum smacked too much of the Establishment, of silver spoons in tea cups while the poor and disenfranchised struggled on.

I rented a room in the slums for a few months while I saved my pennies. I had no parish in California, and no prospect of one. But I had my New York connections, and, anyway, California was warm and bright. One might become a bum and still survive. And so in 1960, with no more than one hundred precious dollars in my pocket, I became a genuine emigrant determined to become an American citizen as soon as possible and bound for San Francisco, the earthquake city that a BBC documentary had recently described as *The City That's Waiting to Die*.

HELP!
1961–1968

Though it was not yet called a "gay" capital, San Francisco had long been a haven of outcasts. It guards the entrance to an enormous bay nearly the size of Greater London and once thought to have been discovered by Francis Drake. After gold was discovered in creeks rising in the Sierra Nevada, prospectors poured through San Francisco from all over the world. A few of them grew very rich; nearly all remained poor and returned to the city to die. Meanwhile the millions of dollars in gold, but mostly silver, that had been panned, sluiced, and dug from the Sierra had built the city up. It had become a city of invention: a Scotsman, Andrew Hallidie, designed cable cars to climb the steep hills; a dry-goods merchant, Levi Strauss, cut rough pants from sailcloth and riveted them together to make hard-wearing jeans. But the city's new citizens were mostly poor. Tiny shacks sold for thousands; beggars abounded. Then on April 18, 1906, an earthquake brought buildings tumbling and broke the water mains, leaving the city defenseless against the fire that virtually destroyed it. Yet it was here in 1933–37 that the Golden Gate, as the entrance to the great bay was called, was spanned by what was then the longest single-span suspension bridge in the world. Only cold sea fogs spoil this lovely location with its long history of triumph and, as I was to learn, also of tragedy.

When I arrived in 1960, the city was the home diocese of Episcopal Bishop James Pike, a former lawyer, raised a Roman Catholic, who was attracting to his cause many a maverick priest. He had stated that the concept of the Trinity was outmoded, and this heresy had caused big waves among the Christian establishment around the world. Those in the know seemed to realize, if only vaguely, that to take one stone from the self-consistent and utterly intradependent structure of Christianity might eventually bring it all toppling. Church "order," as the Anglicans liked to call it, had already been compromised by the long-lasting shock waves of the Reformation, and Pike's attack on the Trinity seemed to have turned the Episcopal diocese of California into another religious frontier.

My arrival in San Francisco had not been greeted with the enthusiasm that had been accorded me when I arrived in New York. Pike's heresy had upset many of the local clergy, who did not appreciate the presence of another rascally troublemaker. However, the generous Suffragan, Bishop Millard, offered me a part-time mission parish north of San Francisco. I did not know and had not been told that San Francisco was a liberal town with a solid but still closeted homosexual population. Yet by responding unconsciously to visual clues I also found myself a small room in the Tenderloin district, not far from a bar where "drags" hung out. At that time, bars were (as they largely remain) the only places where gay people could congregate in safety, but the police would raid even these hangouts, arresting any patrons who were without proper identification or whose gender did not seem to match the picture on their driver's license. They also set us up with decoys who would tempt us to kiss and caress them so as to be able to turn us in for engaging in acts of public indecency.

While working in my mission parish I continued to broadcast to London, this time as a West Coast correspondent. My stories covered events of interest to a British audience and I found so much was happening in California that I was rarely at a loss for something to talk about. Scientific discoveries like salt-tolerant wheat; court cases such as those of the Manson "family," the Symbionese Liberation Army, and Patty Hearst, each considered "the trial of the century"; curious inventions such as edible cloth and talking tombstones; and bizarre events like "stomach bumping" or "frog racing" were all greeted with such enthusiasm that I was eventually syndicated in New Zealand, Australia, and Canada. In Australia I became a "science correspondent," just as in Britain I later became a Hollywood correspondent and was flown down every week to interview stars and talk about new movies. Since I was not expected to spend more than the weekends among my parishioners, I found I had enough time to earn such a living. It did not make me rich, but it kept me alive. Moreover, broadcasting new information seemed preferable to an endless study of the bible.

As for my rural parishioners, they wanted Father Mayes to provide spiritual security and the age-old rituals that confirmed it. They appeared to despise the pluralism that I could now see was an important aspect of American religious thought. The fact that there existed whole religions that ignored Jesus and preferred some other divinity, and, what's more, were practiced by millions, was dismissed as irrelevant. Indeed, that religious freedom is established in American law, regardless of belief, seems even now not understood or taught by the churches, which assume that the god in whom their coinage states they trust, along with the god by whom the one nation is thought to be protected, is not only Christian but also the same god they happen to believe in themselves.

So I celebrated Communion each Sunday with less and less enthusiasm. On Saturday nights, like any heterosexual married priest who enjoyed his sex life, I would try to meet other gay men whose warmth and affection made up for the coming Sunday ice. The only place to achieve this was the downtown YMCA where the corridors were well-known lovers' lanes.

The necessary furtiveness of such temporary liaisons angered me. Only the frisson of risk made them tolerable and helped to counteract the aggressive heterosexuality of my parishioners. One Sunday, for example, in a more accomplished, but no more effective repetition of the incident with the British soap-dish lover, a pretty young wife met me after mass, pushed me into the bushes and smothered me with frenzied kisses, her hands tearing at the buttons of my cassock. American heterosexuals, it seemed, were far bolder than were homosexuals, and I could only wish I had the nerve to do the same to some of the husbands. Other parishioners, knowing I was a "pervert," ordered their children to keep away from me. All this while some spouses told me in confidence, though not in the confessional, how much they hated and despised each other. It was a parish where seething hostilities finally came to a head when my landlady, an elderly social worker, warned me to leave the place before things got worse. Looking back, this flock were the oddest bunch, much like people on a wagon train bound together by the slenderest religious threads, not much liking their minister but putting up with him as best they could and as I did with them.

Certainly, as a parish priest I was unsatisfactory. My ever-expanding world seemed so very different from their world, and far more exciting. I thought solutions for their problems would have involved their escaping from the hidebound formalities which constrained, even enshrouded, their lives and to which they appeared to me to cling so desperately. Of those who lived there, I got on well only with the doubters and the pagan husbands who, even so, found it "strange" and "suspicious" that I agreed more with them than with their pious wives.

Some who had hoped for "higher," more Anglican, ceremony had abandoned the local Catholic church in favor of the new-found "father," but found me already a broken reed. Others, liking my apparently democratic ways, preferred me to the local Congregationalists but found me an unwilling convert to the popularity contest that democracy enjoins. In truth, my own thoughts and desires obtruded too much upon the faith I was required to preach, and though I cared for my tiny congregation, it was only at the arm's length at which they held me in turn. Accordingly I encouraged them to abandon their ambition to form a parish of their own and instead to join with another down the road whose priest was cast in the traditional mold. After two years of service, I did not seek reelection.

In the meantime, after an unsuccessful attempt by conservative bishops to unfrock him for being heretic, our maverick bishop married yet again, and became oblivious to all questions except his own personal problems which had been deep-seated and chronic. He carried an intellectual burden that seemed beyond the powers of his colleagues to understand, or maybe they understood too well where such meddling would lead. His struggles with himself ended some years later after experiments with psychic seances. He was found broken and dead at the bottom of a rocky cliff in the desert near Jerusalem, even as his son, who long had problems I had been invited to help solve but never could, took his own life in a New York hotel room. The new bishop, Kilmer Myers, was a quiet, contemplative man without Pike's energy and seemingly at sea in the intellectual maelstrom of the time. That I had great plans seemed to trouble him even less than it had troubled Pike. I was introduced to him as I had been introduced to his predecessor, and that was that.

One day, I was called to the telephone in the diocesan house. It was Ernie, the vicar of the House Church. He had been invited to give an honorary sermon in Grace Cathedral and now, after delivering it, was on his way back to England where he had become dean of Southwark Cathedral. He wanted to talk to me. We had not met since his parish letter, and with some misgiving I agreed to chauffeur him. I did not know it at the time but he was ill and soon would die.

Together we sat in the lounge of the San Francisco airport. He said with much hesitation that he had long wanted to apologize. He was, he said, very sorry.

I comforted him.

"But it was true," I told him, leaving unsaid the fact that an apology, far from putting things right, underlined the shame his words still seemed to imply that I should feel, a familiar problem with such "accusations." One is "accused" of being criminal, whereas to be described is harmless (witness the cultural implications of being accused of being a Jew).

Not long afterward, as if to add injury to insult, I learned with dismay that the minister who had accompanied Robert Newman to Britain and who had originally invited me to the States had been murdered while on a speaking engagement, allegedly by a handyman he had picked up, although this was never proved. He was found in his bedroom and left a wife and family. Respected though hitherto he had been, his name seemed to have been immediately obliterated from church records. An indefatigable worker for civil rights, he had already been threatened by the archconservatives in Congress, so that it is not impossible that he had been set up by his enemies.

I did not know what to make of his death. The way it had apparently been hushed up reinforced prejudice and pain, rather than allayed them. For, whatever the truth of the matter, there was no doubt that there did exist gay men who for reasons of safety or societal pressure had married and raised a family and were now finding that as society grew slowly more tolerant and their familial obligations had been at least partially met, they could no longer honestly bear the strain of continued pretense. Some, indeed, had even achieved a new happiness, though often at great emotional cost, while some abandoned themselves to a sense of freedom they had never thought possible. At the same time, others took terrible risks and died violent deaths, or, after bitter divorces, took their own lives out of guilt, or from despair at the time they considered they had wasted.

It was a situation into which I might easily have fallen myself. Long before, while a guest at a relative's elaborate wedding ceremony, I once said to my parents that marriage was the most important act of a person's life. I remember how pleased they had been. But I now saw marriage, developed by both church and state to protect property and maintain an imposed moral order, with its simplistic definition of family, elaborate rituals, idealistic vows, and legal entanglements, as something left over from another age. Traditional marriage encumbers us with exaggerated expectations of a dream world in which couples live happily ever after. The pretenses and denial often demanded by such a fantasy can cause pain of many kinds; to free oneself as carefully as possible from their illusions is likely to be the healthier, and in the end happier, course. We need more honest approaches to marriage and a definition of family in keeping with our newfound facts of life. Now that there are reliable organizations and communities providing support for gay people, they need to declare themselves. Numbers alone are no guarantee of acceptance by tyrants, but they can be very persuasive.

I supplemented my meager church income not only with my broadcast reports but also with acting engagements on Pacifica Radio's nonprofit station, KPFA, in Berkeley. The corporation had been founded with funds left by Lewis Hill, another hero who had hopes of preserving peace in the midst of the cold war. He was a tragic figure who had been wealthy as well as a Quaker. Like many in the Society of Friends during the Second World War he had served as an ambulance driver; he and two friends had determined that after demobilization they would match war propaganda with pacifistic publicity. When Hill died, his plan envisaged building a communication network of radio stations and perhaps journals, so as to reach a broad spectrum of the general public.

The Pacifica stations may have been the freest stations in the world. They invited all kinds of people to broadcast, some who matched their liberal philosophy and some who did not. Plays, talks, music of all kinds, personalities whom no one would permit to publish, archconservatives, crypto-communists, all had their chance. Their programs were, in fact, what broadcasting is supposed to be about: communication, unfettered, uncensored, and at a tiny fraction of usual costs.

Religion, too, I now saw largely as a matter of communication. Traditional doctrine holds that a priest is little more than a conduit for divine messages. Then, too, perhaps the very give-and-take of communication is communion at its most practical and meaningful, the essence of religious observance. Accordingly, I determined to continue broadcasting. In doing so, I thought, I must be contributing in some way to the development of the human mind; and the soul (presumably my chief concern) must depend upon the mind for something. Yet the more I considered the question of the relationship of the mind to the body, the less certain I became about the soul. It was an uncertainty made all the more troublesome when I came across some dismaying facts about my new city. San Francisco was considered an ideal place to visit by travelers from all over the world. It far outdistanced New York, Paris, and London. But I soon learned that all too many of these visitors came not to cavort but to die.

In 1960, when I first arrived, San Francisco suffered from the highest suicide rate in the United States and the second highest in the Western Hemisphere after what was then West Berlin. No one knew why these two cities had this high rate or whether it might be a statistical artifact, the result of figures suppressed in other countries by, for example, Catholic or Muslim families, doctors, or politicians. Some researchers argued that like West Berlin in those days, isolated and surrounded by a hostile East Germany, San Francisco was also an island; that those who came there initially hoped for a happier, more successful life, or at least rescue from whatever troubles had beset them elsewhere, but had been disappointed; then, cut off from support systems hundreds or thousands of miles away, they had nowhere left to go. Before them lay the waste of the ice-cold Pacific Ocean and at their backs only fiery deserts named for salt, cacti, and death itself.

The stigma that has traditionally attached to those who take their own lives and are henceforward the "unquiet" dead still colors nearly all explanations, medical as well as religious, of suicide. Condemnation of them has remained largely inflexible and absolute, as if they have committed an unnatural act whose implications other humans cannot tolerate. It is said that among the Tiwi, for example, the suicide is thought to endanger the tribe because the tribe must have somehow brought it about.

But such acceptance of blame is shared by hardly any other societies, although their efforts to distance themselves from suicidal acts suggest they suspect they are at fault. People may, indeed, be *driven* to suicide even though others are loath to accept responsibility, preferring to blame the victim for weakness or lack of will. Modern chemistry has discovered that chemical imbalance may lie at the root of the deep depression which often results in suicide, something indicating even more clearly the unreasonableness of the moral code that lurks unacknowledged at the bottom of much opinion on the matter. Even when pain is the cause of the act, the suicide is liable to be accused of impatience or selfishness. The argument that there can be no reasonable justification for taking one's life because things eventually improve is spurious. One has every right to choose not to wait. Life is uncertain.

There may seem to be many good reasons to anticipate the inevitable and bring to end a life led largely in hopeless physical or mental pain. Furthermore, belief in immortality of the soul might make death far more attractive than life. As Dostoevsky once put it, none of us asked to come here and we may not enjoy the experience. Suicide notes confirm that religious beliefs in divine injunction, like medical oaths to preserve life at all costs, are not necessarily persuasive. Gay people, for example, are specially vulnerable in this way.

Unable to change their sexual orientation, condemned not to a week or a moment, but to an entire life of frustration by an ignorant and unsympathetic majority, they must suffer a situation that neither medical opinion nor religious dogma are able to ameliorate. Only by wrenching their lives to suit the demands of the majority can they manage to maintain a semblance of well-being, as did my headmaster. No wonder many of my older gay friends over the years appeared to have little ambition, and were certainly not in the change-mode adopted later by younger gay people. Their aim was not to improve the world; they'd given up on that. They aimed simply to survive.

The high suicide rate in San Francisco, like the existence of its homosexual population, was a fact that the city administrators at that time tried to ignore. Most who died by their own hand did not jump, yet a coast guard cutter daily patrolled the deep water swirling around the two magnificent towers from which the great bridge is suspended, looking for bodies which, when found, were invariably announced by the local press as if they were an achievement, boosting what was described as the "suicide score."

Most of those who did jump from the Golden Gate Bridge died not of drowning but of broken bones. At the speed at which their bodies struck after falling from such a height, the surface of water had a consistency equivalent to that of concrete. In its twenty-five-year history since its completion in 1937, the bridge had seen more suicides than it could accurately count. One businessman had traveled all the way from New York just to jump from it. He took off his coat, folded it neatly, left a rambling letter on top, climbed the railing before anyone could stop him, and leaped into the void.

Standing at the center of the great span and looking out and down to the converging waters of the Sacramento River and the Pacific Ocean, it was indeed difficult not to feel the draw to jump out and be free. The salty ocean wind tears at one's hair, the traffic roars its way behind, while on the far horizon floats the beckoning city of San Francisco, a fairy palace of towers and minarets.

Everyone acknowledged that nothing was being done about the city's record of despair. Elsewhere in the country there had been, at the end of the nineteenth century, a religious service in New York called the Save a Life League; a Catholic priest later opened Rescue, Incorporated in Boston; and in Los Angeles, a psychologist had pioneered a research center. In Britain the Samaritans did stalwart work but were also a quasi-religious group. Nowhere in America, in fact, was there a suicide prevention service free of religious or medical demands, and researchers into the phenomenon thought it unwise that they should publicly offer to help with a problem the solution to which they had yet to discover. In San Francisco itself, the city coroner had even publicly stated that not only was there nothing to be done about suicides, they were probably "better off dead" since otherwise, being "sociopaths," they would be a drain on the public purse. The local paper had actually carried a headline, "Suicides? San Francisco Couldn't Care Less!"

Though I put all this in my reports on life in the American West, I felt obliged to do something constructive about what I had discovered. (Broadcasting can be corrupting, making those who talk or show themselves to millions think they are far more important or knowledgeable than they really are. At the same time, balancing this self-conceit, constant interviews with Big Achievers can also erode one's self-respect by making one feel like a parasite.) Accordingly, since the sorry lack of services for the despairing was so blatant, and tired though I was from my researching and broadcasting, from my priestly duties and from walking the streets seeking someone to fall in love with, I decided to get down to the work that I had originally promised to do.

I considered my options. Could people who were so unhappy they wanted to die be reached before they made a final decision from which there could be no turning back? What would an American service that aimed to do this be like? The models so far devised were all suspect as being patronizing and religious. Moreover, many of those in need of help would be gay. Some sort of anonymous service by telephone, for example, seemed indicated. To such work I thought I could give a good deal of my life. Conversations I had with those who ran other social agencies round the town made clear that it would be a lonely endeavor, but one that was essentially worthwhile. Guy Wright, an influential local newspaper columnist to whom I confided my intentions, wished me luck and added as he took down the details, "You haven't got a hope!"

My cheap single room in the Tenderloin exposed me to the street population. I learned that among the suicides of San Francisco were many, young as well as old, who being homosexual had been rejected not only by their own families but even by their own kind. These would be especially difficult to help and I thought long and hard about how to do it. Professional help by way of official rescue services might not even exist.

The foolish suicide laws still on the books were largely the result of Judeo-Christian doctrine and continued to burden all who might wish to help suicidal people by imposing upon clients and helpers alike a need for the strictest confidentiality, even anonymity. The police arrested any who were discovered attempting to take their own lives and threw them in jail along with drunks and prostitutes: a paradox not dissimilar to the age-old compromise between spiritual and secular sanctions that had burned heretics for the good of their souls. I thought back to my guilt-ridden headmaster and how no one had been able to help him in his extremity. Though surrounded by intelligent, caring colleagues, in an institution dedicated to education and well-being, yet he found no one to pull him from the abyss. I also remembered Bishop Pike and his son, whom I had been unable to help in time. The hurdles in the way of getting help were many and complicated.

It did not seem likely that suicidal people would think of themselves as criminals, or mentally ill, or even sinful. The two professions, medical and religious, that might otherwise be thought appropriate to assist them were far from ideal as immediate sources of assistance, precisely because of the public belief that they condemned suicidal intent. The public might be wrong, but any plan for helping would-be suicides would have to take "where they are" into consideration, or it would fail. And, anyway, neither profession had yet shown any inclination to give assistance beyond gathering statistics.

Then too, so far as gay people were concerned, professional advisers, too often being what we now describe as "homophobic," were likely to be causing, if not suicides, at least as much misery as they were preventing. Churchpeople, and clergy in particular, present their faiths and their dogmas as reasons for prolonging life, while physicians and therapists are obedient to their Hippocratic Oath to preserve life at all costs, regardless of how miserable it might be. Although either profession would have provided a safe haven by being within the law, it was clear that a public alliance with them might fatally compromise the outcome.

It was thus important that any service that I might devise should not be known or perceived to be either religious or medical. Reluctantly, the bishop appeared to acknowledge this and permitted the diocesan attorney to draw up legal papers of incorporation which provided for the two required additional directors of record, Clifford Horton, director of the Seamen's Center, and Howard Freeman, the public relations officer. Thereafter, these were required to show no further interest and remained ghost directors, later severing all relationship. I was then on my own with a penniless organization called "San Francisco Suicide Prevention," an unfortunate title suggesting forcible prohibition, but one whose connotation of anticipation described what we would be about. It would need to take a working title, doing business under another name. Suicide prevention services known as such are now well established across the country but there were none in 1960, no other service against which to compare what we hoped to build.

My eventual plan was simple and I was surprised that no one had thought of it before. I decided to talk it over with a friendly psychiatrist working at the city clinic. Like the columnist, she shook her head doubtfully.

"The wish for one's own death is not only irrational, it's as if the organism was actually working against itself."

"And that's why you say it must be evidence of mental illness?"

She pondered this. "Certainly of imbalance."

"Ah, yes," I remembered, "in Britain coroners invariably describe suicidal death as being due to an 'unbalanced' or 'disturbed' mind. But this assumes," I continued, not so easily put off, "that death is not a valid choice. Whereas it's easy to think of circumstances such as torture or terminal illness, or even altruistic acts such as a mother protecting her children, when to select your own death or a painless conclusion to it all might seem the most sensible, even a virtuous solution: legitimate, even healthy. Durkheim, remember, felt obliged to include altruism in his list of 'causes.'"

The psychiatrist looked hard at me and waved a dismissive hand. "That wouldn't necessarily mean it was not an unbalanced decision, even under duress. Such an act might seem very unwise given the chance of second thoughts." She frowned. "And anyway," she went on, "the death on such occasions is usually brought about by someone or something else. The man who dives into a stormy sea to save a drowning child all too frequently drowns too. Such an act may be 'heroic'; it is also foolhardy."

"Perhaps what's needed is someone to sort such choices out before they're made."

"But that's what psychiatry does, or tries to."

"Yes, and so do the clergy. But surely to talk to a psychiatrist you must first have come to the conclusion that you are 'unbalanced,' which most people don't like to do. In the same way, to want to talk to a priest, you must have already decided you are contemplating a potentially sinful act. In other words, you must have already taken a judgmental step in either of those directions."

"It's true they don't come to us," she replied ruefully. "Most people prefer to talk to the bartender or their hairdresser, so I'm told. And physicians don't like to have suicides on their record. They immediately ship them off to the hospital because they're bad for business."

I shook my head. "Yes, business. The clergy want you in their flock and shrinks charge money."

She bristled at this.

"Remember we have a sliding scale."

"Of course. And it was Freud, I think, who said fees are part of the cure. But because you have to ask them about their income this becomes another hurdle to getting help."

It was the conditional nature of the help, as of the "salvation" being offered, that had paralyzed the professionals. I struggled on, irritated by the indifference I was encountering. The professionals, despite their expertise, seemed to have done nothing about a most appalling problem of human misery that for years had been breaking records!

I made an appointment with a social worker who knew the local communities and might be expected to have found some sensible answer. At first he sounded hopeful.

"I will admit," he confirmed, "that most people do not get the help they need; either because they don't seek it, or because they don't think they need it. And even when they do think they need it, they still don't get it; either because they can't afford it, or because—"

I anticipated him. "They don't know where to go!"

"Exactly. And who's to tell them? How many people, especially elderly people, can even find their way around the telephone directory, let alone go knocking on doors?"

"And if you're suicidal, you probably don't have the energy to do so anyway."

"Right. Look at your homosexuals. They're in an even worse situation, especially when they're teenagers. We have a difficult enough time with heterosexual kids who don't want us to tell their parents. The law wont let us help them without their parents' permission. This makes it virtually impossible to help kids who are homosexual, even if they're prepared to admit that they are perverts."

I stared at him. "Perverts?"

"Certainly. That's the official description. That's what they'd be labeled by whoever dealt with them. 'Suffering from sexual perversion.' That's even what their parents call them if they ever find out. Of course they don't get help. They'd rather die. And get this! Many parents would rather have them dead. And tell them so!"

This certainly seemed to make nonsense of the mental imbalance theory, especially if people who could treat their own children in this way were judged to be sane. It also showed clearly enough that psychiatrists who claimed, often energetically, that their profession did not pass moral judgement on its clients, nevertheless defined mental illness in terms of standards of normalcy, and their definitions were liable to reflect not scientific findings but merely the current mores of the day.

On the way back to the Tenderloin, I ruminated on these and other very similar conversations with members of the helping professions. The idea for an intermediary listening service using the telephone now seemed definitely to be justified. But its apparent simplicity belied hidden complications, as I soon discovered when rehearsing with a research psychologist plans for selecting and training the staff of volunteers who would be needed.

I explained that the telephone number would be published as a service for those who were "thinking of ending it all." The word "suicide" would not be used. Anyone could call us for a dime or less and we would listen to them, try to find out what was needed, and refer them on. No easy answers, no quick decisions, and no pressure. We'd be playing the same role between troubled people and the help they needed that priests were supposed to play between their flock and God, except we wouldn't have any ulterior motive of our own other than to be of use.

He pursed his lips. "You'll get depressed people, lonely people, but not necessarily suicidal people. People may talk of dying but never take the final step. Most who threaten suicide don't follow through. It's a fact."

"But of those who do kill themselves," I countered, for I had done my homework, "most have tried before."

"True. But once they've made up their mind, they frequently express euphoria. They feel better, even happier, thus lessening the chances that they'd call your service." This also was true.

"Wasn't it Doctor Johnson," he reminded me, "who said the decision to die removes all constraints of law and makes a man so powerful that nothing society can do to him is worse than what he has already determined for himself? It's essentially a selfish act."

"Now you're talking like a psychiatrist. You mean 'selfish' in a technical sense, but I can think of many situations when it's far from selfish and very likely would confer great benefits on others. Those ugly parents of homosexual children, for example, would welcome it. And wealthy old parents might think it a gift to their children not to spend their money on unproductive medical care."

Crucial, fundamental questions about whether to live or die reach into the depths of existence itself and have been explored by great thinkers down through the ages. They are not questions to be fobbed

off with ritual, medication, or preconceived notions, but deserve careful and honest thought. Indeed, Christian church fathers, confronted
with the martyrdoms of so many saints who elected death rather than
betray their faith, expended much effort attempting to resolve the fate
of suicides. They reluctantly determined that whatever others may do
to you, to lay hands on *yourself* is what constitutes the sin: it is an act
of despair that cannot be rewarded and the commission of which
requires special prayers for the soul, just as, until recently, the church
denied suicides burial in consecrated ground. It was a view of existence that I rejected, but that many still held, and as I had discovered
it was echoed in medical theory.

Thus, for legal as well as other reasons, confidentiality was essential. But the useful mechanism of the cheap telephone call only half
guaranteed a solution. Those answering the telephone would need to
identify themselves in a way that did not compromise either the callers
or themselves. It was obvious that my own credentials for offering
such a service might be questioned if I were to be named, and I turned
to our lawyer for advice. He was sitting in a dark room in the heart of
the Diocesan administrative offices near the cathedral.

"Unless you are prepared to identify yourself in your rightful
authority as a priest," he told me, "the service will be attacked as
unprofessional, if not actually illegal."

"But that would mean abandoning all pretension to objectivity.
We'd get only churchpeople calling and certainly no homosexual
people."

He seemed not to hear me and went on, "You must remember that
America is a country where life has been hard and the people tough.
Among those determined to take their own lives are likely to be some
for whom a gun is the instrument of choice." He looked at me and
frowned. "I hope you're not thinking of visiting these people?"

He had raised another important issue. Would we never see our
clients? According to the statistics I had gathered, men rather than
women used guns. Women preferred to die by ingesting pills accompanied by stiff drinks of alcohol. A closed garage with a tube carrying
carbon monoxide into a car interior ran a close third to these methods, while elderly people sometimes attached tubing to a gas stove
and thence to plastic shopping bags tied over their heads with a rubber band. Jumping from the Golden Gate Bridge or from other
bridges or upper storey windows was a well known but actually less
popular way. Our lawyer, however, was correct: guns were also used
and could be turned against those attempting rescue.

And although it was clear neither I nor my assistants intended to visit or see our callers or to play an intrusive role of "rescuers," our callers might wish to see us! Accordingly, as a further guarantee of anonymity, it was determined I would use a pseudonym. But what name to use? Would suicidal people seeking help for the most momentous decision of their lives be encouraged to open up to "Rick," or "Billy," or even "Kevin"? The professional advisers I had gathered about me were now fully in the spirit of the experiment and cudgeled their brains.

"How about Nigel?" asked someone. This was rejected immediately.

"Michael's nice, or even Tom," suggested our sociologist.

"Tom! Are you kidding? I'd never call up a peeping 'Tom.' Besides, what about 'doubting Thomas'? That would put me off!"

We wrangled on until it occurred that we needed a name with the correct associations, a metaphor for courage and good hope. Suddenly I thought of a famous Scottish monarch who returned to battle after watching a determined spider overcoming obstacles on its climb up to its web.

"How about Bruce?" I asked. "Solid sounding monosyllable, not too familiar, suggests strength . . . ?"

So "Bruce" it was, and "Bruce" did I become.

And with this rather tentative, not so say naive, plan, the papers of incorporation with both a formal and working title were completed. The organization was to be entirely voluntary. No one was to be suspected of receiving an income from the suffering of others, so there was to be no pay or recompense of any kind. To emphasize this point, there was to be at first no executive director, as existed in other professional services. Instead, though I was in fact the executive, I insisted on being identified as director of volunteers. Executive directorships were usually paid positions and the title would suggest precisely what I was attempting to avoid—the criticism that we were making money out of people's suffering. We thus became the first volunteer citizens' hot line in America.

Our next task was to determine the location for our telephone. My broadcasting work was increasing and would enable me to pay a reasonable rent. And since it was essential that the service should be as professionally organized as possible, it was important that the location be within easy reach of day and night restaurants for volunteers, and in order to encourage professional alliances, it should be both clean and dignified.

San Francisco has many neighborhoods. Suburbs cover the hills to the ocean and the great port with its cranes and dry docks had been decaying ever since its wartime role as a naval base. Wealthy families from whom some of our daytime volunteers might be recruited lived up on the hills and overlooked the city with its Chinatown (known for its elderly male suicides), the sleazy Tenderloin that housed a struggling gay population, and Polk Street, or "Polk Gulch," where gay teenagers hustled and killed themselves. The tawdry main artery of Market Street split the city in two, the business section on one side, workshops and warehouses on the other, one end at the water's edge and the other in the hills.

During the 1950s, mainline churches in metropolitan communities across America, taking their cue from evangelical sects in poor city neighborhoods, had tried to stem the youth drain by renting derelict storefronts where, to attract the young, they opened coffee houses, or even cabaret theaters. The director of a Seamen's Center invited me to tour such locations, taking me down into the derelict areas of Hunter's Point where he would throw rocks through the remaining plate glass windows "just to be able to say he'd done it." This exhibition, if nothing else, showed me without his intending to do so that storefronts were certainly not the answer to my problem. Too public, they invited inquisitive passersby into what had to be a confidential service. What was needed was a comfortable but reasonably priced office, if possible hidden from view, where selection and training could take place in private.

After several wearying weeks of search, I had almost given over finding anything that could be turned into an inexpensive headquarters, however small. Then, one morning, making my way home, I noticed a "for rent" sign in a brown brick building known as Marquette Apartments on Geary Street near Polk Gulch. The heavy front of the building, the carefully polished brass plate, the solid, reliable appearance, and the clean windows were all promising. I did not like the idea of an apartment but it seemed there was no choice. Geary Street runs through the center of town, a busy commercial thoroughfare at one end which then calms down as it enters this more sedate part of town, near coffee shops but untroubled by tourists or panhandlers. It was also well lit. Volunteers might come there without fear, even at night. But although the place might be suitable, I had already suffered too many rebuffs to expect much. The peaceful but dark hallway of fumed oak and pine dating from the 1920s smelled of polish and cleaning fluids.

The short, balding, bespectacled manager who answered my bell asked me what I was looking for. Something small, private, and inexpensive, I told him. He took me down a short flight of stairs leading off the hall into what was obviously a remodeled basement which had been partitioned off into several small rooms, their doors opening out into a general area; a dark, forbidding place like a wartime underground shelter. He opened one of the doors, revealing a tiny room into which light filtered from a transom window near the ceiling at sidewalk level. The wheels of vehicles and occasional feet could be seen passing by the dirty glass. A camp bed stood along the far side, with a worm-eaten table. A worn carpet covered the concrete floor. It was certainly small, it might be private, and it could be fixed up. Its rent?

"Thirty dollars a month."

"I'll take it." I was tired and could afford it. "Can I have it on a month-to-month lease?"

He looked me up and down. As had happened before, my accent, or perhaps the clothes and college tie that I had hoped would encourage, had put him off. He was holding the papers of the lease in one hand and his eyes narrowed suspiciously. What was someone like me taking a little room like this for?

"You'll be living here . . . alone?" His voice rasped.

"Not 'living,' no. But we'll be here at night."

I saw my chance slipping away, as he made to put the lease back in his pocket. If he was worried about my morality, any mention of my real purpose would more than frighten him, as it had frightened even professionals.

"Who's 'we'? And what d'you mean, 'not living'?" he asked, shaking his head.

I began to explain, without telling him anything. It was to be an office; people would come and go . . .

"People? Come and go? No, no, I can't . . ." He prepared to show me out. I could see what he was thinking. I must be a pimp.

I decided to come clean. More days of fruitless searching stretched before me. This tiny place was becoming more important, more appropriate, the more we talked. It was warm, a bit smelly perhaps, but there was a space for files . . .

"It's for a service . . ." I began hopefully.

"A 'service'? What sort of service?" His brow wrinkled.

"Volunteers will come to help . . ." There was nothing for it. "Help suicidal people." The dreadful word had been uttered.

I hastened to reassure him.

"By phone—to get them help. We don't see them," I concluded, cheerfully.

He said nothing; just looked at me. Then, extending his arms, he slowly turned over his hands.

"You mean like this?" he asked. Two ragged scars ran across both wrists. Oh, my, I thought, and nodded.

"Yes," I said. "Like that." I had come full circle.

He walked across the room and looked up at the window, feeling in his pocket as he did so.

Drawing out a pen, he said, "You can have it for half price. And good luck to you."

We were off to as auspicious a start as might ever have been wished for.

By the 1990s in San Francisco, at work in their prestigious office building, the two hundred volunteers of our Suicide Prevention Center would be talking to and referring more than seventy thousand clients every year at a "donated cost" of no more than a few dollars each. It is still an extraordinary example of customized service. Yet its birth in 1961 had been difficult. I had wanted frontier work and I had found it. Moreover, its planning and development were fascinating.

The room was quickly cleaned and furnished. The telephone company installed a red telephone, my one concession to the excitement I felt at getting something done at last which might be of actual use. The friendly, though pessimistic, columnist came out with an encouraging piece that included his own office telephone number for would-be volunteers; and I planned a manual for their selection and training.

Few of the professionals I talked to seemed to understand that the task to be accomplished was both more complex and more simple than might be imagined. The art of listening was the key ingredient; an art that turned out to be in short supply. Many volunteers, otherwise friendly sounding or especially knowledgeable, seemed to feel obliged not only to talk, but even to offer what they themselves considered good reasons for living. Several therapists offered to take part—a psychiatrist, some psychologists; so did a few clergy of various denominations, all of them sonorous with advice, and oozing professional charm. Like the women who bubbled over with enthusiasm at the romantic chance of saving lives, none of these had the touch I was looking for.

Clearly, too, some of those applying to volunteer were themselves suicidal, a difficulty which was always to remain something of an anxiety, but not something I feared as much as did some of our colleagues. One morning the executive director of a mental health association, in an attempt to assess what was going on, visited our little office, now furnished with donated curtains, chairs, desk, and cabinets. I was still selecting volunteers and had begun training them while also testing a professional answering service to route the calls to volunteers who had already been trained. When the telephone rang, he sprang back, his face ashen.

"There's someone bleeding on the end of that line!" he cried, his face working.

"Maybe," I said, "but now there's someone answering it."

I was surprised at his shock and suspected what later proved to be the case, that he might well be a candidate for the service himself.

"Which would be better," I asked him as I picked up the phone, "evidence that someone cared—or silence?"

Another would-be volunteer claimed to be ideal because, she said, she had attempted to take her own life three times and had gotten over it. She arrived on crutches.

"It's no good," she began. "If you're meant to live, you've gotta live!"

She had thrown herself under a bus, and her right ear was misshapen from an attempt to blow her head off with a pistol.

"No, I won't take coffee," she continued as I offered her a cup. "My stomach's ulcerated from drinking poison." No, I did not take her on as a volunteer.

New ideas have a tough time being accepted, until eventually the detractors come back claiming they too would have done the job if they had had the time. But the work is even more difficult to accomplish when one does not have the tools, a lack which we were at pains to correct as soon as possible by creating them ourselves. To provide a manual, I dug deeper and deeper into my own memories of troubled people facing pain and death. I was convinced that those who have thought of suicide were likely to be far less embarrassed by the subject than would be the volunteers listening to their stories. Thus the subject itself might be named and discussed with callers far more readily than many feared. The embarrassment might all be on our side.

Visits to the research center in Los Angeles and the remnants of the nineteenth-century religious service in New York revealed that neither organization was engaged in dealing with the general public. The Los Angeles researchers were protective of their professional reputation and dismissed volunteers and even a free publicized service as dangerous. Only if help was paid for could the client be taken seriously. Some researchers even insisted that all suicidal people should be locked up in hospital for their own good.

The initial strength of what we had to offer was not only the inherent advantage of the telephone as an immediately available instrument of communication in which power over the call resided with the caller, but also the service's independence. No one intruded on a client's life, for it was the clients who initiated the calls and determined their duration together with whatever degree of anonymity they might desire. Moreover, the service did not judge or assume any position with regard to need or the law. "You're not the police, are you?" was a frequent question, as were fears of "shrinks" and, it must be said, of Catholics. Such freedom was not possible with appointments, visits, or returned calls to identified numbers, all the usual requirements of professional agencies, but ones that we had forbidden. What was more, we could reliably assume that it really was thoughts of suicide that had prompted the call because that was how the service was advertised.

The availability of the telephone in the United States, where telephones are more or less a fact of everyday life, was also critically important. Virtually all agencies and hospitals close their doors at five o'clock, and cannot readily offer assistance either during the night or over the weekend. Yet these are the very times when personal stress is likely to become intolerable. Our telephone lines were always open.

Even many emergency services are available only to people who are prepared to identify themselves, who reside in the same county as the service being sought, and who can in some way guarantee payment. We discovered by means of actual on-site experiments that even in life-threatening situations the only reliable method by which to obtain help from hospital emergency services without actually walking into the emergency room itself was to make a noisy fuss or lie on the floor. We intended no criticism of the hospitals or services concerned. They operated with slender budgets and minimal personnel; but we had lives to save. We also learned that emergency services across the nation were often similarly encumbered by small budgets, tiny staffs, and jurisdictional rules quite out of touch with reality. Emergencies everywhere, unless the police were involved, were situations for which local authorities and their professionals had never been organized nor granted necessary funding. If you were thinking of doing away with yourself, they seemed to be saying, please do so during regular business hours. (This state of affairs had not changed much even by 2000, and partly accounts for the agency's continued success.)

I hoped to commence the service as soon as we had enough selected and trained volunteers to open more than one telephone twenty-four hours a day, seven days a week. Initially, this proved as difficult as it was for the professionals. "Bruce" began with gaps covered by either an answering service or a newly invented machine, both of which transferred calls, but often with disastrous clicking noises suggesting that someone might be listening in. This frightened more timid callers into instantly hanging up.

The first volunteers to finish their training were identified within the agency by numbers, but used their own first names on the telephone. Eileen, ever afterwards proud to have been the first to be selected, was a onetime secretary already used to listening and taking copious, immediately useful notes regardless of emotional strain. Catherine was a trained nurse who, having retired from regular duties, could donate enormous amounts of time without losing her professional calm. Mary was the widow of an army officer, also tireless, never flustered, hitherto untrained but experienced in dealing with crises. She would win over angry callers by telling them she was ready to learn. Jim, our fourth selection, was himself a trained social worker, with yet another schedule to keep, but whose experience and quiet good sense was invaluable during difficult calls. Chuck, our fifth, was a businessman, solid, reliable, careful, and sensitive, who reported that the work had more meaning than anything he had ever done in his life. These five formed part of a small foundational group which was eventually to increase to more than two hundred and included a city supervisor and a state senator.

The early use of a professional answering service to fill gaps in the twenty-four-hour schedule led to an important discovery. As calls began coming in, at first no more than one, then several each day and night, a detailed logbook was kept to the minute with a record of what was said and what referral was made, whether to an ambulance, if one seemed necessary, or to some other professional service. In this way we were able to assess not only each other's ability and to improve the way in which particular situations were handled, but also the efficiency of the many professional emergency services that we had sometimes to call for rescue. These were the services which liked to complain that it was their responsibility to handle suicidal people and theirs alone; that their staffs were professionally trained, whereas ours were amateurs.

To test the efficiency of the emergency services we might be required to use, we utilized my own professional recording equipment and made trial calls from supposedly troubled people to a cross section of the referral sources that advertised themselves as offering immediate or emergency help. We would weep into the phone or be otherwise inarticulate, and sometimes simply ask for help. Sources tested in this way included hospitals, psychiatrists, churches, and mental health agencies; any service, in fact, that suicidal people might be expected to call. The responses were recorded and the results were appalling. Telephone operators, even physicians themselves, were gruff, rude, and impatient, and would sometimes respond with no more than a grunt. Occasionally they even berated the would-be client and then hung up. The responses from clergy were uniformly cloying. Very few of those tested sounded even interested in helping people struggling to articulate their need of help.

The reason for such results was not far to seek, and provided further evidence that our service was valuable, if not essential. Institutions and individual practitioners themselves are usually too busy to spend time sorting out people's problems for them without an appointment. At first even our own panel of professional advisers, sympathetic with their colleagues and anxious to protect them from unfair criticism, proposed that we should respond similarly and abandon the offer of anonymity on the grounds that it reinforced the low self-esteem we were attempting to diminish. Before listening to our clients' troubles, they advised that we should demand their names, addresses, and telephone numbers, and, as usual, ask if they could pay for treatment. This, they argued, would clear the air. But when they themselves had actually listened to callers and experienced their distress firsthand, instead of only reading about it in professional journals or basing their opinions upon experiences with relatively untroubled clients, they came to understand the true difficulty of the referral task we had undertaken. It was simply no use demanding that distressed people immediately become levelheaded and articulate. Such a "snap out of it! stiff upper lip!" approach was precisely why so many in need were alienated from professional help. It had the insensitive overtones of those who just can't understand why others feel bad when they feel well themselves.

At the same time, there was no doubt the argument against reinforcing "suicidophobia" was cogent, and once the city had grown used to our existence, we very soon did away with "Bruce" and our volunteers were permitted to acknowledge the service for what it was: an offer to help desperate people before they took an irretrievable step; in fact, true pre-vention.

There were also practical reasons to dispense with the high degree of anonymity that we had insisted upon. Everyone to do with the service had taken a working name and identified themselves as Bruce's assistants, a system which worked well both among ourselves and for the callers to whom our full names were immaterial. However, because we also allowed the callers to use aliases, our follow-up records quickly became crowded with Bills, Marys, and Joes. It thus became important to persuade them during the course of their call to tell us their real names, and, if in danger, their addresses, just as our advisors had recommended. Sadly, the shadow of the police always hung about such moments and even more so when we were forced to trace calls from those dying in their beds who had changed their minds. On the other hand, cruising police cars were nearly always within reach and were able to save lives because of it. Indeed, because they were so useful, we attempted to train the police force to switch off their sirens when called in by us, and to hide their guns, accommodations they did not like to make.

Always, over the years, as we relocated several times and constantly improved our techniques, the volunteers we accepted for training were never "do-gooders" in the pejorative sense, but were usually drawn from the small number of people in the population who had themselves worked at some time or other in a similar professional field. Such people had empathy for others, were not depressed themselves, and were realistic about life and death. They were called upon to be utterly reliable in their shifts, to be unusually patient with their callers, and always to keep a level head despite emergencies. Not surprisingly, we found that nurses, especially those trained in psychiatry, were often ideal volunteers. Such a team was hard to come by but eventually became the most trusted staff in the city. We knew we had finally been accepted when professionals themselves referred their own clients to us because hospitals and physicians were able to do little else than send suicidal and depressed people on an endless runaround, hoping perhaps that they would land in someone else's lap. Our staff were required to stay with a caller all the way and could afford the time to do so.

The importance of the training manual was such that no volunteer was permitted to handle calls until three months had been spent learning procedures, listening to simulated calls, and being tested by carefully vetted professional advisers. Special training had also to be devised for certain situations the staff might have to face. We would never snatch up the phone when it began to ring, but always waited two rings before answering. This gave both caller and staff time to breathe. The caller had summoned up courage to make the call, and staff needed time to gather their wits. In a famous call later used as a model in the training sessions, the volunteer, after picking up the telephone and identifying the service, could hear only sobbing. She continued to listen without interrupting until at last the caller breathed deeply and asked, "Are you still there?" "Yes," replied the volunteer quietly, "I'm still here."

We recorded tapes by means of which trainees could learn about the various dynamics of taking calls from distressed people. We showed that the opening words and their intonation were crucial to the subsequent success of a call. Winning the caller's trust and finding out information essential not only for making an appropriate referral, but also for evaluating the lethality of the caller's situation, also took considerable practice. Lethality was determined according to responses to key questions introduced, seemingly at random, in the course of the conversation, designed to reveal whether the person had suffered loss of any kind; had readily available means for taking their life; had already made plans to die; had selected a location in which to die; and so on, including any history of dependency on drugs or alcohol. Depending on the answers to such questions, services could be alerted or described and referred to the caller as needed.

During training it was also essential to weed out volunteers who might be prejudiced against gay people, who pitied them, or who had hang-ups about sex of any kind. Although they might claim to be free of prejudice, the tone of voice such people used would often belie them. One volunteer who never finished training was unable to break her southern habit of using the word "Negra" for blacks, now African Americans. Another whom we let go would inadvertently refer to gay people as "pansies"; correcting himself only made matters worse.

In order to help relatively unsophisticated volunteers improve their performance on the telephone, I devised many training tapes, one of which exposed them to, among other information, the vocabulary of intimate sexual activity sometimes used by callers in their extremity. The trainees would be given this tape along with others in the usual run of their training period, and would settle down to listen expecting only professional jargon. Soon their faces would blanch as they heard words which had never passed their lips and which often they did not know the meaning of. Once they had been exposed to such language, they did not repeat the experience of one volunteer from the early days who put down the receiver saying she was not able to handle the call because she had "never been spoken to in that way before!" The temptation to abandon a caller was sometimes great, and not always for reasons of propriety or prejudice. Sometimes the most difficult callers to talk to, find out their problems, and refer them appropriately were well-educated intellectuals who had thought out all the options and who, though they claimed to be in search of sophisticated answers, actually needed only a shoulder to cry on.

One day, a small group of professionals paid a visit. They were led by one of the two directors of the Los Angeles research center who, being a Freudian psychologist, was naturally suspicious of both my religious background and of volunteers, and attempted to take control of our successful agency in order to dismantle it. By then we had considerable clout in the community and despite the undoubted brilliance of our usurpers, our own professional advisory board were powerful and not prepared always to assess suicide in terms of mental illness or to write off trained volunteers as useless; the attempt to disable us was rebuffed.

When I had received our first grant from the San Francisco Foundation, I could only whisper our gratitude. The director smiled and replied, "Exciting!" As indeed it was. Grants, like advancement, were rarely given to openly gay people who—unless they had sold their souls to further their ambitions—lacked the wives, husbands, and children still considered essential for joining the truly "successful" ranks of society. So now we had funds, and we applied for more with increasing success.

Our volunteer staff grew rapidly. The conspirators had sought to destroy the service by renaming it the "Pacific Institute for Living" and making their own research into a national headquarters. Instead, with more annual grants from a variety of sources I opened or helped start similar centers in all the counties of the greater Bay Area. As if in response, the researchers subsequently formed a national association which, as is often the way with associations, drained energy and money from local services while returning little immediate benefit.

Almost invariably the work was satisfying, even uplifting, especially when the callers evinced gratitude for the relief that had been offered, and when our training enabled the volunteers to grow in understanding so that their experiences became an invaluable asset. Eventually visitors, nearly always professionals such as nurses, physicians, and social workers, were eager to undertake our specialized training and quickly found themselves caught up in what must have seemed to them a strange new world.

Eventually we occupied an entire small building with sufficient room to take calls, receive and interview prospective volunteers and supporters, and develop the three essential months of rigorous training. The walls of the reception area carried pictures of well-known suicides from Socrates and Cleopatra to Romeo and Marilyn Monroe, a gift from an admirer who recognized the complexity of our task and the very issues raised by suicide as a rational proposition. (In fact, the pictures conveyed conflicting messages and were finally returned.)

The daily life of the center was exhilarating. In the background you would hear a low buzz of conversation from the service area where two or three members of the volunteer staff were taking calls. Above their heads was an enormous board covered with agencies' names, telephone numbers, addresses, and hours of operation. Sometimes the names of key professionals would also appear or disappear as they became known to be available or rejected as unhelpful or inefficient. Along with these was the list of "walk-in" agencies where appointments were not necessary, and of places offering free food, lodging, and special assistance for the disabled. Maps showing the locations of all these places were also pinned up for easy referral. Old people often needed help finding their way around, especially when they couldn't see or read. Each of the agencies and services to which clients were referred had been visited and researched. Many brochures were found to be incorrect, out of date, even misleading, and the locations themselves hard to find or reach, with many stairs, or down some hidden cul-de-sac. Accordingly, screwed to another wall was an enlarged map showing directions. Dominating the room was a chart with the numbers and shifts for the ever-increasing staff of volunteers.

Training took place in the next room. Around a table, several men and women wearing headphones would be taking notes while listening to a tape played from a special carousel. In one corner a trainee would be being coached by Hazel, our new supervisor of volunteers, who was not only specially trained in handling unpaid staff but also highly knowledgeable about the agencies and services to which they gave referrals.

After two years we decided to permit a small group of specially trained psychiatric nurses to visit selected callers, so as to provide a valuable assessment against which we could measure our responses and the referrals we had made. Accordingly Hazel, along with Marion Kalkman, the director of nursing at the Medical Center of the University of California; Jerome Motto and Marjorie Folinsbee, our resident psychiatric advisors; and Helen Wolford, the chief of the Psychiatric Nursing division, selected and trained a team of visiting psychiatric nurses. Working in pairs, they were to take calls, offer to give counsel free of charge, and, on receiving agreement, visit selected callers and report back from the field.

The experiences of the team were sometimes as hair-raising as they were revealing. Careful explorations of filthy corridors in slum apartment buildings; visits to hotel rooms with ambulance personnel close behind; blood; guns at the ready; weeping relatives and violent spouses; all this confirmed not only the difficulty of the task that our organization had originally undertaken, but also how accurate our volunteers had been in their assessment of callers' problems and how hard it was for them to get the help they needed.

With my parents, 1937

Londoners sheltering from bombing and sleeping in an Underground station during the Second World War, 1940. (COURTESY OF THE LIBRARY OF CONGRESS, PRINTS AND PHOTOGRAPHS DIVISION; BRITISH OFFICIAL PHOTOGRAPH FROM THE OFFICE OF WAR INFORMATION)

Wardens' Post in London during Second World War, 1941, with gas masks within reach. (COURTESY OF THE LIBRARY OF CONGRESS, PRINTS AND PHOTOGRAPHS DIVISION; BRITISH OFFICIAL PHOTOGRAPH, FROM THE OFFICE OF EMERGENCY MANAGEMENT)

Stroking Cambridge college crew at the Royal Regatta, Henley on Thames, 1953

With Anthony, his mother and brothers vacationing in Cornwall, 1952

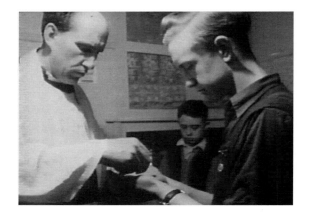

A House Church mass, Halton, Leeds, 1957. The celebrant is Father Ernest Southcott. (COURTESY OF ROBERT NEWMAN; FROM ALF GOES TO WORK, DIR. ROBERT NEWMAN)

Wire and concrete barriers erected across roads linking two housing developments in Halton, Yorkshire, 1957. (PHOTOGRAPH BY ROBERT NEWMAN, COURTESY OF ROBERT NEWMAN)

The "Right to Sing" riot, Washington Square, New York City, 1958. I am wearing the striped sweater. (PHOTOGRAPH BY ROBERT W. BONE, COLLECTION OF THE AUTHOR)

With NASA dresser, wearing astronaut suit at Langley Air Force Base, Virginia, 1959 (NASA PHOTOGRAPH, AUTHOR'S COLLECTION)

Racially mixed farm employees of Koinonia Farm, Americus, Georgia, 1959. (COURTESY OF LENNY JORDAN)

First office of San Francisco Suicide Prevention Center, 965 Geary Street, San Francisco, 1961. The grill of the basement room at street level is in the lower center of the picture.

On the red telephone at the offices of San Francisco Suicide Prevention Center, 1963. Volunteer staff are in the background. (COURTESY OF THE LIBRARY OF CONGRESS, PRINTS AND PHOTOGRAPHS DIVISION, LOOK MAGAZINE COLLECTION; PHOTOGRAPH BY DOUGLAS JONES)

Members of The *Coits* in drag, 1970. Peter is wearing white and seated in the front. (COURTESY OF PETER VAN DER KAR)

KQED-FM was founded in 1969 in a restored Victorian church on Divisadero Street, San Francisco. (COURTESY OF KQED ARCHIVES)

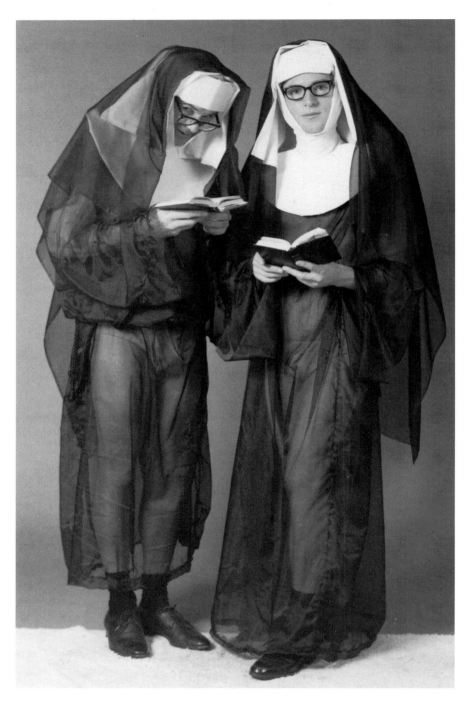

With Peter as "see-through nuns" at the *Coits* annual ball, 1970. (PHOTOGRAPH BY
COLEMAN STUDIO, SAN MATEO CALIFORNIA)

With Peter in 1985. (AUTHOR'S COLLECTION)

Board meeting of National Public Radio, Alta Mira Hotel, Sausalito, California, June 22-23, 1970. From bottom left, clockwise: Sharon Broyles, CPB Secretary; Bernard Mayes, chairman; Marvin Siegelman; William Siemering partially hidden; Albert Hulsen of Corporation for Public Broadcasting; Richard Estell; Karl Schmidt; Frank Gillard of British Broadcasting Corporation; Joseph Gwathmey, vice chairman; Nathan Shaw; Donald Forsling. (Absent: David Platts.) (COURTESY OF NATHAN SHAW)

Candlelight march
in San Francisco
mourning the assas-
sination of Harvey
Milk, 1978. (VIDEO
STILL BY DONALD ECK-
ERT, SAN FRANCISCO)

David carrying his banner at the Parsonage high mass, Grace Cathedral, San Francisco, August 1983. (PHOTOGRAPH BY STEVE SAVAGE; COURTESY OF SAVAGE PHOTOGRAPHY)

Volunteer "parsons" at The
Parsonage, Castro Street,
San Francisco. (PHOTOGRAPH BY
JANET BURKS, COURTESY EPISCOPAL
DIOCESE OF CALIFORNIA ARCHIVES)

At General Conven-
tion of the Episcopal
Church of America,
Detroit, Michigan,
1988

With John at a Gay Rights march, 1992

By this time, although other professional agencies were referring their own clients to us, the city government remained unwilling to acknowledge statistics that might either reduce the tourist trade or increase the drain on the community purse, and finally it was the State Mental Health services and the United Way that provided the comparatively small funds we needed.

Nothing was more persuasive in winning such support than our records. There was the old man who locked himself in the bathroom with the telephone while his wife rampaged outside attempting to break down the door; the woman who, in the course of many desperate calls lasting far longer than the limit we had prescribed for "persistent callers," confused us with a story so strange and a living arrangement so bizarre that it was some time before we discovered she was blind; and those who had swallowed sleeping pills and "liquor" and appeared to be dying even as they called us—the rule then was to keep them talking in hopes that when they fell into a coma they would drop the phone, letting it dangle and so giving us time to trace them.

But tracing calls on the old system took time. Few calls were short. It was our rule to find out as much as we could and to treat the reason given for calling as being not necessarily the real reason. No service in the city could afford to spend as much time as we did with our clients and it was rarely wasted. In the case of closeted gay people, the problems in their lives were often so hedged about with guilt and denial that it was very difficult to sort out what they really needed or where to send them. No wonder it was we who provided the only place they could call for reassurance and respect.

Despite predictions of disaster, lawsuits, or even reprisals from self-interested family members, never once did a single case blow up. Moreover, the work was surprisingly uplifting. Volunteers who feared being depressed by listening to people's despair found that helping them had quite the opposite effect.

Night as well as day, and especially on weekends before the major holidays, the center carried on. Indeed, holidays were the busiest times, when the unhappy believe (quite mistakenly) that everyone else is enjoying themselves. When the staff was enlarged to two hundred, we were able to increase the number of telephones dramatically, to help a variety of specially needy people: the elderly, the gay young, non-English-speaking immigrants, and eventually those with AIDS who found it difficult to decide whether to die slowly in agony or to get it over with.

For many years we were the only such service in America, and calls came into our center from all over the country. Only later did our plan and training methods spread to other towns and cities and achieve much the same results.

The city's suicide rate fell slowly, and sometimes even increased; it would decline during the 1990s but increase among the young. Because our telephone number was listed in the phone directories under "Suicide Prevention" we could at least be sure that we were helping very unhappy people, but with such deeply rooted problems that neither our help nor the referrals could guarantee success. Suicide rates are also affected by factors such as unemployment, parental pressures, and prejudice (especially against gay people). As for clinical depression, an especially intransigent pathological state, treatment was not very advanced until long after the 1960s. The Vietnam War, too, was more and more on our mind, and it is a phenomenon of suicide that during times of general suffering the number of those who consider killing themselves tends to diminish. Loss is actually made more tolerable when others also lose, suggesting there is a competitive element even in despair. As a species we do not like to be singled out for special punishment.

Suicide raises important issues, and the religious faith of my training was coming to seem not so much inadequate as inappropriate in the modern world. The lengthening catalogue of agonies our callers expressed, even when they were relieved, raised once again the age-old question of why evil and pain exist in a universe created by a seemingly benevolent god. The traditional religious response, that pain is a punishment, did not make much sense in a world where discrimination, death camps, racism, anti-Semitism, and homophobia were clearly not the fault of their victims. That pain is a test of one's faith might appeal to those determined upon a stoical life of asceticism, but could hardly justify the horrors of Auschwitz. Then, too, hurricanes and earthquakes wreak havoc indiscriminately; so do genetic weaknesses, once thought to be proofs of divine displeasure but in fact quite unconnected to morality. Prayers of gratitude for survival from such phenomena are clearly unthinking, their implication being that the ways of God are not only strange, they may even incriminate him (and in this case it is surely a him) in the death of those he murdered.

Increasingly I knew I belonged to a world from which religion had set me apart. No doubt because of my homosexual orientation, religion struck me as content to teach that human existence occurs by divine dispensation; that all of us, regardless of differences, are answerable for our lives without truly belonging together; that we are not part of the whole, but are merely sojourners, pilgrims. The early teachers of the Christian church, like early Hebrew rabbis, also had trouble with this uneasy relationship. Why, after all, create us?

As many a suicidal caller would cry in our telephones, referring to humanity at large: "What the hell is going on? What are we doing here?" I now felt the same way.

THE CAULDRON
1961-1970

By 1964 one of the information boards at our Suicide Center contained as complete a list as we could compile, from careful research by expert witnesses, of drugs for sale on the street. These street drugs had been proliferating largely due to the burgeoning "hippie" culture. Hippies and "flower children" were the harbingers of an extraordinary social revolution. The war in Vietnam was already underway. More and more teenagers, together with young men and women of draft age, were now to be seen gathering on the streets dressed in whatever clothes they could find. Like doves, they seemed to come from all over America as if to escape from the hawks of the Eastern seaboard. In seeking for somewhere to sleep, they settled first in the great Golden Gate Park and then could be discovered gathering at the intersection of two nearby streets, Haight and Ashbury, which no one had ever heard of before.

I had been making single, lonely love in the YMCA, a conscious violation of cultural norms. But the hippies, as the first phase of this invasion came to be called, were intent upon a wholesale orgy of "togetherness" which, had they known it, was to change the world. The Beats of San Francisco had renounced middle-class morality; the Beatles had worn their hair long; "perverts" wore drag. Hippies seemed to embrace everyone, burned their draft cards, and smoked marijuana. At first dismissed, their life and its style came to be labeled a "counter culture," which struck at the roots of American puritan morality. It was a revolution of consciousness.

It was as if the young had sensed that death was again on the march and unless they did something—they hardly knew what—its armies and atomic bombs would overtake the world. Raised on a long diet of fear, even terror, propagated by their government in the name of democracy, they broke through to a broader, more generous view of existence in which the interdependence of things and beings might be made manifest and honored. They gathered flowers from neighboring gardens and pushed their stalks down the barrels of the National Guard guns brought against them. Some of their new iconography had its origins in Native American respect for the environment, and some in Asian religions that resonate with a yearning to be free of the corseted, repressive Christianities of established Western culture. The hippies wore whatever pleased them, or nothing; and in adopting outlandish costumes drawn from all ages, fashions, and genders, they seemed to reach deep into the well of the unconscious and to draw up from it priceless treasures of acceptance and love.

Yet, as in the days of Thermidor, this revolution quickly became overcast with renewed tyranny and horror. In the end, relief at being freed from parental demands was insufficient. Finding that chemicals could reduce their inevitable anxieties and induce idealistic euphoria, the young took to experimenting with drugs, then to imposing both uniformity of ideas and addiction upon each other, so that within a few months the movement had been permeated by drug dealers and death itself. Older experimenters, infiltrated by adventurers and criminals, found they could transform this naive innocence into orgiastic illusion and make use of it for their own ends.

One day I was seconded to a BBC film crew who followed a gaily clothed young hippie couple down Haight Street, beads and bandanas flowing around them. The boy was hunched over as if in pain and the girl had her arm around his neck. Together they entered the door to a free clinic set up by one Dr. Smith. They struggled up the narrow stairs, and at the top the boy collapsed in a heap. Our camera took in the whole scene: the milling crowd outside in the street below, singing and laughing their lives away, the twenty or so stairs we had climbed, and the distraught couple. The boy was now kneeling on the floor and his shoulder-length hair had caught in his open mouth.

A disenchanted medical student sat behind the desk. He was unmoved. He asked what the trouble was. The girl pulled out handfuls of brightly colored pills, a Pandora's box of "uppers," "downers," "red devils," "lizards," "turkeys"—scarlet, yellow, blue, and green. Like candy, they cascaded onto the desk as she opened her hand.

"All these," she said listlessly. The young doctor's eyes widened in horror. She continued, her young voice breaking, "I think he's ill."

I was reminded of *Dr. Strangelove* and Slim Pickens, legs astride an

atomic bomb, naively crowing "Whoopee!" as he dropped to his own
death and that of thousands, still not understanding what he had
done. American innocence again. And as if to confirm it, on our way
down the Haight toward Ashbury, another young man passed us in
the crowd. He was very handsome and walked appealingly barefoot,
a sari wrapped around him over a pair of riding breeches. He was
chanting, "I love everyone! I love everyone!"

I could not forbear to ask him, "Do you love me?"

He shook his head. "No, man!" he replied. "Everyone!" Strange
are the ways of cognitive dissonance.

Slowly the dream faded. Long lines began waiting at bank counters. They were cashing checks mailed them by ever-loving parents.

Professionally objective though I tried to be, I found myself caught
up in the revolutionary fervor. Soon I discovered that even my own
perception of reality as something long understood could no longer be
taken for granted.

I had been invited to teach a course in humanities at the California
School of Fine Arts, now the San Francisco Art Institute. During the
early 1960s the students of this institution were nearly all hippies,
many with considerable artistic talent. The final seminar of the year
was conducted in a windowless basement room beside the studios,
and since it was something of a celebration, the students were already
"mellow" with marijuana. Indeed, pot was smoked everywhere, by
students and faculty alike, on this occasion supplemented by red wine
and homemade cookies. I had selected one of our brighter students to
deliver a paper and she had chosen for her theme "The British Influence upon American Art Forms of the Twentieth Century." But
although this interesting subject was illustrated by slides and record-
ings of songs by the Beatles, it was being delivered in a monotonous
voice as joints were being passed from hand to hand.

The little room quickly filled with marijuana smoke and it occurred
to me that unless I took some refreshment I would fall asleep under
the influence of the pot and be unable to evaluate the paper. I was
accordingly offered some cookies, of which I ate six or seven, the marijuana apparently acting as an appetizer. The cookies, however, far
from being an antidote to the pot, had been laced (as I later learned)
with LSD, and the more I munched the less grasp I had on what was
happening around me. Finally, I had no option but to leave, still not
knowing what had taken hold of me.

On attempting to rise, I discovered that my legs weighed several
tons and were several yards long. It took approximately six days to

raise the left leg and then another six days to raise the right leg. To relearn the art first of rising and then standing took fully six weeks and was followed by yet another challenge: how to walk across a room, making my hesitant way among students lying or sitting on the floor. My progress was exceedingly slow—"deliberate" would be the word for it, each careful step measured and its future location in the scheme of things given due consideration. Tottering through the door and down the corridor to the telephone to reach help was a nightmare. I laid my hands on a telephone and slowly dialed the number of Peter, my new boyfriend.

"What's wrong? You sound funny."

"I've been given some drugs. Please come and get me."

Now the seminar room receded in time and memory to the state of some long-lost dream. Where had I just been? Who were those people I was with? What was this place? Had I really called for help?

Time stretched endlessly into past and future. For forty-two years I walked the street outside the Institute being leered and pointed at by pedestrians who clearly went out of their way to reproach me with angry and accusatory faces. During one eon I managed to reach a seat in a nearby park. Clutching my hands to make sure they were my own and not someone else's, I noticed they were the hands of a completely articulated skeleton. As I flexed the fingers and worked the bones, I could see that each one was in good working order. This did not frighten me, I remember, but after attempting in vain to count the number of bones to prove that drugs can promote X-ray vision, I struggled to free myself from an overwhelming desire to lie on the sidewalk even as an oncoming police officer, with a stare menacing immediate arrest, advanced toward me. Accordingly, I rose with all the dignity I could muster and slid off down the street.

Peter, a strawberry blond from Hollywood, eventually arrived on his mission of mercy and found me collapsed on my knees, with both arms embracing a utility pole. The ride back home in safety reversed the paranoia: houses became palaces, their colors resplendent; my tiny bed a couch of feathers and lamb's wool; time began slowly to contract.

The following morning, still with only a tenuous hold upon what we call reality, I was due to fly to Hollywood to interview Rex Harrison on the set of *Doctor Dolittle,* his latest movie. I managed to reach the airport and hire a car without arousing suspicion, but when I finally arrived at the sound stage, I was much the worse for wear.

I waited for Harrison as he repeatedly failed at a seemingly easy scene. The takes were endless and he apologized profusely when finally we got together. "I'm so sorry," he said. "I've had a terrible night."

"Can't be worse than mine," I replied.

"Why?" he asked, "what's wrong with you?"

"I was given a big dose of acid and had a bad trip."

"No!" he cried, slapping his thigh. "Tell me ALL about it!"

And after he led the way to his dressing room on the other side of the set, me still on watery legs and he muttering "Fascinating! Positively delightful! Just fancy!" we discussed the uses of lysergic acid, mescaline, and other mind-altering drugs, and how they enable us to see visions, dream dreams—perhaps even pass on information mind to mind, and one day control the movement of objects far away. It was an experience I was anxious should also be discussed by our professional therapists at the Center. Although the development of drugs to alleviate anxiety and depression had still a long way to go, I had seen how the effect of molecules upon the working of the mind might alter our thoughts, our attitude to life, and, of course, our beliefs.

At this same time in the mid-sixties, my priestly life was invaded by another, slower revolution that was gathering momentum as more and more other gay people prepared to declare themselves. Despite our growing numbers, or because of them, this was not without its backlash. At the Paper Doll, a bar among the coffeehouses of North Beach owned by a hospitable and generous hostess, we enjoyed free meals on Thursday nights, while at the Black Cat the resident "Empress," José, would often sing us his theme song which concluded, "God save us nelly queens!" It was always a rousing performance, and established our identity in the face of continued raids by the police. Indeed, those bars where the owners welcomed our patronage were still our only available gathering places, and our attendance was always accompanied by the fear that we might spend the night in jail. Lesbians with short hair who wore pants were still careful to carry with them some evidence, however small—a powder compact or a bra—that they were women; while drags carried a cigar or, taking a big risk, offered to unzip to prove they were men and not breaking the religious law, still on the books, that was employed to harass us for masquerading as persons of the opposite sex.

Lesbians at that time were even more withdrawn from society than were gay men and much in need of an organization of their own. Two women with whom I struck up a warm friendship, Del Martin and Phyllis Lyon, were busy incorporating the lesbian Daughters of Bilitis and having a difficult time of it. These were bold spirits who were slowly raising our self-esteem and enriching our perception of ourselves. Certainly it has often been the lesbians who have made all the difference in our battles with the law and religious prejudice.

As the movement slowly grew in strength, so physical relationships became more possible. Celibacy, even when preached by my monkish mentors, had never appealed to me either as a personal discipline or as a virtue. The cold intellectual aspirations of the Platonic lover clearly sprang from Plato's own stern and fantastic ideals that forced him to deny the body, the existence of which I preferred to celebrate. Moreover, sexuality, with all its mechanisms and sensations, held increasingly few fears for me; it was rather a phenomenon to be shared. Its original function of propagating the species was only one of its relations to the complexities of human life. Love seemed to me far and away more important. Another man in my arms brought me closer to happiness than could almost any other experience. The Christian mass was a supposedly simple, generous act of love, but one that my disconsolate congregation had been anxious to keep to themselves. I would remind them that it is at its best on the battlefield, where the mass is permitted to be celebrated by anyone using even ditch water and whatever crumbs may be found in a dying man's pocket. The church may preach that such a generous love is acceptable to God only under fire; but the lives of homosexual people were always under fire. And it was with such minimalist thoughts as these that I kept my faith alive, attending clergy conferences, and only occasionally preaching.

But preaching about love was difficult. We homosexual people, who had always lived on the edge, were noticing that even as we found ourselves, we were also the target of increasing violence. Several times I had been hit in the face for a glance or move of admiration, or jeered at from trucks. "Fag!" they would scream, handsome faces leering out the window. In a reversal of machismo, these men feared being admired by other men. Their masculinity was primitive, established and defined by sex with the female. At such moments we would feel just as Jews or blacks feel when attacked by thugs. Yes, we would think to ourselves, we *are* "fags"; it was an insidious poison which, for the moment, lesbians didn't have to put up with, and it seeped into our nightmares. In the days before civil rights there was little recourse in a culture where police, lawyers, judges, and juries all believed that one deserved to be insulted. The more successful one was in reaching responsible positions or achieving prestige, the more careful one had to be; the more defenses one had to erect; and the more deception was required to appear to be normal. It was no wonder gay teenagers took their own lives. If we did not take our own lives, others seemed ready to take them for us.

I was not living with Peter at this time for we were, in the old-fashioned term, still courting. Nor were either of us so heavily in love that we forbade ourselves from meeting other potential lovers. Coming back from my duties at Suicide Prevention, I invited a young man to my apartment. He followed me in and, unknown to me, left the front door unclosed behind us. I served coffee and during our conversation began to hear low voices apparently coming from the next room. I rose to find the furniture being carried out through the front door to a waiting truck by three men, two white and one black (who appeared to be the leader), and a pretty blond youth.

Not immediately comprehending the enormity being committed, I protested, but was thrust to the floor by the largest of the three while the youth immediately pushed me down, knelt on my chest, and held a six-inch stiletto to my throat.

"You're gonna die, man," he snarled. "You're gonna die!"

Perhaps it was my anger at being duped, together with a certain fatalistic view of a situation that could have occurred at any time, but in a foolish reversal of values I found myself less concerned for myself than for my broadcasting equipment, my livelihood, which, even while I was pinned to the floor on my back, I could hear being ripped away from the wall. As my American host's own life had ended, I saw mine closing without purpose.

The hand that held the knife was raised to plunge it in when the telephone rang.

The kid had murder in his young eyes but he hesitated, proving that murderers do, in truth, play with their victims rather than immediately despatching them. I seized my chance. "It must be my friend down the street. He must have seen you come in . . . I'd better answer it. He's a policeman!" I lied, still British. It was a long shot; a scene from a "B" movie.

The telephone was insistent and the big man, his arms full of my clothes, looked worried. A muttered conversation took place, consisting of growls and barks. The big man picked up a lamp.

"Hurry it!" he shouted, and ran back to the bedroom to collect more. As the telephone stopped ringing, the kid again raised the knife. He would probably thrust it in just before they left. The blade was narrow and wouldn't leave much of a mark. I attempted to reinforce their fears.

"You'd better hurry. He'll be up here!" I was good at seeming to join the enemy. They were now taking my belongings out through the back door, the front apparently being too risky. Then the telephone began ringing again.

The kid's face was close to mine, summoning up courage for the final lunge to do me in. The bell was now very loud in the rapidly emptying apartment. They did not have enough experience to pull the phone from the wall or even take it off the hook. Again I joined the enemy. I could hardly breathe with fear and the knee in my ribs and tried to nod the kid away.

"You'd better get out," I croaked, "That must be him!" It was more likely to be my producer inviting my comments on life in America.

The big man reappeared with the two others, all three with their arms full of shirts, ties, my overcoat, underclothes. The phone continued ringing and it broke their nerve.

"Get out!" said the leader, dropping his load, and made for the kitchen door. The others followed, seemingly leaving the kid behind. I expected a sudden thrust with the knife, but now he was scared of being abandoned. The others tore open the kitchen door, rushed out, and smashed through a small picket fence that ran between the apartment blocks.

The kid, still holding his knife, hissed, "Next time, man!" then jumped to his feet and followed them.

I heard a truck roar off down the street, tires squealing. Still trembling with fear, relief, and rage, I thanked the telephone, and called my friend down the road. He wasn't in.

I did not thank God. His role in all this was clearly ambivalent and my rage grew. Why should natural acts of flirting and sexual ecstasy, enchanted offerings on the altar of love, always be under threat of violent death? True, such a lethal combination is the stuff of tragedy and romance, but it's very wearing. Since laws with origins in religious piety were, and still are, so written as to encourage murder and mayhem against us, it was once again apparent that if criminals did not get us, the law aimed to do so, taking up where the hoodlums left off.

I thought back to my parents living quietly sedate, orderly, heterosexual lives. They would blame me, of course, for provoking the attack. What should I tell my producer when he calls? That America is alive and well? That Congress has everything under control and in God we trust? Impossible to reveal to them what happened, for in my producer's circles, also, queers were anathema and I would never be asked to broadcast again. To that extent, I was still a closet case, and ashamed of it.

Nonetheless, I had been lucky. Tens of thousands of us have had knives, fists, and boots in our faces and many more have died from beatings and bashings. It was also a time when the medical profession, the courts, and the churches had not only declared homosexuality to be a mental disorder, but even justified crimes against us as the natural outcome of what was then characterized as "homosexual panic." (The term "homophobia" had not yet been coined.) Moreover, if the homosexual victim remained alive, he or she was charged, as Oscar Wilde had been, and jailed, in some states for life. Accordingly, I did not call the police. Oppressed people know when to let sleeping dogs lie.

However, as I picked up my belongings from the floor and rescued pieces of my broken equipment, I knew that I was not yet doing enough for our cause. It was clear, as never before, that the less one did for it, the more one supported the enemy. So I first joined the Mattachine Society, then going through hard times for lack of members; later, a newly formed Society for Individual Rights, the first gay organization that was openly political. That was where I had met Peter.

Peter was a member of an organization that called itself the Coits, after the phallic Coit Tower which overlooks San Francisco Bay. They enjoyed wearing drag and contributed much money to social causes. Peter was not a "drag queen" as such, but ever since moving north from Hollywood had adopted several of their witty, pseudofeminine ways of speech which, to tell the truth, he knew I did not like. But he was a wiz on clothes and fabrics. For several years, I incorporated his knowledge of them during my reports to London on Oscars night; he would whisper to me what the stars were wearing.

I had never known drags before and found them warm, friendly, often shy when out of costume, and generous to a fault. It was Peter who reminded me that they were essentially political, in that the act of pretending to be a woman struck deep into what our species has ever thought itself to be, and called into question values and meanings built into what we name civilization. Thus the exaggerated style adopted by drag queens in their dress, makeup, and mannerisms is at heart a brazen act of defiance, a revolutionary stand, not merely against the law, but against all that such laws stand for: a morality derived from fear of the unknown. Drags were our icons, our standard-bearers in our battle with the heterosexual world.

Not surprisingly, serious drags were and still are rarely casual or careless about their preoccupation. Indeed it can often become an obsession. It was as if, and not always unconsciously, they understood the importance of their role in the gendered world in which we were forced to live. Entire savings would be spent on expensive outfits, seemingly to outdo each other in the mimicry of women. It was not that they wanted to be females; they, like all of us gay men, wanted to be admired by other males. In a significant undermining of this aim to catch a man, their models were strong-minded female movie stars who had never tired of putting each other down in the endless competition to win one. The preference for biting sarcasm and bitchy repartee that I at first found distasteful I later realized, under Peter's coaching, had a "subtext." Yet semiotic world though it was, it was also an intense, even frantic, dream world, wherein one wept if a hairpin was lost or a brooch mislaid, or when upstaged by a rival.

Meanwhile, we macho men who were drag escorts wore drag of our own—elegant evening dress complete with tails or leather chaps and chains, sporting colored handkerchiefs according to a special code I learned much later and which indicated what kind of sexual activity we preferred: red for tops, green for bottoms, yellow for water sports, black for S & M.

One of the most elaborate events in town was the Crowning of the Empress. This still takes place in hospitable bars and local halls in rural and provincial cities, usually where gay rights are still in question. It was a ceremony reinforcing the much older description of the participants as "queens": contestants would gather from far and wide wearing entire wardrobes. Almost to a woman (or man), they had demanding ways and would not be satisfied until they had gathered about them a group of admirers among whom they could hold court. Nearly all were in their twenties, though some were quite elderly and had worn drag for much of their lives. Together, they would engage in tireless and often witty banter. Bertha, for example, would arrive at a dinner party wearing a new exotic hat trimmed with pink lace, only to raise his arms, flex his muscles and greet us in stentorian, truck-driver tones. "Greetings, Men!" he'd say, at which the rest of us, some resplendent in high heels, pancake makeup, and powdered wigs, would growl, "Hi, Man!" and get on with the latest gossip.

But drag was not easy. Liniment and aspirin eased aches and pains caused by strapping pectorals tight enough to produce the plumpness of breasts, or by sores resulting from the stays of corsets and buttock boosters. Later, as the battle for gay rights gathered strength and took on more defiant expression, traditional drag gave way to "gender fuck," which required that the drag queen, no less bedizened, should also wear a mustache and cease to shave his legs.

Peter, raised among the Hollywood set, was thirteen years younger than I. He danced with panache and had thrown over the most handsome man on the floor to be with me. For a whole year we would meet in a coffee shop and talk, make love, and then talk some more. It wasn't until that much time had passed that I suggested we live together. And only then that I dared come clean.

"I have to tell you something," I ventured with the deepest sigh. Would he turn away, write me off as so many others had? I had tested the waters and he seemed sensible enough. Not that I would myself have welcomed the news.

"What? You can tell me anything," he said with his charming smile. "I've seen it all, you know," as, of course, he had.

"I haven't told you before because I thought you might not want to see me any more."

"Oh, God!" he looked at me in mock surprise. "You've murdered someone! Oh, well," he went on nonchalantly, "I've met them too. We'll have to find you a lawyer."

"No, not as bad as that. I'm a priest."

Gales of laughter greeted this.

"You're not! Ho ho! He he! A priest! Oh, I'm sorry. Forgive me. I've never had sex with a priest before! Will I go to hell?"

It was a satisfying yet difficult marriage. Raised among children of the rich and famous, he was far more worldly wise than I, and having slept with men, movie stars among them, since he was fourteen, understood the gay scene long before I knew of its existence. Both of us were needy yet shy, and both had been raised in families where affection was rarely openly expressed.

Many gay people suffered similarly. The strong-minded might adopt another persona, the less aggressive shrink into the background or join the heterosexual majority even to the point of marriage and children. The most wounded might become unstable and even suicidal. For the pressure to conform with the straight world was overwhelming, omnipresent, ever insistent. Even more dispiriting was our sense of alienation. I felt this most keenly. It was reinforced daily, hourly, in books, newspapers, on television, in movies, even among conversation with heterosexual companions who often had not the slightest inkling what it means to be Other. Life for us was thus an obstacle race in which the prizes of returned affection were few. Only as more gay people identified themselves have the chances of a stable, happier life improved.

The new life I was introduced to by Peter and his friends seemed to justify the famous description of San Francisco as a delightful city with all the attractions of the next world. Wearing a tuxedo I would escort my mate, an incarnation of Kathryn Hepburn dressed in pink chiffon, a strawberry wig, and an immaculate complexion. We would attend occasional balls along with other drags, guarded by the local police; they had learned at last to protect us from tourists, who for the most part saw us as freaks and took pity on us. Peter never lost his sense of humor and would climb aboard a hired cable car to wave his bespangled gloved hands, blowing kisses at adoring (and, so credible was he, unsuspecting) tourists, including the heterosexual men, or casting flowers to the multitude. I was very proud of him.

Only three times did I attempt drag, once as a witch in Greenwich Village, twice as a Mother Superior when I looked more like a dragon than a nun. As a concession to my inability to look feminine, Peter abandoned his curls and dressed as Sister Gotlieb. I became Mama Mia. To improve upon the forbidding convent style we appeared as "see-through" nuns in black chiffon gauze with nothing much underneath. We were perhaps among the very first Sisters in a long line of convent drags that was born among a wonderfully imaginative group of singularly attractive young men calling themselves the Coquettes and reached its apogee with the Sisters of Perpetual Indulgence who bore outrageous names such as Sister Clitoris and Sister Cunnilingus. These toured the town on roller skates, spreading alarm and despondency among the religious. Deplorable as such activity may seem to some, its ostentatious vulgarity was again a thumbing of our communal nose at all the pruderies with which society had burdened itself in law and custom. As we paraded and danced, we seemed to cast aside centuries of superstition.

Clearly, my devotion to religious tradition was beginning to wear thin. Drag attempted to subvert structures predetermined and established by authorities themselves considered divine. Jewish and Christian priesthood forbade such practices as idolatrous pretenses abhorrent to the divine will, a prohibition strictly reinforced by later Puritan traditions of simplicity. As a result, the Western male—though in other centuries he has dressed himself colorfully and once wore wigs—still brushes his hair but leaves his calf-enhancing high heels and makeup to the female and does not permit confusion of gender without penalty. Indeed, a telling measure of the deeper meaning of drag is the horror with which heterosexual males in the West now view men wearing makeup. It is said that the Afghani tribesman, with his younger male lover at his side, may wear kohl to make his eyes seem more beautiful and compelling; likewise the ancient Egyptians and the males of many indigenous people throughout the world will

paint their faces either to improve their looks or to frighten their enemies; but never the modern Western male, except at sporting events.

Thus, viewed from the sidewalk, the drag who struts and postures,
scorning ridicule and demanding attention, may excite fear even while
she fascinates. She is a creature of the imagination, built to break
down and rampage through civilized pretensions, making nonsense of
what hitherto was held sacrosanct and inalienable. As we expected,
our demonstrations were frequently attended by fundamentalists
announcing both our own doom and the End of the World.

Peter, of course, had put his finger on a vital question: would he go
to hell for making love to a priest, and would the priest lead him
there? That is how we've been raised to think of love, even though
what people report of the church and what the church actually
teaches are rarely the same. Yet the best the church could offer was
forgiveness, and even today true acceptance of sexual adventure as a
necessary fact of life is hard to find, let alone reconcile with what
passes for traditional doctrine. And by 1970, the questions raised by
rampant sexuality were never more apparent than in the "tubs" that
suddenly began to flourish.

Steam baths, "Turkish" baths, and massage parlors have been
around for hundreds, if not thousands, of years. Often condemned or
suppressed by the somatophobic Western Christian church, they had
survived both among Muslims and in Eastern Orthodox countries.
Moscow, for example, has steam baths and hot plunges as a public
service to tired businessmen. Thousands visit them on their way home
from work and even subject themselves to the ancient rites of flagella-
tion and scraping to cleanse the skin and revive their flaccid muscles.
Long identified as "Eastern" or "Turkish," these institutions have
nearly always had a sensual, homoerotic flavor to them, and sometimes coteries of secretly gay men would meet there to be together,
flirt, and find partners.

In San Francisco, these bathhouses, or "tubs," as they came to be
called, were more enterprising; they included luxury lounges, restaurants, exotic saunas, and even floor shows. One of the more tastefully
decorated that I patronized sported a whirlpool. It appealed to me
because it was designed in the style of a Minoan palace, complete with
a labyrinth surrounded by tanks of exotic fish peering out at the
naked bodies swimming beside them. It was a service that enabled
young and old to find in a more civilized way what society had forced
for so long to be hidden.

The tubs offered a variety of erotically charged situations that were
contrived by means of areas specially designed and equipped to cater

to a variety of fantasies. One room might be in semidarkness, its walls lined with rough bunk beds as in a military encampment. Another might sport revolving starlights to illumine heaps of decorative multicolored cushions among which men with exquisite physiques, oiled muscles a-gleam, would offer their bodies to be caressed. There might also be a "torture" chamber equipped with chains, ropes, and mediaeval stocks. There was always a room arranged with either pews or pillows before one or more television screens showing continuous videos of sexual encounters. One room was nothing but a series of walls with spy holes, or holes at various levels through which a penis could be poked, inviting attention.

In my favorite establishment there existed a complicated maze, the labyrinth, with only an occasional fitful lamp to illumine one's path, and many an abrupt dead end leaving a passionate clinch the only way out. Usually on several floors there were also long corridors lined with doors leading to tiny rooms assigned by number, each complete with a bed, a lamp, and a lock. People would enter their rooms, lie provocatively on the bed leaving the door open, with their colored handkerchief draped around the doorknob to give a clue to their wares or their interests.

The lighting throughout such establishments was always dim, except in the orgy room, which was plunged in stygian darkness, and from which only groans and sighs could be heard to indicate that it was inhabited. The actual baths themselves might include a complete swimming pool and a series of steam rooms, sometimes with their own maze of secret corners and hideaways in which couples could coalesce hidden from view in clouds of warm steam, beneath endlessly dripping ceilings as in some underground cave. One would sometimes come across a friend or even a closet case emerging from the mists. The etiquette on such occasions was to smile benignly and pass on one's way without comment since embarrassing mistakes might easily be made. Who, after all, could decipher one's most secret desires, even among friends?

Not all gay men went to the tubs. In fact, the majority did not. Many stayed away either because they felt no need of them, being satisfied with a mate, or for fear of venereal disease which, even before AIDS, was always a possibility. The closeted majority also feared public exposure by friends or coworkers or as a result of police raids, which, until the gay rights movement gained strength, might still occur. But many who did not pay at least one visit were secretly envious of those with sufficient time, money, energy, or abandon to make a regular schedule of them.

On the other hand, those who did so often found not only civilized sexual release, but also moments or hours of such tender, genuine affection that weeks of frustration and nightmares of rejection were thereby made more tolerable than they had ever been. A younger friend once encountered an ancient fellow lying hidden at the back of a bunk bed. He generously embraced and kissed the bony limbs. In a broken voice, the old man whispered that this was the first time he had been kissed by a man for twenty years without fear of reprisals. And, indeed, our culture has taught heterosexuals that it is far more acceptable to kill another man than to kiss him.

I was eager to learn more about these oases of comfort, both for our gay suicidal clients stuck in their closets of desperation and for my own well-being. For there was no doubt that once inside the tub doors and among one's own people, years of fear drained away. The outside world where, as Christopher Isherwood once described it, one seemed to suffer lack of oxygen, was laid aside during my brief sojourn in safety, and I would breathe deeply in sheer relief. Those around must have felt the same for, despite what was offered, most of us did very little but sit or stroll about, visiting the restaurant, "cruising" the steam room. I often went home without a sexual encounter, satisfied merely to have been where one was no longer frightened and alone.

Even in such confined ways, we were finally learning to permit ourselves not only love but also identity. We had been nonpersons for so long, existing only in our secret minds. The most ignorant heterosexuals saw us as abhorrent, engaged in the most unholy orgies their perfervid and perhaps envious imagination could devise. Even the most tolerant never thought of us as better than freaks to be pitied. Taught to regard even their own sexuality as shameful, ours was to them unimaginable. Our esthetic and artistic sensibilities had long been exploited by various professions only to be denied or dismissed. Not until we could establish an identity, discover our "nationhood," could we even be said to exist except as aberrations. Identity, like one's skeleton, was so essential to well-being that its survival became our Cause.

For me there was another specific cause at stake: the body, the home of our senses, the links between the workings of the brain and the rest of the physical world to which it belongs. Love, the desire for union with another, is no less authentic in its physical, erotic, or sexual expression than it is in an intellectual enthusiasm. Derived from the need to create, it is all-pervasive and endlessly variable. From it springs whatever each holds to be desirable and its recognition is a cause in which all humanity has a stake.

*   *   *

After the tubs had been in operation for some years, there sprang up a service known by the cognoscenti as the Cauldron. Its home was an elaborate arrangement of bar and orgy house. Like other meeting places it tried to cater to all tastes. This complex quickly became notorious both for what went on inside and, more importantly, for its serious philosophy. Unlike haphazard orgies among friends in private houses, it was an institution and for some years it had been a favorite among those for whom the tubs were too refined, too predictable. It was located south of Market Street in the same part of town where the streets were lined with manufacturing warehouses and occasional bars, and which, during the day, would be filled with metalworkers, plumbers, and construction crews. At night, when street lamps cast a lurid glow over the empty sidewalks and the shuttered workshops, men would appear in cars or on motorcycles which they would park in nearby alleyways or in rows along the curb. We would wear tight jeans to emphasize our leg muscles and give ourselves a sense of being in the saddle, as it were, unencumbered and ready for anything. Newcomers were advised to wear their oldest shirts since, once inside, they might be ripped from the body in the ecstasy of the moment. We also wore subdued expressions, eyes cast to the ground, taking only surreptitious glances around at others either already entering or approaching from downtown. Among them might be local celebrities in danger of blackmail, while others could be seemingly happily married heterosexual husbands.

Once inside the complex it was always essential to maintain this self-sufficient pose and avoid any old friends who might be present. Chatter, and especially giggling, were invariably counterproductive, and silence, apart from groans and gasps, was the rule. Indeed, even to recognize a friend's presence or in some way to break the essential anonymity of the place was the height of bad manners. So strict were these unspoken rules that it might be said that on entering, we became one flesh, members one of another.

The building itself was a former workshop that had been remodeled to contain the bar, behind which was a series of darkened rooms containing a variety of paraphernalia such as chains, stocks, and primitive handcuffs with which to promote erotic experiences. In one room was a urinal in the shape of a long, grey, rather battered galvanized bathtub. Clients might even sit or lie naked in this tub while others who found this experience erotic would urinate upon them. Urine is not always nor everywhere considered distasteful, and in the frenzy of our frustrated passion for release it was obvious that the God of love embraced everything He had created.

Confronting such satisfactions of erotic need, moralists, of course, saw only indulgence and rampant hedonism, which they viewed with both fascination and horror without quite knowing why. Most people, however, were indifferent to the delights of others, acknowledging the force of the adage permitting different strokes for different folks. Scatological enthusiasms, for example, are far from unknown even in the heterosexual world. Unpleasant and grotesque though they may appear to some, their tabooed expression is far from unnatural. The body's excretions are well known to both attract and repel. But such experiences pose a new critique of cultured mores. The apparent reversion from civilized ways to primitive, basic instinctual desires may be shocking, but only to those who consider themselves removed from their animal natures. Even in condemning what he may describe as the concupiscence of bestial perversion, or lust of the flesh, the moral theologian is merely upholding theoretical structures modeled and codified according to an imagined distinction between body and soul. And it was the correction of such misunderstanding that was the specialty of the Cauldron.

At the back of the building and behind the orgy rooms, though still among or in their midst, was a private area set apart, a semidarkened place, in which a trained social worker was known to conduct meditations. After having experienced the various sensual excitements of the place, anyone who desired could enter and, sitting quietly on the floor, join a circle of other clients who together examined their feelings. The purpose of this exercise was not to purge away sinful lusts, but to accept the precious nature of the body in its entirety.

The leader would introduce those who felt the urge to join him, usually a small number, in a meditation upon the body and its various organs, from the top of the head to the toes of the feet, both inside and outside the envelope of skin in which all the other organs are contained. Buddhist in style, this task would carry the participants, now satiated and relaxed, toward an awareness of and respect for themselves that they had never had before, and toward a recognition of all that goes on inside the body: the flow of blood, the secretion of digestive juices, the absorption and adsorption of nutrients, and the working of stomach, intestines, and bowels. All that is contained in the body became personal, precious, from the tiny organisms that inhabit the eyebrows or the pores of the skin, to the food being broken down in the stomach to be squeezed along the intestines and from which living cells were renewed and energized.

So powerful was this curious combination of sensual expression and enlightenment that clients reported gaining a sense of spiritual

unity and completeness not available elsewhere. Formal religious rituals seemed to pale by comparison, emphasizing as they almost invariably do the separateness of the body and the spirit, and condemning
one in favor of the other. If women had been able to take part in these
discoveries, the revelations would have been more comprehensive and
complete, but women seem to have been reluctant to develop anything like it that I could find. A heterosexual steam bath did exist and
was, I understood, well patronized. It also included much sexual
activity but eventually fell victim, as did our own tubs, to the fears of
AIDS.

My own experiences at the tubs were often condemned both by
heterosexual priests and especially by closeted gay priests who in their
attempts to be accepted were anxious to dissociate themselves from
dissidence of any kind. At a meeting of the nonparochial or "worker"
priests called by William Swing, the new, warmhearted evangelical
Bishop of California, we were asked to identify ourselves. Each man
was dressed as he might be for his particular work, some as businessmen, for example, some as teachers or technicians. Many continued
to wear their clerical collars during their daily work but most wore
suits or jeans.

Each of us was invited to describe his current job. The only women
present were three who had been permitted by special dispensation to
study for the diaconate since, at that time, no women priests had ever
been ordained in the Anglican communion. As each man described his
job he ended by saying that he was married, named his wife, and
proudly numbered his children. When eventually all had had their say,
the bishop turned to me.

It was, I felt, an appropriate moment to stand up for equality. I told
them I was a broadcasting journalist in the evenings and worked full
time at my Suicide Prevention Center. I then reminded them I was gay
and added, "Since each of us has described his lover and the results of
his sexual activity, I will do so, too."

The gasps were audible as I told them of Peter and reported that
our sexual life was without issue even though, as it appeared, we had
been together for longer than any of them.

"But you are celibate?" asked one man, shocked at my daring.

I then felt obliged to defend myself. Should I not touch the man I
loved, I asked: kiss him, enjoy the beauty of his God-made body as I
hoped he did mine, and as, I assumed, they did the bodies of their
wives? This provoked heated discussion. I was asked about the tubs
and whether they could not somehow be suppressed, not because of

disease, which was not then present, but simply because they encouraged the hedonism the others felt was dangerously pagan.

But I was an urgent supporter of the tubs. In 1964 I had joined a group of clergy to help found the Council on Religion and Homosexuality, which attempted to make sense of same-sex desire. Now I explained, as I had then, how important the tubs were to gay people who had for so long been forbidden to have sex; that the tubs were an inevitable explosion of more than two thousand years of frustrated libido, all the more exhilarating for the time it had taken to burst forth. I added that if we continued to bottle up the sexuality of our young people, this effervescence was likely to continue unabated.

Could they say, I asked the heterosexuals among the group, that their sexual lives were entirely and only concerned with producing children? That they had no physical pleasure in sexual activity? And that love was absent from it? Or, more importantly, if heterosexual teenagers had been forbidden any show of affection to the opposite sex, would not a similar explosion of heterosexual libido have been likely? And I added that as for the accusation of promiscuity, the freedom to love should not be confined; a country flower may bloom for not more than a night or an hour, but is no less beautiful for the dropping of its petals. I went on and on: duration was no guarantee of value; a rock may last for ever, but a rock remains cold, hard and unfeeling. One might be forgiven for suspecting that it was not divine law that kept heterosexuals from making love more often; it was fear of pregnancy. True love was open, free from jealousy and the sin of possession. One's mate was not one's property . . . and so on.

From time to time, I could hear the three women muttering agreements behind my back, for it was such a confrontation as I doubt had ever occurred in those holy precincts before. It broke so many rules and upset so much that the heterosexual church took for granted.

Not surprisingly, I was soon taken aside by more than one fellow priest and reminded that concupiscence had been identified by saints Augustine and Aquinas and had long been held a sin. Moreover, the moral theology from which this teaching derived had its roots way back in the words of the God who had created, stocked, and peopled the Garden of Eden, and was not about to give way to novel concepts of reality. Reality, as we think of it, I was told, is a product of disobedience and is of no use in measuring right or wrong. To question this teaching would result in the rejection of God and the authority of His Church, while also causing behavior inappropriate to our profession, which would be deserving of the utmost punishment.

I began to perceive, as I had not before, that despite the consistency of this position and its long history, it was nonetheless based on an idea that was both imaginary and fraudulent. The Garden of Eden had been a dream world; its supposedly peaceful, happy, naive, simple, and untroubled inhabitants were cardboard figures. To claim that such a picture was an ideal from which humanity had fallen and by which human virtue could be measured had long been shown to be mistaken. It could be upheld only so long as one ignored all that had been discovered since; so long, that is, as the imaginary Garden, its impossible inhabitants, and its celebrated Creator also remained unexamined. No wonder any who attempted to chip away at moral theology were quickly silenced; too much was at stake.

The forbidden games in which rival Bedouin tribes engaged may well have been similar to the orgies in the tubs: the worship of pagan divinities who represented passions hidden even from ourselves. The records of Suetonius also tell of coupling among the Roman population and in the Emperor's court. Christians, condemning such abandonment to the ephemeral, mistook its message. They flayed and tortured, slashed and burned, and believed their God did the same. Voyeurs all. Hell became an orgy pit of pain and punishment. But the Cauldron offered love of many kinds. Sex was indeed a witch's brew, or so it seemed to some of my clerical brethren, but a brew concocted of acceptance, not of hate.

Erotic passion is not a darker side of love, merely a different one. To desire to become part of and unified with another in the act of love is not to destroy but to adore, even to worship. The closeted Thomas Mann conjured up a terrible dream for poor Aschenbach, but he was maddened with frustrated love, not hate. Excess destroys; too much heat will burn the steak. Nevertheless, the urgent desire to embrace and worship is a human characteristic and the wellspring of our creative lives. By both careful husbanding and release, it can transform and elevate. To silence, to bury such a force, is to smother life itself.

Yet I knew Christianity still disapproved. And my experiences were forcing me to face what I knew would be condemned by the church. Not only what I did was sinful, but also what I believed, and what I was. I was not ashamed.

Instead I was more and more exhilarated. I had been stumbling across facts of life, of the body, of existence itself, of which Christianity, perhaps religion in general, appeared to be not only ignorant, but willfully so. These were facts that had lain hidden, suppressed and nearly forgotten, for two thousand years, waiting to be rediscovered. I could see why they were hidden: they might very well be dynamite. Being covered, hidden from the real world of ideas and denied the health-giving oxygen of open discussion, they had festered, gathering around themselves unjustified fears and suspicions. But the body in all its needs and passions, in its sheer physicality and essential materiality at one with all the universe, was at last finding its way back into our consciousness. And it was not only the Christian body or the homosexual body that was being made manifest, but the bodies of us all.

WATERSHED
1964–1968

The year I was born, Einstein published his Unified Field Theory. Hubble had already proved the galaxies were on the move. Logical positivism was all the rage. Yet I had opted for the church, an institution that depends for its survival upon a faith with just as much reason as doesn't upset it. My experience of seminary and the rigors of working parishes had left me highly suspicious that we religious people were not concerned with existence, but were the victims of our own illusions. Reluctant to question the real meaning of life on earth except in terms of religious doctrines that we regarded as God-given, we dared not look further. And for centuries we lacked the tools to do so. The theologies we had thought up seemed to explain everything, whereas in fact they were full of holes.

Questions about the human body, what it was made of, what happened to it at death, whether women's bodies were the same as men's bodies, the role of the brain and the emotions, the passions and the appetites, had never been satisfactorily answered. No wonder that in the Christian view, rooted in archaic white heterosexual male moralities, we who have different bodies were anathema. Blacks, browns, and women were permitted at least second-class status; gays, not even that. Either we were already cast out; or we should have been; or we will be.

But by now I was a legitimate American citizen, and felt less constrained by tradition, even religious tradition. I had long abandoned the tiny red roofs and rain-soaked landscape of England in favor of skyscrapers and big skies. Immigrants are rarely completely assimilated, and in a xenophobic, machismo world my accent, as well as my unmarried, childless state, still told against me. Nevertheless, I felt free—indeed, had a right—to question what others were taking for granted.

Such freedom is, to some extent, an American invention. Americans are heirs to the Reformation and to what in Britain is labeled the "Nonconformist" tradition. Yet it remains a battleground. In the 1960s, terms like "authority," "discipline," and even "standards" were suspect, even while equality was losing out to uniformity. It was obvious that America was still an experiment, and though the enormous diversity of the people and the extent of the land gave me hope, yet there was no doubt that without the great anchors of religious freedom and equal protection before the law, the experiment could easily come to an end and sink back into the maelstrom of bigotry and injustice from which it was born. Religion permeated the culture— and still does—yet no one dared discuss it except to recast the traditional faith. Religious discourse remained larded with the rhetoric of evangelical revivals, and nowhere in the world was the Christian bible thumped more mindlessly. Despite the triumphs of science, the lock that fundamentalists held on schools and textbook publishers is still hardly relaxed. Times were changing in the 1960s, but there was an awful lot to change. Even by the 1990s at least fifty million Americans counted themselves bible-believing born-agains.

As the shadows of the war continued to lengthen, they engulfed so many families that hippies too were being swallowed up in mass demonstrations by tens of thousands of quite ordinary people, young and old, who filled the streets and squares in nearly every major American city, protesting what had finally become a national catastrophe. In May 1969 I was rushed to Berkeley to cover a confrontation over a piece of waste land that came to be known as "The People's Park." The University of California planned to build on it, and the disaffected, taking upon themselves the title of "the people," vowed to prevent yet another intrusion into their lives, just as they had done in Washington Square, only this time the police had been reinforced by the national guard, themselves young men uncertain how to handle their own kind. I stood before the BBC camera trying, in vain, to make sense of a situation I hardly understood myself.

The old white heterosexual males were still in charge. But by remaining deaf to the growing cries of rage they were cooking their own goose: the war quickly became an index of everything that was wrong with traditional hierarchical values in which national empire, male authority, and white supremacy were now under siege. Gay people, inevitably caught up in this maelstrom of resentment, tagged along. We too might have revolted had we not been apprehensive lest our seeming allies might turn against us, not wanting to prejudice their own cause in the eyes of their own oppressors. We did not immediately realize we were witnessing a great watershed in American affairs: a long disillusionment with Victorian values which, born in the agony of Vietnam and the Cold War, had become personified in beats, hippies, flower children, and draft card burners. We did not think it might change America, and perhaps the world. Yet the twentieth century was finally finding itself. Nineteenth-century structures were at last discredited; the great leveling tide of democratic values was at last obliterating age-old hierarchies. Just as slavery had become a battleground, now it was our turn.

The gay rights movement had been slow in getting underway, but gay people were eager to throw off the coils of Cartesian morality and at last rejoin soul and body. The number of sexual encounters exploded. Some men, and not a few women, claimed thousands of partners. Our lesbian sisters watched this with envy; they had sexism to fight as well. (In the end, we all fight the same battle against patriarchy.) Certainly the growing political strength and sexual awareness of gay people was reinforced by the revival of women's rights. Women who hitherto had been held, or held themselves, apart from a full life were also being drawn into stimulating and unexpected arenas.

Sexual liberation, women's liberation, and gay liberation reinforced each other, perhaps even depended upon each other for their success. Indeed, the very condemnation of homosexuality by religion and state authorities seemed to have been based on valuing the male over the female. Sacred scriptural prohibitions explain themselves in precisely such terms: the gay man is condemned not merely for lying with another man but for lying with a man "as with a woman" and confusing his supposedly ordained gender. Homosexuality, in confusing the two genders, even making one of them, offends against what is presumed to be a natural state. But it is only an "unnatural" act (if any act can be said to be so) when nature is conceived as having such a rigid structure that a tree should never be made into a chair; and a chair should never be used as a table; and where even atoms should, like my own mother, know their proper place. Such claims were no more than intellectual definitions of nature that took advantage of attributes assumed to be divine as a cover to serve personal and institutional ends. It was, in fact, a ruse to con people into accepting a particular theory of existence that did not hold water. And to maintain it in the face of modern knowledge is to transform into an intellectual hoax something originally constructed out of simple ignorance.

It was also becoming clear to me that the City of God, for example, devised so earnestly by Augustine upon necessarily naive and, I suspect, unexorcised Manichaean foundations, could be only circumvented rather than dismantled piece by piece. Augustine and others had been unable to do more than paste over gaps in their knowledge with honest faith, ignoring what might be dangerously upsetting for fear of punishment. Only modern understanding could set the record straight, reinforced by new discoveries and less narrow perspectives.

Historically, even the aesthetic of sexuality has been encumbered with morality that judged it unfit for public examination. Guilt prevented the senses from being discussed openly or honestly, a silence born of ignorance and fear that permitted the soul to remain high on its imagined perch. Reason, however, reaches out to make sense of human experience and cannot abide such silences with their empty rhetoric. After all that I had been through, the Christian position relating to the human body now seemed to me to depend upon a divine plan that falsely distinguished things spiritual from things material in the style of Plato. Reason demanded a different explanation, one in which bodily functions and appetites were not less important than things of the mind—the mind being a product of the body.

Surely, then, it seemed to me, the needs attendant upon love and sexuality can be an appropriate vehicle for the achievement of human happiness, just as can other appetites. And the aesthetic that is derived from them would be sufficient justification in itself for their enjoyment. As I run my tongue around the well-defined jaw of a man I happen to consider beautiful, I feel the strength of our species, the determination that has carried us generation upon generation through the perils of our planet. When my tongue probes his teeth, meeting his tongue in a delightful intimacy, I draw his body close upon mine in celebration of a unity that transcends time, distance, and the many unspoken barriers that civilization has placed in our path to prevent our ever meeting. I caress firm square shoulders, smooth skin, broad pectoral muscles hard upon my own; strong hands with the tendons of powerful, inquisitive fingers caress my thighs. I trace the bones of the rib cage, I feel nipples, erect, eager. I run my fingers over the skull, the skull of a being formed of atoms that once were born in the sun and have lived in myriad creatures, other humans among them, down the ages. I kiss eyes that look to me like stars and I feel the now hardened erect penis thrusting at me, wanting me as mine yearns to be united with him, and to bestow upon him the very best one human body can give another.

This subjective appraisal escapes the shame imposed by those who cannot share such ecstasies. If the subtle orientation of my sexual equilibrium is unusual, it is no less genuine in its love than are the passions of a more common one. Certainly such excitements are derived from sights, sounds, scents, and memories which together excite subtle chemical secretions, and without which they hardly seem to exist. Nonetheless, they do involve the entire organism, its brain and its body, and in ways which have too long been denied expression, hidden from view as unmentionable or vilified as forbidden lusts, because, as a priest would say, they forgot or denied the soul. Yet if they did not deny the soul; if, indeed, whatever the soul is also rejoiced in them as part of a newly realized view of human existence, what then? Accordingly, I took in my stride experiences which at one time would have shocked my prudery and built a new morality with which I and others would find themselves more comfortable, one determined not by terror but by love.

The massive censorship of homosexuality by past historians, literary scholars, and the so-called "helping" professions actually proved how widespread homosexual desires have always been. And the growing enthusiasm among educated and professional people for a new openness toward sexual matters was suddenly made manifest to me in bizarre and unexpected fashion. One day, between shifts at the Center, I was to have my eyes tested and visited an optometrist to whom I had been referred by my medical program.

I was ushered into the consulting room usual in such places, where large shiny black measuring devices stand ready to engulf the patient sitting in the chair. The nurse indicated this chair and I sat down. With its array of revolving lenses, its variety of telescopes, it was as if I was ensconced in the midst of some time machine. Surrounding me, on the walls, were charts and diagrams. At the end of the room hung the reading list of letters, each line diminishing in size. My chair was brightly illuminated from above while the room itself was in comparative darkness. I could see the vague likeness of a desk and a small sink, but the rest was in shadow. The nurse came and went, came and went. She announced that the doctor would be with me shortly. Then suddenly I felt a presence somewhere near, perhaps behind me, betrayed by the rustling of clothes or a light footfall on the floor. A voice spoke in my ear.

"Place your chin on the rest, please, and look straight ahead. . . . Have you ever been fist-fucked?"

I had been leaning forward to do as I was bid, and for a moment the question gave me pause. Obediently, however, I continued to poke my jaw forward onto the black plastic chin rest and cleared my throat. The optometrist, if indeed it was he, was clearly waiting for a reply. Unsure where this was leading, I answered tentatively.

"Er . . . no."

The door opened quietly and the nurse came in again, carrying some long instrument with a head on it like a rocket. I swiveled my eyes in some concern but the optometrist, without a word, moved from behind me to operate the machinery. He was about thirty years old, all smiles as he twisted first one knob then another, adjusting his apparatus. The nurse left as quietly as she came, leaving her rocket behind on the desk. I was now staring straight into the optometrist's eyes. He spoke again.

"Close your left eye. . . . Thank you. It's a strange experience. Now the other eye. . . . Thank you. . . . I'd never done it before; not fist fucking."

I was prevented from immediately replying to this confession because my chin was resolutely placed on the rest. I lifted it up.

"Is that so?" It seemed the only thing I could say with any degree of decorum. Was I now so obviously gay? I, whom my boyfriends had once mistaken for a police officer? He must have seen me somewhere at one of my haunts.

The nurse returned, this time with some papers. The doctor began whirling his lenses. The nurse left.

"I was at the beach yesterday." Now he was whispering confidentially while he adjusted a bright blue light. "Look into the light. . . . Just walking along among the families on the beach. . . . Look at my ear. . . . Thank you. It was really quite amazing!"

In came the nurse again. She seemed extraordinarily ubiquitous. It occurred to me she was spying. Each time she entered, he stopped speaking, and began playing with the lenses. Each time she left, he began whispering again, not hurriedly but in a strange conversational manner as if I was a confidant, which I suppose I was.

"Now look to the right. . . . I climbed over some rocks and there behind one of them was a man. Stare at the light. Thank you. He was totally naked . . . I mean . . . Look at my ear."

As if on cue, in came the nurse. Meanwhile, this strange revelation, so disjointed, constantly interrupted first by the spying nurse and then by the need to complete the professional task, did not bode well for my contact lenses. The nurse left and the optometrist was whispering again.

"He looked up at me, this man, as I stepped over him. And I mean he was a . . . can you see the blue light? Look straight at the blue light, please. . . . He reached up and grabbed my wrist, pulled it down to his backside and said, 'Put it there!' I mean, he meant it! Are these your present spectacles?"

I swallowed.

"Er . . . yes." Even though by this time I was not unfamiliar with the vagaries of physical attraction, I had wanted my eyes properly examined. Now he was looking at me as one who had just finished an extraordinary tale and hoped for a surprised response.

"Odd!" I managed. I tried not to sound too encouraging but he took me up immediately, holding my spectacles and leaning down towards me in the chair.

"It was like putting your hand inside a leather bag! And, just fancy! No more than three feet away on the other side of the rock was a family! Having lunch! Imagine! Now put this over your left eye. . . . What would they have thought had they known?"

"Did you like it?" It was, after all, the obvious question. Some people like fisting very much. I once knew a—but that's another story.

He hesitated, holding the eye obscurer in his hand. "Not much," he replied. "But I know he did," he whispered, as the nurse came in.

This time she stayed.

Not long after my encounter with the fisting optometrist, I was covering a story on Australian Aboriginal ritual at a museum. The museum boasted a planetarium and before going in I wandered around the back to see how its automated mechanisms worked. Beside the glass cases displaying meteorites of various sizes, a handsome young man was standing. It seemed he was the assistant projectionist and he motioned me through a door into the dark cavernous vault under the auditorium and above which the planetarium's projector was built. The door closed behind us, and beneath the massive frame of the slowly revolving projector and while the audience above our heads was absorbed in their lecture on Mars and Venus, the stars circling above them, we made urgent, passionate love. He told me how much he had longed to make love down there in the dark, beneath the simulated stars.

Later the same day, I spent some time with a small group of Aboriginals who had been flown specially to San Francisco and whom I interviewed only to discover they were nearly all gay. They invited me back to their hotel room where we sat around laughing about the white heterosexual culture which in our different ways we were all managing to endure, and how the traditional heterosexual mindset manages to muddle the sexual messages.

Surely the morality capable of judging such experiences should be one that measures the happiness of the whole being, not adherence to a self-serving theory of paralysis. Augustine's own sexual confusion, for example, is patently apparent, as is St. Paul's. Their emotional needs frequently break through their narratives, which are so contrived as to render those needs harmless by making them invisible.

My experiences in San Francisco were initiating me into a whole new train of thought that could no longer be denied. And once begun, just as the moral theologians had predicted, the eventual conclusion was inevitable. The restoration of the body, of which the brain is a part, indeed the struggle to unite it with all of what is usually described as nature, seemed suddenly insistent, ineluctable.

Nearly all religions and much of religious experience either recommends or hints at inclusivity, the comprehensive gathering together of all that is, in one vast embrace. Even exclusionary Christianity envisions a God who becomes all in all, and the universality of God's presence is a favorite theme of Christian mystics. There is satisfaction and reassurance in such a view of existence, and it responds to what we are learning of the interdependence of the universe and all that it contains.

The principle of unity is nowhere better expressed than in the passions of sexual intercourse. The exchange of bodily fluids, meaning saliva, sweat, sperm, tears, and even, we must suppose, urine and feces, expresses in a localized way a search for unity similar to that proposed by Aristophanes in Plato's *Symposium*. No moral reproach need attach to such exchanges; rather, they are indices of a broad acceptance of existence in its many forms and endless transformations.

Yet Christianity's disposition toward such unity has been unequivocal: it is wrong, even positively evil, because it accepts too much and fails to distinguish between the supposed will of God and human obligation toward God. According to this view, evil is represented by or inherent in the body and all material things, and will be punished in some way, either now or later. A bottomless gulf yawns eternally between those who observe this ukase and those who do not. From this gulf, extending in all directions, cracks and fissures separate men from women, animals from humans, material from spirit, the body from the soul, and earth from heaven; they divide races, classes, religions, vices, and virtues. Hierarchies and dominions are dependent upon these chasms that fragment, favoring one over another, and endlessly diminish everything in a veritable ecstasy of distinction, so as to maintain the pinnacle of God. But if God really is all, how can this be?

That the distinctions cause more trouble than was ever caused by pain itself is ignored in the clamor of competition for God's favor. In

the loving embraces of the tubs, when all artificial postures and pretenses could be dispensed with, one seemed to experience something
of what supposedly less sophisticated cultures remind us are the
essences of existence. Compared with such experiences of natural,
uncontrived, unpretentious beauty as might be found in the woods,
beneath the stars, in the midst of a storm, or when the meadows are
silent beneath a fall of snow, whole libraries of controversy fall silent.

It was borne in on me as I pursued this theme, perhaps as a result of
my journalistic excursions into the realm of science, that should by
chance the sun suddenly glow hotter than usual, or should an errant
flare shoot from its surface in our direction, our planet would burn up
or dissolve, leaving behind not a single trace of Christianity, humanity, or any living organism. From such a vast, earth-consuming cata-
clysm, not a shred of what we were or might have been or hoped to be
would remain. Only some molecular, atomic, or particulate memory,
an irreducible, ineradicable pattern of what existed, might survive.
The grand cycle in the reaches of eternity would eventually cause
some other dispensation to arise that once again included Everything.
But are we not already there? We are separated more by ideas and theories than by facts.

Discussion of the body also and inevitably raised questions about
Jesus. What of his body? Indeed, the meaning of his body is critical to
Christian thought. He was, Christians like to say, not only divine but
"all man," with a penis and human desires. The Christian fathers
found an intellectual explanation of his essential physicality in his
supposed moral power of suppression, in divine attributes of self-control, and finally in the *magnum mysterium* of divinity itself. Such
things as defecation, urination, ejaculation, and all the other bodily
functions, were no doubt discussed but secretly, foreshadowing the
self-censorship with which the churches approached the discoveries of
the twentieth century. After all, it is not impossible that Jesus himself
might have been gay, as well as Paul, his too-ardent theorist. And why
should they not have been? It is as credible to claim that they were
Caucasians and knew arithmetic, or had red hair or blue eyes. It has
long been obvious that this would explain the insistent Gospel reference to "the disciple whom Jesus loved." The reluctance of theologians to deal with such embarrassments suggests a preference for
denial over facts. Jesus, they say, seemingly in his defense, was a creature of his time—thus unmasking their god for what he was, an animal like ourselves.

THE LYCEUM
1969–1972

*W*e were once supposed to have been perfect and were then thrown out of the Garden because we learned too much. It took time to discredit this theory because we knew so little. Only since the beginning of the last century have we been able to gather enough accurate information about existence to know what to believe in. I was still learning. But it was not the preacher in me that led me forward; it was the journalist. The preacher would have set my thoughts in concrete. For example, I had to force myself to abandon the addiction to prayer: it assumed what I was trying to research.

For years, working at night and whenever I could filch a few days off, I broadcast almost daily, mostly for radio and sometimes for television news and documentaries. So much was changing, and I enjoyed the work immensely. The laser had finally been perfected; Alan Shepherd had followed Yuri Gagarin into space; the Beatles and Elvis had revolutionized the sound of popular music; salt-tolerant wheat was perfected; atomic power stations were being built; Freedom Riders began the long struggle to end America's apartheid; the President had been assassinated; and in August 1965 I could be found in a rented car driving across broken plate glass through the Los Angeles suburb of Watts where thirty-four deaths, thirty-nine hundred arrests, and the burning and looting of two hundred shops made it the worst riot in Californian history.

I received fan mail from various foreign audiences but was unknown in American broadcasting. This bothered me. I felt I wasn't pulling my weight and so volunteered as an actor and an announcer at two noncommercial radio stations in the Bay Area, KPFA and KXKX. Then in the fall of 1968 I received a curious telephone call. It was from the Ford Foundation, at that time one of the wealthiest in the country. Would I be willing to attend a private meeting to discuss the declining state of American radio and television?

The meeting was to be held somewhere in New York state at a place called Suffern. I gathered it was to be kept somewhat secret and was told little of its purpose other than that it had to do with the future of broadcasting. A stretch limousine was waiting at Kennedy Airport. "Step inside!" invited the chauffeur, and alone I was whisked into the night. The huge chauffeur remained silent, and when the long journey finally came to an end I found myself in what seemed to be a luxury compound, where I was put to bed. When I woke, I was taken to breakfast and on into a conference room where I was briefed.

Those around the table were a curious bunch. There was Robert Swezey, a handsome southern gentleman who had been the president of a commercial television station in the South and who was introduced as representing a newly formed Corporation for Public Broadcasting, about which I had heard only whispers. There were three other presidents: James Day, an urbane and friendly fellow, who ran KQED, the oldest educational television station in the country, operating out of a rat-infested warehouse in San Francisco; Hartford Gunn, an ebullient former radio engineer who had cobbled together WGBH, a combined television and radio operation in Boston; and Sy Siegel, the ambitious president of the Broadcasting Foundation of America, an educational network headquartered in New York that mailed a mixed bag of taped programs around the country.

One or two others were from the Ford Foundation, and then there was Frank Gillard, a courteous, intelligent Englishman of considerable authority in Britain, whose voice I recognized from his despatches during the Second World War and his coverage of royal affairs. He was now the director of the BBC's radio networks and had proposed an imaginative and far-reaching plan for their massive reorganization to include Britain's first local stations. Also expected, although he appeared only briefly and then to predict that FM radio would never come to anything, was Fred Friendly, a celebrated and acquisitive producer from the commercial Columbia Broadcasting System. He had worked with the famous Ed Murrow and was well liked in Congress.

"You know about the Communications Act of 1934?" I was asked.

"Yes, it's been amended with an addition, called, I think, the Public Broadcasting Act."

"It's Johnson's best effort yet," said someone else. "It'll change broadcasting in this century!"

"I'm not sure about that," said a third man, shaking his head and looking sad. "But it'll put the record straight."

They then discussed hearings that had taken place prior to the passage of the Act. These had revealed not only gross ignorance in Congress about broadcasting itself—how it worked and what it was supposed to be or do—but also anxiety in both Houses over the constitutional implication of using public appropriations to fund the modern media. It seemed, in fact, that the new Act, however well-meaning, was thought by many to be an infringement of the First Amendment that guaranteed freedom of the Press; the thin end of a wedge that would lead inevitably to a State propaganda machine.

However, as all those present admitted, not even its most determined detractors could deny that the American commercial system had become a gold mine for its owners. The three commercial networks were reaping multimillions every year from advertisements, very little of which they seemed to spend on programs. It was one of the most profitable businesses in the commercial world. And in becoming so, American radio and television programs, their content controlled and constantly interrupted by sales talk for products from soap to hemorrhoid ointment, had become a laughingstock. In hopes of appealing to an entity described as the masses, writers, directors, and producers of radio and television programs were churning out what the chairman of the Federal Communications Commission had described as a "wasteland" of rubbish, the shame of a civilized nation. His 1961 speech, supported by the report of a special commission created under President Lyndon Johnson (himself the owner of a commercial radio station), had finally provoked change. Our meeting was one of the results.

Ironically, the stumbling block to ending, or at least mitigating, the commercial orgy by any means other than a voluntary housecleaning was the American constitution. As the critics of the amendment to the Act had pointed out, the First Amendment prohibited interference with freedom of speech by any part of government. This Amendment had been carved in stone and for two hundred years had successfully prevented the use of public money to infiltrate the American consciousness. To fool with such a foundational structure was to enable tyranny and invite public wrath.

I had been silent through the discussion and it was time I put in a word. "But the American press isn't free!"

This provoked stares of reproof. I was taking pot shots at a sacred cow. However, I went on.

"The media may be free of government control, but this has

allowed private interests to shackle them just as tightly as any government could. They're tied up to the point of strangulation! From what you tell me, you can't invoke either national security or the so-called public good. Even the Voice of America is beamed only toward potential enemies."

"But that's why we're here," said Swezey, the southern gentleman. "We're here to loosen the knot, and to do it we can use the educational stations."

In America these had traditionally been considered the birthplace of broadcasting itself, the laboratories of the scientists and inventors who had theorized the very existence of radio waves, developed them, and made them useable. They had had a long and difficult struggle to survive, even while planning for just such a network as we were discussing. Before he died, the man who was to have been the chairman of the very first commercial educational radio network had been the president of the University of Virginia; stations housed in educational institutions like his had been in receipt of special title appropriations as part of the commitment by the government to science and invention, and operated on reserved frequencies.

"They're used to train commercial broadcasters, disc jockeys, and so on, but the Act doesn't say so, and nor does the appropriation for funding educational technology. They're restricted only from competing with commercial stations."

"Who was it," asked the Englishman, "who said you're building an American 'Lyceum'? That should be the way of it. Your unions have supported it and, if I remember correctly, local leaders were brought in to say they'd welcome a new educational system. After all, it's a good way to reach minorities with quality programs."

I looked at him. I knew that in Britain, "minorities" meant Colonials, and "quality" implied an elite. Did he really understand, I wondered? It was he who had invited me and he now expected my support.

"Remember, my company will honor our pledge of a million bucks," said the CBS producer. The commercial networks had no fear of "quality" programs that were likely to reach only small audiences.

"I only wish they hadn't called it 'public.'" This from the president of KQED, which had invented on-air auctions to raise extra funds. "They'll think it's paid for. It will make it much more difficult to raise funds. We can't improve things on auctions alone."

At this, the New York man broke in. "It's gonna be a darned hard struggle anyway, without the public breathing down our necks."

I could see Britain was upset at this. "But won't you be serving the public?" he asked. "I mean, isn't that what your new Act implies; or does 'public' refer only to the source of funds?"

The president from New York looked sad. "Here in the States," he growled, "the term 'public' carries a truckload of responsibilities. It could mean that anyone who wants to be heard or seen must be allowed on the air. It also means the government pays."

Even the Englishman looked aghast at this. Had he expected the public to be those special private elites that inhabited British "public" schools such as I had gone to?

"See what I mean?" the New Yorker went on. "That word was the only description the Administration's lawyers could find. They must have taken it from the regulations on interstate commerce. They did mean that anyone could broadcast. What did they know about it? And Congress thinks of it in terms of funding and government control. Goddamn word! It'll plague us down the road, you mark my words."

Yes, we predicted it. The amendment to the 1934 Communications Act that had ordered the new corporation to be formed required that its directors were to be appointed by the president of the United States. This immediately made it a political football, the very thing the critics had warned against. To insulate actual programs from politics, the corporation was to form two additional autonomous corporations, one to build a full-fledged radio network with freedom to produce and distribute, and another to distribute television programs but, as the individual stations had lobbied for, *not* to produce them. Strangely, neither of these organizations was permitted to actually broadcast. The funds would filter down to them, and then to—

"To the stations! We will still have control of it!" cried the former Boston engineer.

Britain paled again. "But the stations are autonomous, aren't they? They'll never get it together."

Missing the somber implication of that statement, drawn from bitter memories of endless national negotiations, the various presidents grinned. They were station managers themselves.

"You bet they are! That's our only hope. If any bureaucrat tries to tell me how to run my station, I'll run him out of town."

"You mean," said I, "dispersal of power, decentralization."

"That's the key," agreed the southern gentleman with a sunny smile.

"I keep forgetting," the Englishman went on. "Your country is so vast. Our networks have only a single source."

"And you produce the best programs," said the Boston man, an

Anglomaniac. "Sure you do! We'll buy your programs and put them on the air. Set the pace, raise the standard right away."

"But won't British voices . . ." I began.

"What else do we have? It'll take us years to produce our own shows."

There was no gainsaying this, yet I thought of my experience in Georgia. Certainly, second runs, as they're called, at fees far below original production costs, would show what might be done, but would such programs play in Peoria? I said as much but again indulgent smiles spread around the table.

"We must have quality programming. Without quality programs right at the beginning, we're dead in the water. The Act even forces the new television organization to buy its stuff," Gunn continued. Then, pointing round the room, he went on. "And, anyway, where else can we go for programs but to Britain?"

Britain raised a deprecatory paw.

"Radio, of course, is different," said another voice, a television man. "No one cares about radio any more. It's a lost cause."

This time the Englishman looked startled. After all, he was a radio man himself. "I wouldn't say that. In Britain we still produce thirty radio dramas every month. At drive time our commuting listeners even match television's prime. And once you have FM up and running, that'll make all the difference in quality. Anyway, aren't we here to talk about radio?"

"FM? No way! That's ten years down the road, if then." The commercial people had done their job well. Keep these turkeys out of FM at all costs until the commercial networks had grabbed the better frequencies.

Television was another matter, and the talk quickly turned back to it. But if the new organization turned into a showcase for prerecorded British productions with British accents and British class structures, they would be watched by only a select few. They certainly would not play in Peoria and they'd be open to charges of elitism.

"Elitist? Of course we're elitist. That's what it's all about," was the reply I got. So it really was the archbishop and the Prayer Book all over again! Anticommercial animus, combined with Anglomania and lack of facilities, was likely to submerge their overall strategic objective before they had even begun. So much for the trusted American genius for infrastructure!

The session ended with my flying back to San Francisco with Jim Day, the president of KQED. We sat together in first class seats, both rather dispirited: I, because the meeting and the participants had shed a sad new light on American attitudes to culture in general and broadcasting in particular; he, I suspected, because he had hopes of heading the production of programs for the new television system, a prospect which, unless he was able to outwit the meaning of the Act, was unlikely.

Then, turning to me over mounds of ice cream, he asked, "Want a radio station?"

"Why not?" I replied, not taking him seriously. It was the kind of remark that I was learning Americans liked to make. "Which one?" There were more than fifty working radio stations in the San Francisco area alone.

"The one owned by the Presbyterians. KXKX. It has an educational license. We're buying it. You take it over and then design the new radio network." He laughed. Was he serious?

Had they decided it over drinks while I was walking the terrace attempting to figure them out? I had kept my thoughts to myself, otherwise they would never have agreed upon it. They had seemed to dismiss their educational station colleagues and they wanted an alliance with Britain, using British foreign correspondents. Such reports would provide additional income for Britain while providing the new public network with comparatively cheap, albeit "classy," material from all over the world, giving it the desired "quality" edge over the commercial competitors. I would become a "public" broadcaster.

"I thought you had all written radio off."

"Not me," he returned. "Want it?"

I thought. It was a generous offer. Moreover, it would open up yet another view of the world beyond that offered by suicide and the church.

"You remember I'm a priest?" I reminded him. "A worker-priest, really."

"So much the better. Just don't preach on the air," was his reply, not an entirely satisfactory one. But I was rapidly coming to the conclusion that there was a certain chaotic element in American life, the downside of its much-vaunted freedom.

To help build an American Lyceum was no mean purpose, incorporating educational, cultural, and even philosophical aspiration. In a time of revolutionary social change, the modern media were likely to play a significant, even a provocative role. Religion had become increasingly regressive and unresponsive, when its inspiration should have animated something more appropriate to contemporary needs than parochial security. Also, I had learned a new phrase from the American station managers: some things had to be placed "on the back burner" to await later fulfillment, a culinary way of dealing with responsibilities that needed patience.

I talked it over with my own board of directors at Suicide Prevention, among them a judge whom I much admired. "Radio?" he scoffed. "Radio? What a waste! You should be a lawyer. Radio's junk!"

"But think what it could be," I countered. He was unrelenting. Like most Americans, he had no experience of what I considered to be the real thing. What's more, he had never heard me on the air!

Accordingly, in 1970 I handed over Suicide Prevention, now ten years old, remaining only to preside over a Bay Area–wide conference of five additional centers, and in its place accepted the "gift" of a radio station with a catchment area of some hundred square miles and millions of potential listeners. As I hired staff and began planning programs, my life changed almost immediately.

Only slowly were people hired to run the new umbrella Corporation for Public Broadcasting. After a long search, John Macy, a commanding presence with long civil service experience behind him, was brought on board as president, and Albert Hulsen put in charge of pulling the educational radio stations together. Later, with Churchillian affectation, Macy liked to call me "Mister Radio," but first, presumably in fulfillment of the Suffern plan, a national poll of so-called educational station managers resulted in the election of six who then elected three "members at large," of whom I was one. We were to be a planning group under first Al Hulsen and then John Witherspoon, the manager of a station in San Diego. Together, we were to act as midwife, as it were, of the new radio baby.

As usual with such undertakings, preparation was needed before the new corporation could even be said to exist. So far we did not even have a name for the new enterprise, and spent much time trying to find one. An "American" or "United States" network sounded misleading, smacking of government control. "National," a possible alternative to these, seemed colorless and reminiscent of commercial enterprise. Nor did the term "public" appeal to us for the same reasons that had been advanced at the Suffern meeting. For a long time, the only part of our title we could agree upon was "radio," but even this was, as Ben Franklin would have said, self-evident and thus unnecessary. There was also much discussion as to whether we should include the terms "broadcasting," "network," "company," or "corporation," and also whether two or four words might not be better than three. Finally, however, we settled for simplicity, and for want of something better agreed that when finally it was incorporated, it should come into the world as "National Public Radio."

During this planning stage I was vice-chairman and was anxious that from the beginning we establish as a principle of operation that the network would be democratic, one in which all Americans could be said to take part. Representation in the development and future programs of NPR, as we quickly came to call it, seemed to me critically important for its success. This was not only in keeping with the turbulent times, it was something I seemed naturally to believe in. After all, people like me had a stake in being represented. At the same time, like an old-fashioned "leveler," I was uneasy, even antagonistic, at any signs of class domination. I well understood the enormous advantages of a centralized operation such as the BBC, with its total editorial control and its determination to give the public what it thought they should have, but I was determined that if I had anything to do with it, NPR's programs should be drawn not from a single home base but, in full agreement with the Suffern group, from the stations it served; it should be not only representative but also decentralized. All groups, minorities, and localities should have their say. Only in this way, I thought, could the network have any value as a truly new way of broadcasting and help change the world. And at our next meeting in San Diego, I said so.

Talk then turned to the location of our headquarters. In keeping with the principle of decentralization, Denver was proposed. But though it might eventually have been linked electronically with the rest of the world, that admirable city was still too far away from the action for daily reporters to survive. Los Angeles and New York, two other likely options, were peopled respectively, we thought, with entertainers and salesmen, both anathema to our constituencies. No one seemed to like Chicago ("too cold") or Boston ("too much") and we almost selected Philadelphia before the need to be on top of events forced us to choose the District of Columbia—"headquarters," someone said, "of the world."

Meanwhile, with a greed not lost on us, the television group now under the direction of Hartford Gunn was eager to control the entire government appropriation set aside for radio as well as for television. Gunn chose not to limit his horizon, and his own board of managers, eschewing the obvious in favor of ambition, accordingly called themselves the "Public Broadcasting Service," expecting one day to engulf radio as well. Indeed, the aggressive, often arrogant, tactics of our television counterparts were frequently to enrage us. We were also to learn that the board of the umbrella Corporation itself knew nothing, and seemed to care even less, about radio. It was many years before we realized this blindness was a blessing in disguise.

Then, at four in the afternoon of March 3, 1970, four of us— Richard Estell from Michigan, John Witherspoon, Ralph Nicholson representing CPB, and myself from San Francisco, met in the offices of the Corporation for Public Broadcasting in Washington, D.C., to formally incorporate National Public Radio. After a meeting that dealt with some preliminary business, John Witherspoon, who had been chair of the planning group, and William Kling, a board member from Minnesota, were almost immediately absorbed into CPB, and I was hoisted into the driving seat as chairman to put our plans into action.

It was an intimidating responsibility for one so new to the field. As an upstart, I felt uncomfortable. But apparently that was what had been intended. The educational radio system had been creaking in every part for many years and new approaches were desperately needed; it was why the Public Broadcasting Act had come into being in the first place, and why I, with my quite different experience of broadcasting, had been invited to join in. But it was an onerous task to ensure that the key principles that we had laid down were built into the very foundations of this newly born organization.

We were a congenial and hardworking group that was composed originally—to the shame of the industry—only of men. Many of them had been part of our planning team. There was my vice chairman, Joseph Gwathmey, a tall, energetic, deep-spoken Texan. There was Richard Estell, with myself one of the four original incorporators, whose readings of books on the air already commanded an increasingly widespread audience; Donald Forsling, who had replaced Witherspoon and whose quiet meditative presence was often to calm our too-great enthusiasms; David Platts, a lively maverick from Florida; Karl Schmidt, who saw more clearly than could I the difficulties of the task before us; Marvin Segelman, whose Pacifica station in Los Angeles had been setting new standards of on-air representation; and Nathan Shaw, whose programming in Philadelphia was to set legal precedents. Finally, there was William Siemering, who had already thought up some novel programming plans.

It seemed somehow appropriate to hold the first session of this new board in some exotic place off the beaten track. Accordingly, I flew them all by helicopter to Sausalito, California, where I now lived. Once a Portuguese fishing village and later an artists' community, Sausalito sits snugly on the side of the hills in a tiny bay on the Marin side of San Francisco's Golden Gate. It was also the home of "Sally Stanford," a former madam who in the early part of the century had grown wealthy entertaining the "nobs" of San Francisco. And it had been to the springs of Sausalito that San Franciscans once sailed to escape the terrible fires that devastated the city following the 1906 earthquake.

In this pretty and salubrious environment we could review our options, set our priorities, and with any luck begin the selection of our first president. The blue expanse of the great San Francisco Bay spreading outward in the sunshine might inspire and encourage us to embrace the challenge and chart such enterprises as might help change the world for good. Beneath widespread cedars, surrounded by palm trees, and with the Pacific headlands behind us, the whole continent really did stretch out before us, faced as we were with a weighty national responsibility. And indeed, before we left that delightful spot we unanimously passed a motion from Karl Schmidt that NPR recognize itself as "an instrument for social change." This was no small declaration in an America burdened by Vietnam and demonstrations in the streets. It was a theme that was to inform all our discussions and decisions. Like good radio people, we rejoiced at being called to respond to the political and social turbulence of the time, and had little inkling of the battles we would soon be fighting at every level merely in order to survive.

During these early meetings we established decentralization as an immediate working principle. It was a policy for which I had long argued and received strong support. But it was difficult to achieve. On the one hand there was the need for a central controlling or guiding editorial stance, and on the other the urgent needs of station managers scattered throughout the country who had been struggling for years to keep their stations alive on the tiniest budgets. The small government appropriation that was to be NPR's lifeblood seemed enormous by comparison with local budgets and the managers wanted it distributed among themselves. At regional conferences we were forced to explain that, fairly distributed, it would amount to no more than half a microphone each.

At the same time, we knew that if NPR was to be truly public, the vast extent of the United States and its varied populations demanded that our programs include material from as many stations as possible, none of which could produce programming without additional funds. We and Al Hulsen, our Corporation adviser, who was devising the first highly controversial Standards of Operation, were to struggle for some time to come up with a working formula that would solve this difficult problem in a fair and practical way and help Peter to contribute to Paul.

It wasn't long before we had to hand over much of the nitty-gritty working responsibilities to a president. There was an initial preference for someone well versed in lobbying, but we were also attracted to the idea of having a well-known broadcasting figure at the helm. In the end, the physical task of actually building the network took precedence over both these considerations, and the board selected Donald Quayle, the accomplished former head of our national association, supremely versed in technical know-how. His quiet confidence and unassuming ways were well known and well liked. Even more important, at least to me, was his unhesitating agreement with the need for an essentially democratic service that would value material drawn from all over America.

Together, Quayle and a board committee then reviewed what he had discovered might be an appropriate starter-home in Washington, D.C. Any building we chose would need to meet complex technical requirements. The difficulties would be enormous. These were the days before satellites and computers were still primitive. And the negotiations for leased land lines could be crippling, financially as well as technically.

But our president knew his stuff, and with surprising despatch our growing facilities were moved to a newly designed and specially modified building on M Street at the heart of downtown Washington. (To our chagrin, it was also to house an arm of the Secret Service. Perhaps, we thought, we should have chosen Denver after all.) Quayle worked fast, and it wasn't long before there was enough electrical cable in the building to reach to Los Angeles and back several times, all hard-wired to the most up-to-date equipment that our slender means could buy.

It was then time to determine what kind of programming would serve our constituency of the entire nation. Again, our working principle of decentralization would be critical to its success. In a decision that we never regretted, our president selected one of our own board members, William Siemering, to be in charge of this aspect of our operation. He was a shy young man, more like a monk than a traditional broadcaster, and he had already done much thinking for us, presenting a draft plan during the earlier sessions before the incorporation.

Our board insisted that the programs we offered not only set as high a technical standard as possible but also be both representative of the nation and acceptable to a sufficient number of stations to justify their expense. Some hoped we would also feed programs in the arts, especially since the stations themselves would necessarily continue to broadcast local news and their own preferences in music.

"They already have the world's finest orchestras on disc; they don't need that from us," I said. But I was wrong. Concerts broadcast live are very often more successful than recorded music because they achieve what radio does best: instantaneous communication of events as they happen. We also discussed our chances of mounting a daily soap opera, an idea that greatly appealed to me as a way to reach less cultivated audiences. Radio had made its mark with soaps in the past and might do so again. In Britain, *The Archers* had been running for thirty years and was actually a vehicle for agricultural news. But, as the term itself implied, soaps were too "commercial" for my fellow board members, and I was reminded that, like full-fledged drama, they are expensive. What the stations really wanted was news and current affairs. This I understood. My own news editor was tired of newspaper clippings and "rip-and-read" material taken from the machines of the Associated Press, however reliable. We wanted something live and under our own control.

We talked about all this informally at the board level even while Bill Siemering was trying to pull something coherent together. What we needed was a mix. For years I had been contributing to a morning news and information program on the BBC, and at my own station I was now broadcasting news and music in a magazine format similar to that being offered by the Canadian system and the Christian Science Network, a very professional organization.

However, the strength of such a magazine program would necessarily depend upon contributions by reporters and correspondents out in the field at the local stations. This posed difficulties because the stations, especially those housed in educational settings, usually relied on disc jockeys who were student volunteers. I pushed for bringing local station staffs into Washington to be trained, but this was a plan that Quayle was able to implement only later with local centers operating on independent grants. Moreover, as our president quickly pointed out, it would appear as if we were competing with the local stations.

Coverage of foreign news was, I remember, an even more difficult problem. The only English-speaking reporters we might be able to use in other countries were BBC employees who spoke with British voices, a sound that would undermine our claim to be American. Some did not care about this. "We're supposed to be an agent for change," we were reminded. "We need something different." Quayle's team thought of a solution: if an hour of hot news was going to be difficult to achieve, especially if it was to include items from abroad, why did it have to be hot? I agreed. They were taking themselves too seriously. Why couldn't it include the kind of thing I broadcast: background pieces, local color, strange occurrences, everything and anything with zip and humor?

"Did you know someone has invented talking tombstones?" I asked.

They stared.

"Tombstones with built-in tape recorders which play your last words, or if not your last words, some last message by which you'd like to be remembered. The BBC snapped it up like hotcakes. I even found a variant: tombstones with built-in film clips of the loved one's face which glows as it speaks. Or here's another: clothes made of sugar with nuts for buttons and licorice for laces. You can eat them as you go along. We must have humor."

"That sounds too trivial," said someone. "Too—dare I say it?—too commercial." They laughed, but I thought them wrong, nonetheless.

"Anyway, would the stations be able to find such stuff?" I was asked. "They don't yet have the staff or the experience to do so."

This was certainly true. In fact, not only were local stations not up to contributing much, but when their managers did manage to mail in stories, often recorded on domestic machines with poor quality, the voices were usually those of students, so young and unconvincing that although they were less offensively aggressive than were their commercial counterparts they failed to sound reliable. We were to suffer from this weakness for years until, in effect, the station staffs grew older and their voices could compete.

But it seemed I had made a point, and it being agreed that our key program should have a magazine format, Don Quayle invited suggestions for a title. Stale descriptions like "Radio Roundup" or "The Six O'Clock Show" were offered; finally Siemering's staff came round to "considering all things" and "All Things Considered" was established—a title that enabled us to cover our lack of hard news with a variety of material. Soon we also learned that Schmidt's university production group at the Wisconsin station had developed the now well-known musical signature phrase for the magazine, capable of being performed on a variety of instruments, even cups and saws. We were on our way. *All Things Considered* not only survived, but over the years it has received many awards and grown increasingly stronger, and by the turn of the century its audiences ran into the multimillions, limited only by the capacities of individual stations.

Unlike public television, which to avoid Congressional criticism encumbered its schedule with animals and the trials and tribulations of the British aristocracy, it seemed that we had aimed straight at the all-American ear. Quayle's increasingly experienced and creative team even discovered the wonderful voice of Susan Stamberg, who projected just the edge of warm authority we needed, as did other now-famous women's voices like those of Cokie Roberts, Ann Taylor, Nina Totenberg, and Linda Wertheimer. These and a series of engaging male voices, like those of Noah Adams, Bob Edwards, and Robert Siegel, eventually helped to give us the enduring broadcast equality we were looking for. We hoped that eventually the local stations would match them with talent on their own staffs.

By careful maneuvering and perhaps because we were prevented by tight budgets from overplaying our hand, we had managed to lay a firm foundation as well as steer a course in keeping with the revolutionary spirit of the time. NPR gradually increased the amount of material it was able to feed its members and this soon increased their audiences far beyond expectations. Among the network's prime achievements were the principles upon which it had been originally constructed and the production values that continue to inform its programs.

As an increasingly visible national service, it was to weather some difficult times, especially when we were faced with the top guns of the Nixon administration. In order to ward off funding cuts, we were forced to develop stronger alliances with community leaders and, later, to improve station representation. From time to time, as the organization grew, there were also enormous fiscal problems. But, looking back, it can readily be seen that the strength of the foundational work was critical in enabling the network not just to survive these crises but to flourish. In fact, NPR can be said to be one of the most significant, reliable, and influential communication systems now reaching into nearly all levels of America's daily life.

I had been running my own San Francisco station according to the same principles we had discussed at the national level. Our overall strategic objective was to spread accurate information. The station was housed in a former ballet school which, in an irony not lost on me, had once been a church. It enjoyed all the architectural characteristics of a church, complete with arched windows and a nave. The side chapels had been turned into production offices. I might have been back in the past. Our union engineer virtually rebuilt the electronics from scratch because, like nearly all the educational stations, this one had originally been cobbled together from obsolescent hardware donated by commercial companies earning tax benefits. I pulled in a couple of gay colleagues expert in drama and music and hired an expert director to run programs to be broadcast live from the streets.

Our success was derived from what we called Street Radio, which opened with *Day Break,* during which news from the Associated Press was recast to match the spoken word. This was followed by *Morning Break,* in which hosts, women and men chosen from among the town's various community leaders, were invited to run their own shows from outdoor locations on the downtown sidewalks. Their microphones were hooked up to local telephone lines.

The programs opened at hours when businesspeople and other workers were taking breaks. The hosts would take pedestrians aside and invite their opinions on politics, social welfare, and recent events. Whereas commercial networks dared not open their microphones to the public for fear of offending their sponsors, Street Radio had no sponsors to antagonize and we permitted the public their freedom. Moreover, the hookup by telephone lines was inexpensive. Listeners could also call their questions in and even answer people out on the street. Despite the often chilly weather it was an enormous hit, a format whose informal, friendly way gave the people a chance to be heard that they had never had before. San Franciscans learned how their city worked and how they could help make it run better, and took part in discussions that even the board of supervisors listened to.

While Street Radio was broadcast during the day, we invented Tribal Radio for the evening hours. This schedule, like the daytime format, also fulfilled an FCC requirement that stations broadcast programs which satisfied "the public interest, convenience and necessity." Later, when the Commission added a well-intentioned but perhaps unconstitutional and therefore toothless ruling that all stations "ascertain" local needs and problems and respond to them on the air—an expensive, time-consuming process—we were easily able to comply. Other stations, being devoted almost entirely to music, struggled to include problems with local drains, traffic patterns, and housing, subjects that our programs dealt with as a matter of course. It was a requirement that revealed once again how out of touch the FCC bureaucracy was with the very world it was supposed to regulate and how powerless it was to change it.

Tribal Radio matched the public interest in innovative ways. First we divided the cost of running the station, including electricity, into a price per hour. Then we permitted any bona fide nonprofit group capable of raising enough to pay for their share of the costs of transmission to apply for air time. Once accepted on a first come, first served basis, each group was given basic training in how to produce and edit programs and was granted one hour on the air each week until the evenings of the entire week were filled. Even foreign-speaking groups were allowed their time, each representing its own community. The programs, being placed back to back, encouraged competition and also provided immediate evidence that we offered a balanced schedule. The *Israeli Hour* (in Hebrew), for example, was juxtaposed with the *Palestinian Hour;* the *Polish Hour* was placed next to a program produced by a rival Polish group who at that time regarded themselves as less "indoctrinated."

A major weakness of Tribal Radio was the fragmentation of the potential audience, especially when programs were produced in different languages without a generous leaven of authentic music that would otherwise make such programs attractive to more than their specialized audiences. Such programs were also of interest to the xenophobic FCC, and our lawyers advised us to obtain verbatim translations in case someone was calling for the downfall of the Republic.

We had other more serious dangers to deal with. Since nearly all the programs on Tribal Radio were broadcast live, the participants in the Israeli program were bound sometime to meet in the same studio as the Palestinians. Both groups turned up armed with guns, which they kept in their hands until their rivals had left the station. The *Irish Hour* also caused anxiety, but in London, not Washington. We were honored with a visit from a British consul who had to be told this was America where people had a right to speak out, as did he. Curiously, he rejected the offer. The gay community also put together a program but, as with many such attempts by gay people at that time, its following was too small to sustain the cost and, moreover, the police still waited to pounce on information that might lead them to arrests. Other programs offered helpful hints on gardening, health, how to make and offer tea (on the *Chinese Hour*), what books to read (on the *Literary Hour*), where to get good Armenian food, how to speak French, and so on. After some hesitation, we finally accepted religious programs, including the black-owned *Voice of Islam.* It was a practical adoption of pluralism that appeared to give everyone a place.

Such programming had never been heard before, not even on Pacifica's freewheeling station across the Bay. It had its drawbacks, but it had a hundred faithful audiences and it balanced the books. It naturally caused misgivings among our lawyers, who searched the regulations for loopholes. But the philosophy was sound. It was truly public broadcasting and achieved this by fulfilling the original 1967 plan that all minorities be served. The format survived for some years, brought fame to the station, and was copied at other stations around the country. It success was due, in part, no doubt to both the rising costs of professional broadcasting that it undercut and the growing fragmentation of the mythical "mass" audience of the 1950s, a splintering of society that was brought home to me not long after I had been translated into the executive level of the sister television stations. Television was another world entirely.

Our stations' board of directors, mostly elderly, wealthy, and white, were fearful of alienating the public even though most of them served merely for the kudos obtained from doing so. They once sought to escape from public harassment over a federal cut in funds to minority programs. Accordingly, they announced the location of their next public meeting, but secretly gathered for lunch in a private room on the upper floor of a small downtown restaurant.

The groups whose funds had been cut quickly found us out. The door to the room burst open and they appeared, together with their families, dressed in ethnic costume and waving sticks and guns. The elderly directors cowered to the table, their heads driven slowly down into their soup by the howling mob crowding against them. Using epithets with which only my Suicide Prevention volunteers would have been familiar, insulting the splendid birthrights of their victims and their well-known family names, the demonstrators hurled abuse and threatened immediate dismemberment of everyone at the table.

Spoons and forks that had been so genteelly raised to mouths were suspended, trembling, in the air. No one dared to take a single bite or say a single word. The slightest move implying more interest in food than in minority rights was met with renewed shrieks of derision. Crying babies and elderly parents were thrust forward directly onto the table for all to view as evidence of the injustice being perpetrated before their very eyes. There was only one solution: order more food and invite them all to lunch!

Commercial stations were hardly ever forced to deal with such situations. In an irony of misplaced accusation, our demonstrators failed to see that the poor had been made poor not by the government but by the wealthy commercial class that exploited them. Instead, they regarded government as the solution, and saw its economies as the cause of their plight. Certainly revolution was in order, but our onerous title of "public" made educational broadcasters easier meat, especially when many of our directors were representatives of the commercial class itself.

Inevitably, bowing to this kind of need, we attempted a television experiment similar to Tribal Radio but with far less satisfactory results. Large sums were obtained and distributed among local ethnic and racial minorities to make their own television programs. Most of these groups confined themselves to dance, song, and talk, but an enterprising Chicano group, made up of several extended families under a talkative leader, opted for political drama. Dramatic work on television is far from easy, but the Chicanos demanded total freedom coupled with veiled threats to bring the station to a halt unless they were granted permission to produce a play. However, without training, such a project was bound to fail. After twelve months they had no more than five minutes in the can, which I asked to view. They switched on the projector.

The scene was set inside a hut seemingly in Golden Gate Park that was meant to be a submarine. A character dressed to look like a cross between Che Guevara and Fidel Castro faced the audience and spoke. Every sentence was larded with "motherfucker" and other bold expletives. I turned to the producer.

"Under present FCC rules we can't show it."

"Why not?" he demanded, feeling for his holster.

"The audience would turn off, and we would lose our license."

"What audience?" He waved his arm around a room crowded with wives, children, and babies on whom much of the money appeared to have been spent. "This is our audience! You mean the gringos. Yes, they would turn off!" But was it not the gringo audience they were trying to reach?

I demanded the same discipline of our radio DJs who sometimes happened to be hippies who would turn their backs on the microphone. They seemed unable to understand that the art of broadcasting, being a medium of communication, necessarily includes an audience. Bound up with themselves, they had forgotten their purpose. Film directors sometimes make the same mistake.

By this time, the Nixon administration was determined to cripple what it conceived to be a "liberal" press, and chose as its whipping boy public broadcasters. Indeed, the irony of the public broadcasting story is that the very impetus in which the concept originated served only to limit its development. Public television knew exactly what the public wanted but seemed determined to make sure they didn't get it. Accordingly, it came under siege by the very Congressional critics who demanded freedom from Congressional intrusion—it was as if they had known full well that they themselves would be the ones to interfere. They were not against propaganda; they simply wanted their own propaganda. President Nixon, for example, through his minion, Clay Whitehead, demanded an end to documentaries and lower pay for news anchors whose views he presumably did not agree with.

This immediately raised questions as to whether our vaunted "public good" was a viable concept. If it meant no more than the good of whoever happened to be in power, then even seemingly benevolent organizations such as the BBC were as dangerous as the Red Cross. The demand for "high standards of excellence" would be used to manipulate the people's will in ways no less self-serving than those of commercialism. But in America, as I had long learned, the very idea of established standards was anathema; discipline a dirty word; and even accountability easily abandoned. Indeed, many Americans who were idealists seemed loath actually to demand the best, preferring only to hope for it. Their concept of total freedom seemed in the short term more often to produce chaos. I used to think that unconditional benevolent support is likely to result in dependent people, and that only an intelligent balance of interference and freedom determined by a fully representative body can maintain a creative public enterprise. Today, I am not so sure. Private benevolence can be critical to success, while public committees bog down in compromise. In an egalitarian society the ability to come up with an ideal mixture of support and standards itself depends upon education. A committee of ill-informed people can do great damage and quickly become a burden on the public purse. At the same time, the freeing of information from control by commercial interests that define operational success as financial gain is critical to societal development. Truth, whatever truth may be, requires a more reliable determinant than fickle profit making.

As a journalist and broadcaster I could not help but think about such things, and as a priest no less so. Ignorance is a threat to the public good, one for which only those dedicated to knowledge can provide an antidote. Once upon a time, churches ruled the media of their day. Should educators rule them now? But even educators seem to find it impossible to "let it all hang out," and censorship, especially in the field of education, drags a society back into darkness. Find a decorous, discreet, and genteel society where certain words must not be spoken and certain subjects never openly discussed, and you'll find a shrunken, pusillanimous, ignorant people, a people frightened of itself.

Our fear of the body, for example, our somatophobia, overshadows our culture; I wondered where it began. Perhaps it was no more than the fear of unwanted babies that made the laws and frightened us into this strange, unnatural submission, so that, in effect, gay people inherited the oppression meant for others. We all suffer from its tyrannies. The media, especially, where information is stored for all to use, are among its most egregious victims.

*   *   *

I had helped set up a communications network of which we could be proud. Its success over the years suggests that educated America is increasingly ready to abandon myths and hearsay. Broadcasting had allowed me to search for truth more effectively than ever before. The battle for the restoration of the rights of the body continued, but in the meantime, I believed I was providing more significant service in that fight than I had ever been able to do from the pulpit. The various celebrations of communion by which so much of Christianity puts great store seek to unify existence only to separate it into the sacred and the secular. The very doctrine of transubstantiation, which sought to bind these two together indissolubly, failed to do so. It now seemed to me that the molecules of the bread and wine are sufficient in themselves. Theologians had predicted this might happen if I pursued my course, and I will admit I wondered whether my rejection of church teaching was merely an excuse to enjoy what it had so long forbidden. I had to justify myself or somehow return to God, if, indeed, I had ever left that sanctuary.

CHEMISTRY
1968–1976

*M*y broadcast reports on radio and television now covered an enormous quantity of ground. The list of subjects eventually ran into the thousands. Demonstrations, riots, discoveries, and inventions provided much material by which I tried to keep up with the times and make a living. Nonprofit work is far from well paid. Even the chairmanship of NPR was required by law to be voluntary. But the zany counterculture of the times made it all worthwhile. Indeed, I flattered myself to think that because I was being heard and seen in many places of the world, I might be responsible in part for San Francisco's growing tourist trade. My research on behalf of ABC's *The Science Show* broadcast in Australia and the South Pacific helped me considerably in my new assessment of religion, existence, and the world we live in.

One day I was standing next to Arthur C. Clarke in the Jet Propulsion Laboratory in Pasadena, California. We were awaiting the arrival of the first detailed pictures ever seen of the surface of Mars. It was 4:53 PDT on the morning of July 20, 1976, the seventh anniversary of Earthlings' first visit to their Moon, and the Viking Lander would soon unfold itself and feed back its long-awaited digitized signals. No one knew what to expect.

I turned to Clarke who, like myself, was glued to the television monitor where the picture would soon be displayed line by line, just as it arrived.

"What will you be looking for?" I asked him.

"A ninety-degree angle."

I knew what he meant, even though the atoms in the aggregate of many inorganic molecules form ninety-degree angles and can often look as artificial as anything built or carved by intelligent hands. But he had his famous monolith in mind.

Scientists all over the world and perhaps some unusually percipient churchpeople were anxiously awaiting the truth. It had taken years to plan the experiment and weeks more for the "site certification" teams of four hundred experts to examine the radar readings and decide where to land. The planet is from two to five billion years old and its surface is pockmarked with craters. The location finally determined upon was the Plain of Chryse, a flat area, vaguely identified by optical telescopes and originally named by Schiaparelli. It lies among giant mountains tens of thousands of feet high. Radar signals bounced off the area by the Arecibo Observatory in Puerto Rico had revealed rocks and holes as small as twenty-two centimeters across but few large depressions or boulders.

Immediately on landing, the computerized program on board Viking had begun checking its senses: the mirror, the engine, the anemometer, the magnet, the sieve, the chromatographic sensors, and so on. Almost immediately, two slit-eyed camera eyes had opened, ready to gaze in stereo and color at whatever lay before them. Suddenly, with several clicks and whines, a short metallic stump had unfurled what looked like an umbrella, or perhaps a sunshade, just as if on vacation at some beach. This was the receiving dish antenna. Then, with further whines and clicks, two more gawky arms extended, each nobbly with measuring devices, one to test the air, and one to sample the soil. No one saw anything of this, except perhaps the Martians. Only the data streaming into the nearby Mission Control room signified that all was well.

The famous author-scientist beside me, very tall, thin and erect, was silent. Grouped around us were other journalists from foreign countries, some with cameras and recording gear at the ready, others with notebooks and pencils poised.

The signals were even now arriving back on Earth three minutes after they had been despatched, after traveling thirty-five million miles at the speed of light. They carried a quantity of encoded information. Would the Martians be discovered living safe from radiation at the bottom of the immense canyon five miles deep, or in the caldera of the giant volcanic mountain, Olympus Mons, three times as high as Mount Everest?

The variegated line of light and dark crept slowly across the screen and stopped. It would require many lines to make the full picture. We were in for a long, maddening wait. Clarke's eyes never left the screen before us, then lifting his long chin and speaking in his light Somerset accent, he said slowly, "History in the making." It was indeed.

Yet when representatives of the human race had at last reached the Moon and finally divested her of her divinity, and although more people watched that event than had ever watched any event in the world's history, it had not rocked traditional religious faiths. Now that we were watching the outcome of what might prove to be an even more momentous voyage, would humanity once again turn its back, unable to process the information? Certainly, apathy is frequently consequent upon intellectual indigestion; and an organ without the wherewithal to make sense of unrecognizable stimuli will ignore them. At the same time, minds that are both capable of responding to, but also threatened by, new stimuli may also deny them, as gay people knew to their cost.

The Martian landscape was now much more apparent on the screen: a vast plain of broken, jagged rocks protruding from and loosely scattered over what appeared to be light brown sand. It stretched to the horizon and seemed a lonely sort of place. One could almost hear the wind of carbon dioxide whistling and moaning over the desolation.

Finally, a corner of the Lander itself appeared so that we could orient ourselves more readily. The camera was aimed directly from the Lander's platform. Soon orders from Earth would turn it left and right. To watching Martians this would have been a frightening sight: a strangely shaped, awkward being with its club feet, one corner sporting a metallic umbrella, and two skinny arms, one pointing upward, the other pointing at them. Then they would see the two narrow eyes, glittering through their slits and swiveling this way and that as if on the lookout for reprisals.

We on Earth continued to stare up at the screen, hoping, despite the possible consequences, to see signs of living intelligence, the builders of the celebrated "canals." We scanned the rocks. What was that down there, amongst the shattered lumps? A recognizable shape with . . . a right angle? Could those circular structures half buried in the surface be the remains of a staircase? Were we looking at the aftermath of a great war, some ancient atomic holocaust?

The following day, Mission Control reported that Viking's robot arm had also been successfully extended and the camera had turned to watch the process. The apparatus for testing the soil had taken thousands of hours of detailed work. It was composed of as many as forty thousand working parts carefully fitted into a box not much bigger than a gallon milk carton. There were tiny ovens, pantries, bottled gases, Geiger counters, valves, a sunshine lamp, circuits, drains, and tubes, all tested to withstand extremes of heat and cold. The apparatus for this single experiment had eventually cost more than $30 million to build. Its chemistry was refined and its mechanisms were ultra-sensitive. It was, in fact, a perfect miniature laboratory that was as reliable as humans could make it.

It had been found that even a simple operation of obtaining soil samples on Earth was a thousand times more difficult for an automated machine operating under computerized radio orders than it was for human hands. Various devices to obtain and test samples of soil had been tried and rejected, including one that shot projectiles trailing sticky strings to which particles of soil would adhere and which could then be retrieved. But if digging and retrieving were difficult, the laboratory testing had been the result of months, if not years, of research.

That given the correct formula, life could occur elsewhere in the universe had already been elegantly shown in 1953 at the University of Chicago by Stanley Miller and Harold Urey. Methane, ammonia, water and hydrogen, subjected for no more than a week to lightning in the form of a high-frequency spark, produced glycine, alanine, and alpha-amino-*n*-butyric acid—organic molecules capable of forming the basic constituent of life forms as we know them. This revolutionary discovery had opened up a whole new field of "exobiology." By 1959 Miller and Urey had also shown that, contrary to expectation, not even oxygen was necessary to achieve the correct molecules.

Tests of the Martian soil were crucial to the Lander's purpose, which was to see if life on Mars existed, had ever existed, or could exist. The soil was collected in a scoop at the end of the arm, which slowly retracted so that the scoop was over an aperture on top of the testing device. The scoop was then turned so that its contents fell into the aperture. The aperture was covered with a sieve so fine that only particles of soil smaller than two millimeters could get through it. The particles were then heated in a tiny furnace and the fragments swept out by a blast or "stream" of helium into a column lined with coated glass beads where organic molecules would be trapped. The column was heated to release any organic molecules and vaporize them. The vapors were then ionized and focused onto an electron "multiplier" tube. This generated electrical impulses that were measured, converted into digital signals, and transmitted. The entire process was repeated nine times. And, surprise: the radioactivity in seven of the tests revealed the presence of organic molecules sufficient to account for the possible presence of anywhere from one hundred to one thousand bacterial cells.

The soil was also tested to see if by adding a sort of soup to it, microorganisms might be encouraged to perk up and emit telltale gases as a natural result of metabolism. And again, a "labeled release"

mechanism did detect a fairly high level of radioactivity as if from biological causes. Then, after adding carbon dioxide, under a xenon sunshine lamp, followed by incubation with krypton and 0.5 cc of nutri-
ent, the resulting gas was analyzed. All this took place in the tiny
laboratory on board.

The printout back on Earth showed possible evidence of organic
compounds: not only oxygen, but also neon, nitrogen, argon, and carbon monoxide. True, the process of testing itself might have
accounted for all these but not for the high amount of oxygen, which
was as much as fifteen times greater than it would otherwise be. Even
more significantly, when the soil was heated in the tiny furnace to
500°C, the mechanism also detected what could even be water. Since
there was no evidence of actual cell growth, these results were strange;
but they were matched by tests made with soil taken by the next
Viking during the following month.

As all these significant figures were received back on Earth and
relayed to the world, a curious melancholy spread among us journalists and scientists also. No canals had appeared, no right angles, and
there was no one to be seen who might conceivably be identified as an
actual Martian. The curiously high amount of oxygen left everyone
wondering what it meant, but that was all. Thus the official judgement was "inconclusive" and encouraged more than one scientist to
state categorically that the chances of molecular structures coming
together in the correct formation to establish life as we know it are so
infinitesimally small that any expectation of this happening more than
once in the universe was no better than wishful thinking. But considering the size and extent of the universe, such a dismissive statement is
highly suspect itself. There was perhaps a religious tone to it.

Several years later, while one of the two Viking craft was still capable of sending back monthly reports and pictures, one of the scientists
who was part of the Viking team showed me a sequence of pictures
taken by Viking's cameras. One side of one of the rocks which lie in
the soil in full view of the cameras had changed color! Could this
change be due, he asked, to the seasonal colors of living lichen such as
exist on Earth? And if another experiment known as the Wolf Trap
had been allowed on board, would it have been able to detect something that the other three experiments had missed? Of course, no one
could yet tell. It is not unlikely, however, that meteorites similar to
that found in the Antarctic and possibly originating from Mars millennia ago will also contain polyaromatic hydrocarbons which would
confirm the Viking findings and so further increase the chance of
neighbors elsewhere in outer space.

And, anyway, what is life? It can conceivably spring from a variety of atomic structures. By the 1990s there were several alien machines on the Martian surface, standing silent and derelict among the scattered debris of several others. In the immensity of the universe tiny organisms on a pinprick planet of a minor star had reached out to a neighbor and found only rocks and sand. But a close-up of a patch of Death Valley would not disprove the remains of a Rome or a Manhattan somewhere else. And when our sun has breathed its last, our home too will look the same way as does Mars: pockmarked with craters, its waters hidden in the rocks and nothing to show that humans or their history had ever existed. With our planet still teeming with life, it is difficult enough to find evidence of dinosaurs, and they ruled the planet for several million years!

My Mars adventure, like the Moon exploration, had brought a new dimension to my philosophical and religious thoughts, one that was not to be easily gainsaid or ignored. We had built machines that had finally been able to show actual places in space, real locations. So long as they were merely names attached to points of light in the night sky, the stars could, with slight adjustments, be incorporated into traditional cosmogonies. Or they could even be ignored as mysteries with little bearing on actual life or existence in general, the secrets of which would be revealed to us in some God's good time. But now things were different. Places like Mars actually existed and could no longer be dismissed as something of no concern to us. The universe was not merely a word but under scrutiny. Moreover, we were in it and part of it. In Gertrude Stein's useful phrase, there is a "there" out there, where once there were only undefined "heavens." The Christian church, and all other religions, must some day come face to face with the eternity of space, the particulate composition of all things and, more importantly, their interdependence.

During the late 1960s, the possibility, or rather likelihood, that humans will one day visit and even live on other planets was taken very seriously by scientists, many of whom were working hard to provide life-support systems at NASA's Life Sciences Center in Menlo Park, California. They had shown, for example, that lunar soil brought home from the Moon was fertile and that given adequate protection it would be possible for a human colony to live there. Much of such work was secret, for it was feared that a hot war with the Soviet Union might well be fought in outer space and that the outcome would depend upon the ability of astronaut-soldiers to survive. It was thus essential not only that space suits withstand wear and tear but also that chemists find or create portable and digestible food for astronauts.

The chemist in charge of one aspect of this research, Jake Shapira, was a slender, intense middle-aged man of wide-ranging interests and imagination. At this time many Americans, not realizing what was at stake, were attacking the expenditure of so many millions on space research. It would have been better, they said, to have taken Voltaire's advice to cultivate our gardens than to have eaten the apples of knowledge. Jake, however, was having none of this. Overlooking his desk on the wall of his tiny office was an immense Oxfam poster advertising the plight of the starving peoples of the world. "I put that up there," he told me in a dry voice, "to remind me why I'm here. From this research will come benefits. My business isn't bombs. It's food."

I realized that my interview had been arranged as a public relations ploy, but was still interested in seeing what results the operation had produced. Jake led me out of his office across the corridor, down to a set of double doors similar to his own. They opened onto the brilliant glare of a vast laboratory, as if we had walked into sudden sunshine. Row upon row of glass retorts, test tubes, gas jets, electric furnaces, more and more glass, glittering and bubbling, stretched out beneath a seemingly endless ceiling of fluorescent lamps. White-coated scientists moved quietly here and there, some bending over microscopes or peering at flasks gurgitating and glowing with strange colored liquids, others writing careful notes in books and ledgers.

Jake beckoned me over to a group of retorts. Glass tubes ran from one to the next. In the first, what looked like water bubbled quietly beneath a Bunsen burner. The next was attached to a reducing column and thence to another retort. The third contained a beautiful orange liquid sparkling with tiny bubbles. Jake reached over to the third flask, unscrewed it from its attached assembly, and held the flask up to the light. Then he turned to the wall where a Coke machine was standing and pulled out a paper cup, into which he poured the orange fluid.

"Try it," he said, offering me the cup with a broad smile. "You can sue NASA if you die."

I took a big breath, and with a farewell glance around the laboratory, accepted the cup and put it to my lips, paused only a fraction, and drank. It was a delightfully fresh drink of fizzy orangeade.

"Good?" he asked, then went on, encouragingly, "It's nutritious."

It was also, I told him, very refreshing. What was it?

"Well, you see, it's like this," he began, almost apologetically. "Perhaps I should have told you beforehand, but then, it would have spoiled the experiment and, being a scientist, I wanted to have an honest assessment."

I must have looked strangely at him, for he embarked on a long history of astronauts and the difficulties attendant upon long voyages. "There's a limit to what you can carry," he said, pouring himself a cup of Orange Something. "Have another," and, offering me another beakerful, he continued. "It's just not possible to cart barrels of beer or cans of Coke back and forth to the Moon. At least, not yet. And we've found that even water gets difficult to drink after a time. But what else do we have? So," he went on, throwing the cups into the trash and putting the flask carefully back into its seating, "I went to work on their wastes."

"Their 'wastes'?"

"Yeah. You know. Urine and feces. They're a real problem. They're very heavy and everything you extrude from the spacecraft is something lost, irreplaceable."

I stared at him as the truth sunk in.

"And . . . that . . . ?" I said, looking at the flask from which I had just drunk not one cupful, but now two.

"That's the genuine article. Transformed, of course, into its chemical parts, chemically altered and, as you might say, 'purified,' and fortified with vitamins, along with some flavor, color, and carbon dioxide to make it palatable. We found that making it yellow like lemonade was too close to home. But they can stomach the orange. It came down to being a philosophical question, in the end. A spacecraft is a closed system just like the Earth, or, for that matter, the entire universe. Everything goes round and round and round for ever. Until we finally acknowledged that fact, and put the waste back into the system, we kept getting stuck with it."

We returned to his office and had a hot cup of reassuring coffee. He reached for a cardboard tube from behind his desk, and pulled out what seemed to be the plan of an enormous dome.

"This is a Buckminster Fuller dome impossible to build on Earth because it's so big. This is for the Moon." Then, pointing to rows of green blobs along the floor of the dome, he said, "Enough food to feed the world."

He looked up at me, his face quite serious. "We'll do it . . . eventually," he insisted. "We may have to."

Later, I learned that the building of such a lunar facility had already been given a budget. It included the construction of a space station at the libration point midway between Earth and the moon to which rock from known asteroids could be catapulted and then smelted down in solar furnaces to form composite materials from which the skeleton of the dome would be formed and erected. The space station itself was one of several plans that an imaginative physicist had proposed as the foundation of what were virtually entire space colonies. These ingenious dreams took various shapes. Some were toroidal or donutlike, and slowly revolved around a central core where the sun's energy was to be collected and distributed; others were more conventional, no more than long corridors connecting clusters of spheres in which particular work could be conducted. They were all immense, many miles long or wide, and in the drawings looked like floating cities. Some even included artificial landscapes complete with rows of tiny houses, pastures for cattle and sheep, and hills and rivers full of fish. The feasibility of such grandiose schemes had been calculated by earthbound experiment, some of it in great tanks filled with water. Much seemed to depend upon the freedom with which it was assumed that engineers could work and buildings be erected without the constraints imposed by gravity. Ore mined from the asteroids, for example, once impelled in a particular direction, would keep on moving and could be easily halted wherever it was needed. Girders, heavy on Earth, once manufactured out in space, would be weightless, while roofs would be capable of stretching vast distances without collapsing.

Perhaps the most intriguing part of these plans was a solar power station that could beam sufficient energy down to Earth to satisfy the electrical needs of entire continents. However, as I discussed each of these proposals with the scientists involved it became clear that, despite their futuristic glamour, they might well cause as much international tension as they would relieve. Self-supporting space colonies could easily hold Earth's governments to ransom. Tens of thousands of space colonists acting autonomously and with the Earth's food, or especially its energy supplies, under their control, could demand whatever they wanted. I had even raised this issue with Jake.

"But what else would they want?" asked Jake, generously spreading his hands. "They would already have everything they needed. There'd be nothing else we could give them." It was the naive American again.

"Power corrupts," I answered. "They might want us for slaves and use Earth as a concentration camp." Perhaps I had imbibed the American fear of tyrants, but Jake only shrugged. Yes, he admitted, it was possible. Hitler, after all, had had everything he wanted.

Nonetheless, such dreams are likely to come to pass eventually—no doubt with occasional nightmares among them—under the sponsorship of some world government with slowly increasing needs. The vision of astronauts dancing on the Moon will not readily be forgotten, and not for nothing are young humans fascinated by other worlds to explore.

My visit with Jake Shapira lasted several hours of publicly funded government time, but I had confirmed an important lesson. Recycling was a key to understanding life on Earth and perhaps even existence in general. Aristotle could think only in terms of starts and stops, measures and movements. He had not grasped, had in fact abandoned or ignored, the hunch of Heracleitus long before, that "everything flows." Likewise, Plato in his *Theatetus* attacked this view of existence as flux on the grounds that what is at rest cannot also be in motion, but we now know different. For Plato it appeared to be simply a question of the difference between perception and what he called knowledge, a difference that has bedeviled philosophy ever since.

On my way back to San Francisco I began work on a novel in which humans had abandoned a long-derelict Earth and continued to survive in an immense artificial colony, ruled by tyrannical priests, only to have it disintegrate in an overwhelming catastrophe so immense that evolutionary history had to begin over again from its primary molecules.

CONFRONTATION

1970-1980

In the 1970s, Lester Morgan, a young sociologist, predicted that within ten years a gay platform would be on the agenda of every political candidate in the nation. At the time, he was training the first self-acknowledged gay men and women in the San Francisco Police Department. And since Suicide Prevention had provided evidence of police insensitivity to gay people, I was asked to tag along to show how they should deport themselves when dealing with both their future fellow officers and also the gay public.

The real reason why, despite dire predictions of rebellion by straight officers, gay and lesbian applicants were finally admitted into the police force in San Francisco was the administration's fear that as their numbers increased, gay people who were prepared to come out of the closet might turn on their oppressors. But the growing unrest was not confined to gay people. Nonviolent marches for racial equality had finally broken the national conspiracy of silence regarding the rights of all minorities and more than half the human species. In fact women would eventually begin marching. Even Native Americans had taken back the island of Alcatraz and sued to protect their ancient burial grounds. Chicanos and immigrant farm workers, long exploited and ignored, were also on the move.

These various large fragments of the body politic were noisy with constant debate over tactics and strategy, for where all have a say, few like to listen. The noise they made was the turbulence of a coming storm that would confront everyone with demands to choose which sides: that of the exploited underdogs, or that of the established males, the landowners and entrepreneurs.

Thus it was with much trepidation and yet with a heightening sense

of importance that some gay people began breaking out of their closets. Taking chances with their jobs, they too organized a march. It was
not to be a parade but neither was it to be violent, and with the police
chief on our side, permission was obtained in June 1970 to march
down Polk Gulch to City Hall. Peter and his friends were some of the
sponsors.

Few of us apart from drag queens had dared to show ourselves as
homosexuals in public before this. And only by way of drag had we
been at all obvious. That men in business suits and women in flow-
ered dresses would openly acknowledge that they loved people of the
same sex was revolutionary. It was not likely that such an event had
ever taken place before. Research in European court records of previous centuries reveals what seems to have been almost unanimous condemnation of any outward display of group solidarity on the part of
sexual outlaws.

"Are you going?" I was asked. "There'll be several thousand of us.
It might get rough. We'll be in full drag: Mavis is wearing that
sequined thing with the vegetable hat."

"Of course I'm going."

"You must wear your collar." So I dressed politically in a dark blue
suit and clerical collar, something I had not done for some time, and I
felt awkward in them, alien.

Polk Gulch was lined with people, some obviously supporters, a
few tourists, the local shopkeepers, and shoppers attracted by the
"Gay Marching Band" that had only recently been formed. Local
commercial television crews had found themselves salient positions
from which to catch distorting views of freakish clothes and behavior.
It was a bright sunlit day but the crowd on the sidewalk was largely
silent. Those of us walking slowly down the center of the street felt
every eye upon us. Some of us carried placards, some flags, some bal-
loons—anything, in fact, to help hide our self-conscious nervousness
at being so obviously on display. Like politicians, we felt constrained
to smile foolishly, even wave at nonexistent cheers. Otherwise, we
stared straight ahead, glancing awkwardly at those watching us
slowly pass by.

I remember I noticed, as if for the first time, the painted lane mark-
ings passing beneath one's feet, how hot the tarmac got to be in the
sun, that here and there the road had been patched with different sur-
faces, and that manhole covers had different designs depending on
where they were cast. Eventually you overcome your embarrassment
and force your head up to look around to see familiar storefronts for
the first time from the center of the roadway, and above them, open

windows with faces peering out. Occasionally a hand waved encouragement or a voice shouted words you couldn't catch.

At such events, you start out with a group within the crowd, but as the pace quickens or slows the groups tend to break up. Peter, with his fellow Coits, was somewhere far ahead and I soon found myself walking next to a middle-aged woman in a dark brown dress. She was carrying a rough piece of wood to which was nailed a large piece of square white card. On this had been written in black capital letters: MY SON IS GAY AND I'M PROUD OF HIM. That a mother had dared to take such a brave stand was astonishing.

Slowly we moved down the center of the street surrounded by men, women, boys, and girls arm in arm. But after half an hour, as sometimes happens in such marches, the group following us had slowed to cheer a supporter on the sidewalk and the contingent in front had increased their pace away from us. We two, the mother and myself, found ourselves walking alone, exposed to the full gaze of a growing crowd to the right and left.

Still gripping her sign, the woman began walking closer to me and finally grasped my arm.

"Do you mind?" she asked, "I'd feel safer."

And so we walked on, both of us encouraged by the physical contact but feeling more and more conspicuous, me in my collar and she with her sign. Her pace began to slow and her hand dragged on my arm. I offered to carry the sign, even though it did not identify me correctly and I was unwilling to detract from her presence as a mother, as defiant a stand as any we could take, sending a powerful message long before the parents of gay people were organized. Then I noticed that tears were running down her face. Her arms were trembling. She gazed about as if in terror. Suddenly releasing my arm she put her hand up to her face. The sign wavered in the air.

"Oh my god!" she whispered, "there's a television camera!" She turned to me in an agony.

"If my husband sees me he'll kill us both!" I assumed she meant herself and her son.

She thrust the sign into my hands. "I can't go on, I really can't! You don't mind, do you?" she pleaded, and ran off down the street, then into the crowd. I was suddenly ashamed of being an American, until I remembered that the woman was an American and it was only because this was America that we were marching at all and I became proud again.

On such occasions, as I knew well, television camera crews, being creatures of the current cultural norms and under orders to bring back

something worth looking at, would take pictures that exploited heterosexual myths of faggots flaunting their freakish lifestyle, making
nonsense of the truth that we existed everywhere as a simple fact of
life. Their producers believed that to have done otherwise would have
resulted in complaints from sponsors or from consumers of the sponsors' products; or, more likely, that if they gave us what is called
"sympathetic" coverage, they would have been suspected of being
faggots themselves.

We took comfort in the knowledge that any coverage is better than
none. We had been invisible for a long time and were grateful that we
might even be seen at all. But it wasn't our increasing numbers that
justified our claims. Even a single gay person would have been sufficient reason to demand equality.

Inevitably, the march became an annual event. Once we marched
through Sacramento, the state capital, in the pouring rain. We demon-
strated in front of City Hall, and, years later, finally marched, fifty
thousand strong, the length of Market Street; at the commencement
of this event, I and Susan Bergmans, one of the first ordained women
clergy, concelebrated a truly mass communion in a parking lot among
the waiting floats. Our drag balls, too, became more lavish than ever.
So much so that back in Washington, we were eventually to be listed
by the Director of Emergency Management (no less a person than
John Macy, the former president of public broadcasting) as another
dangerous element in need of surveillance.

At one of the drag balls held to celebrate our public appearances in
the mid-1970s, I received a call from a handsome BBC television journalist and a rising star in Britain much celebrated for his coverage of
foreign news. He was vacationing in San Francisco, largely, he told
me, as the result of my daily despatches, which had encouraged him
and his Marxist lover to come there. This cheered me, for I had been
wondering about the value of the media in spreading the good news.
We invited him to the next drag ball, to be held in a labor union hall,
where Peter was to display his talents as "Crystal" accompanied by
her usual consort.

On the night of the ball, our two guests sat shyly at the back of the
hall near the exit. They feared a police raid and their proximity to the
street was "just in case." The drags that year were spectacular. Mavis
appeared in purple ostrich feathers and a full-length sequined gown.
Laura (who later became a real woman) was resplendent in tight-fit-
ting, snow-white, bosom-enhancing satin. Michelle, trying for the title
yet again, was Athena (or was it Aphrodite?) sprung "fully armed"

from Olympus. She had surrounded herself with dancing boys and waved a wand from which hung glittering stars and multicolored stripes. The hall was filled with strangely tall women, their high-flown hairpieces piled one upon another and topped with roses, gilt, fruit or even doves. Drags in flowing fabrics bedizened with stars, spangles, and silver were accompanied by handsome men of all ages, some in uniform with swords, some in scarlet, nearly all in tails, and many wearing top hats. As Mavis passed by, her competitors giggled.

"You've dropped another carrot, darling!" they cried, ecstatic. Mavis was suitably furious.

Permeating this magnificence, pulling us together, making of us one vast proud family, were the music and the lights, now bathing us in glowing colors and flooding us with full orchestral climaxes and lightning flashes of red, white, and blue. We were, after all, celebrating basic facts about the psyche of all humans, releasing it from its long bondage and rejoicing in the rich variety of life of which it is capable; a psychological, aesthetic, and political extravaganza!

Finally I found our guests. The Marxist looked sad. The older man was weeping.

"Never," he began, "Never, in my life have I felt so free!" I thought of the mother and her gay son. Had something begun at last, maybe around the world? But within a year we learned that both our British guests had taken their own lives.

The United States, urgent with individualism, its hybrid vigor born of massive immigrations from lands where bitter hatreds and terrible wars are seemingly the rule, is still largely rough and tough. Americans are impatient of completion and maintenance. They are ever looking to get ahead, and as they urge their way forward, violence of one kind or another is never very far away. On November 27, 1978, I was in Washington, D.C., on network business, when the mayor of San Francisco, George Moscone, and Harvey Milk, our first gay supervisor, were assassinated. Their murderer, Dan White, himself a young conservative supervisor and former police officer, had evaded the metal detector by climbing through a back window with his service revolver. He entered the mayor's parlor, argued with him and shot him three times; then after making his way down the hall to Harvey Milk's office, went in, took aim at Harvey, who was holding his arms out to protect himself, shot him four times, and then leaned over the body and fired a final bullet into his head.

In the uproar that immediately followed, it was finally Diane (later Senator) Feinstein who, surrounded by police, made it to the front door of the Town Hall and in a choking voice announced the tragedy to the crowd that had rapidly gathered outside. No one could believe it.

Harvey had campaigned several times before finally being elected. The gay and lesbian community, its power strengthened by precinct lines newly drawn to match the city's growth, had worked hard on his behalf. He was a colorful, sometimes intemperate, but always dedicated politician, able to win the votes and pockets even of union leaders. During our annual parades down the center of San Francisco he would sit on the front of his limousine, waving his arms, calling for us to pull together, something we were not used to doing. He was a Jew, but like many gay leaders he had little use for those churches that continued to withhold support, hoping to ride out the storm. "Don't trust them," he seemed to be telling us, "Trust me!" One of his final pleas was for gay people to work for equality on the frontiers of society, especially rural areas, where gay people were still aliens and outcasts. It was a challenge I was to take up for myself.

The news of his death was paralyzing. AIDS was not yet apparent in the community and violent death, especially assassination, seemed to rock the foundations of all that we had been building. Though it was not unexpected, once it had occurred it was difficult to comprehend except as a thrust to the heart of all we stood for. Would it mark the beginning of a pogrom or witch-hunt against gay people as had once occurred in Boise, Idaho? The fact that Harvey was not the only victim, and that the mayor, a much-loved Democrat known for his support of gay rights, had also been murdered, did not reassure us that this was not a private vendetta. I immediately flew back to San Francisco to broadcast the story and join the mourning.

"Can you be objective?" my London editor asked me, suspiciously.

"You think straights would be more 'objective'?" I asked him angrily. "I won't cry into the mike, if that's what you mean." Yet objectivity was to be an important question at the murderer's trial and confirmed our suspicions that in our battle, as in the battle for women's rights, so-called disinterestedness was a myth. For my producer, sympathetic coverage even in the tone of voice would necessarily be biased. Our mere existence spoke louder than what we said.

I arrived back to find the Castro, by now our neighborhood, stunned and silent. Black banners hung from upstairs windows, shops were closed and displayed black-edged notices; flags floated dejectedly at half mast. Everyone, even those who had never liked Harvey, spoke of the event only to find themselves grieving. Just as each of us feared violence for ourselves, he had predicted his end in a recording he had made years before. He had called us together, entreated us to fight, never to give in to the monstrous injustice we suffered and had been suffering through the centuries. He had laughed, shouted aloud the convictions that we all shared, made us feel proud of ourselves, and finally laid himself open on our behalf. The comparison with other martyrs was irresistible.

The assassin, a conservative who had won his seat by calling for law and order, claimed the mayor had passed him over in the selection process and had favored Milk. The rage that overwhelmed him was that of a spoiled child in the face of competition. If Milk had been a republican, Christian and not Jewish, heterosexual and not homosexual, and less outspoken, he might have been spared the man's fury.

It took no more than a day to organize a response. On the evening following the assassination more than a hundred thousand gay people of all ages and races met together in the streets of the Castro district, many wearing black, many with black armbands, and all carrying candles of various kinds. As the darkness gradually gathered about us we each kindled our light then moved slowly forward in the direction of the Town Hall. As more and more arrived to join the huge crowd it was as if flickering streams of fire were pouring into the broad street to coalesce in one vast sparkling river moving slowly forward through the darkness, toward the heart of the city. Row upon row, line upon line, we walked; old, young, women, men, massed together with somber faces, each eerily lit from below by our candles. Caught in the slight evening breeze, the flames would gutter, be relit. The faces all around were set and still, unspeaking, and unutterably sad.

The only sounds were an occasional muttering here and there, or a gasp as hot wax spilled onto fingers. To protect their hands, some held their lights inside tin cans; others had made holes in cards and pushed the candles through them. One young man walking near us held a whole box of household candles that he shared around. Some had managed to find only tiny cake candles, which they lit one after another until they all were gone. Some had unpacked Christmas candles in red and green, tall, brilliant in the darkness. One man had found an altar light which he cut in half and shared; made of beeswax, it burned steadily and long.

The sparkling expanse of a myriad tiny flames was protected by the mass of moving bodies around them that ebbed and flowed, now hesitating, now accelerating as mourners do, held back by sheer numbers or filling gaps as they opened. The night life of the city had grown quiet, and surrounding streets were empty. Traffic lights changed their colors unheeded, now red, now yellow, now green; then back to red. All else seemed overwhelmed and brought to a standstill by such an outpouring of grief. Only the long river of light, stretching back to its birthplace, moved slowly forward, never ending.

At one point, halfway toward city hall, among the shifting shuffle of ten thousand feet, a woman's voice broke the silence, quietly singing the ancient Hebrew dirge for the dead. The sad notes in their minor key lifted high above us like a blessing, moving in the air as if kept alive by the flickering of the candle flames below. As the voice died away, another, far away, began humming the melody of the old civil rights song "We Shall Overcome." The humming spread and spread, quietly, reverently, as more voices took it up and, as if in some sad response, the light from our myriad candles glowed and shifted in the cold night air.

The square in front of City Hall was already a dark mass of people silently standing, still unbelieving, remembering. Some still carried lights, but many, as they moved into the square, placed their candles down before a statue of Lincoln that stood beside the steps. As the number of these abandoned candles grew, the mound of molten wax increased in size, its color variegated, red wax mingling like blood with the dead white of the rest, with greens and yellows, while a few struggling flames still bravely held their own before joining others and being finally absorbed. The wax flowed and congealed, stubs and fingers melting down and growing firm. The tall melancholy President gazed down upon this strange votive offering before his feet, as it climbed up to his knees then melted down again.

The quiet, poignant demonstration of misery masked a rage within us all, a rage that not even a giant memorial service in the Opera House could dispel. The assassin's defense argued, grotesquely and without expectation that anyone would believe it, that it been junk food which had caused him to lose his mind. And when the jury brought in its outrageous verdict that this indeed was so, and the judge sentenced the murderer to no more than a few years for such a heinous crime, we all were stunned. We took to the streets again, and this time we burnt and smashed and screamed. Police cars went up in flames outside City Hall. Behind the statue of Lincoln where we had mourned and where the remains of heaped-up wax could still be seen, we broke the heavy plate glass windows and battered down the doors. Then, at last, because we had damaged property, our cause was noticed, though still without effect.

Only slowly did we pull ourselves together. The following year, the annual march carried banners memorializing our dead. An eponymous political organization was formed in Harvey's honor, and with a martyr's scars upon us, we even seemed to be strengthened by his

death. Yes, we might have to die. Yes, we would give our all. What
more important was there in life but our identity, our meaning? A
renewed sense of dedication spread among the gay and, increasingly,
the lesbian community. For lesbians, naturally resentful at the continued male chauvinism often expressed even by their brothers, now had
evidence of a determination that they also shared.

Local religious people, including my fellow priests, who were still
not sure what to do about homosexuality had now been faced with an
event similar to many which in the long history of their various
denominations they had been taught to venerate. Martyrs were precious people, witnesses to faith held against all odds, proofs of a
belief's authenticity. True, this Harvey Milk had been only a politician
and a Jew, the reason for his assassination apparently equivocal—yet
he had predicted his end and had clearly been a man with a cause that
reached far beyond any political interest. Some were even saying that
he had given up his life for his friends: daring, provocative words. Perhaps, after all, it was time to take these gay people seriously.

Churches have often embraced seemingly lost causes, seeing in
them an opportunity both to increase adherents and to practice their
virtues. Some have even taken up the cudgels to fight strenuously
against obvious injustice, regardless of ecclesiastical benefits. My
statement at the Episcopal bishop's meeting, and now violent events
in New York as well as in San Francisco, had caused similar flutters:
"What should we do about the . . . er . . . homosexual problem?" was
debated in city parishes. The question was briefly raised at the Episcopal diocesan conference and then later at General Conventions, but
only to condemn us because we had always been condemned. However, faced with clergy who were openly gay, marching in the streets,
consorting with drag queens and slipping off to bath houses, the situation appeared to be getting out of hand.

It was immediately clear from the many questions raised by obviously anxious parishioners that the people of God had rarely managed to address their own sexuality, let alone same-sexuality. It was
also obvious that we gay people had ourselves enabled this woeful
abyss of ignorance; our silence had helped excavate and maintain it.
Christian moral theology as taught by all denominations over the centuries had terrified virtually everyone about sexuality in general.

There had, in fact, been little improvement on Augustine's simplistic theories. The punishment that his fearful mind had assigned for
erring beyond tradition's restrictive confines had rarely been questioned. Inevitably, as if to ward off even the appearance of such sinful-
ness, the clergy had imposed appalling penalties for homosexuality in

both this world and the next. Torture, burning at the stake, forced castration, whipping, and in the twentieth century even lobotomy masquerading as "treatment" had driven gay people into silence or the invisibility of solitude and half-hearted or miserable marriages. Discovered, imprisoned for years, sometimes for life, too many of us had gone mad. For the young, ostracized and threatened with hellfire, the utter hopelessness of a situation that appeared unchangeable offered only suicide. Not even the philosophies of the Enlightenment with their renewed interest in reason had been proof against such passionate denunciation. Despite attempts since 1900 to repeal Christendom's laws (Magnus Hirschfeld's, in Germany, seems to have been the first), traditional judgement had survived, especially in rural America.

But now it was time to speak out or disappear once more into the shadows, a retreat which those who had already freed themselves could not abide. So many of us had long learned to pretend, to ape being heterosexual, to joke at ourselves along with the rest, it had become second nature. Our admiration for the beauty we perceived had nearly always been surreptitious, guarded, furtive. We would even talk about ourselves behind our hands, whispering what we were. We were so sly we never even admitted to being sly. We had denied ourselves, our true feelings, our real hearts and much of our minds, to the point of extinction. Like other ostracized minorities we had been living secret lives and had learned how to survive, to pretend that all was well, and even that there was no Cause, no need to change the way things were. In fact, we had only "seemed" to be. But now the long age of self-denial appeared to be drawing to a close, and it was time to speak out, and *be*.

TO BE!

1971-1983

During the celebrations in 1976 of the two hundredth anniversary of American independence from Britain, I had been invited by the BBC's education department to travel across the country to meet a variety of Americans and learn their opinions on the current state of the Union; the system of education with which future Americans were being raised; what Americans saw as their future tasks in the world; the state of their politics; and how they spent their leisure time.

It was a formidable task that took me into many U.S. states and walks of life, recording, analyzing, piecing together a coherent picture of life in the United States after two hundred years on their own. I learned many new things about America, and discovered the truth of much that I had previously suspected. For most people, television had become the primary means of entertainment and information. A college education was no guarantee of a job. Race was still an issue. Rights for any other than white heterosexual men still had to be fought for. In fact, America was a nation still struggling forward, burdened by its enormous wealth, its inequalities, and its slowly growing awareness that to be American meant to be different from the people of other countries in ways that neither they nor others seemed fully to understand.

It was also apparent that many Americans were still "churchified." The various immigrant groups that had founded or populated the states had each established a modus vivendi requiring compromise and a respect for the principle of pluralism. Catholics, Protestants, Jews, and Muslims, at war elsewhere in the world, were forced to live and work side by side without killing each other. At the same time,

221

each group held as closely to the beliefs of their forefathers as tolerance by others might permit. Compromise was essential but limited.
Each could agree upon only one thing: their belief in a God who cared
for them. But for each group it was a god who cared for, or favored,
them alone. State and federal laws relating to moral and ethical issues
that might interest this conglomerate God were usually couched in
such a way as to please those who carried the majority vote in each of
the religions. Racial, sexual, and ethnic minorities were still expected
to behave as the majority wished. Thus was the grand American popularity contest maintained by leveling, just as de Tocqueville had said
it would be.

Religious pluralism raises questions about both God and religion
that uncompromising state-enforced faiths seek to avoid. It fosters the
suspicion that differences among faiths are not essential differences of
doctrine but the results of different taste or custom; that despite their
apparent dissension in matters of dogma, they are no more than variants of the same belief and all refer to the same God—the God in
whom Americans officially trust. Under such circumstances, religions
may tend to lose their exclusiveness: the American Methodist, Baptist,
and Roman Catholic, even the American Muslim and Seventh-Day
Adventist, may begin to accommodate and meld into each other, to
the point of abandoning or submerging beliefs and doctrines that
require each religion to claim to be the only true Way. Divinity would
no longer be confined, nor could Christianity of whatever denomination claim to be the exclusive means to whatever might be meant by
salvation. Under such conditions, which theologians of the 1980s
were beginning to explore, divinity itself is called into question, let
alone the religions that attempt to pin it down.

But this inconsistency also seemed to be the much-touted, careless
"American Way." One accepts the implications of many antagonistic
faiths and the new theologies that argue them and awaits the final
explanation at death. Yet this leaves unexplored the critical question
of how Christianity could simultaneously be both the only true way
and the American Way. No doubt Aquinas would have shrugged it off
on the grounds that "all things are possible with God," but such a
response, like the postmodern definitions of divinity, begs important
questions about existence itself for which there might really be
answers. Solutions claiming that different faiths and philosophies
merely consider existence from different points of view are specious.
Existence includes Mother Nature who, far from being the benign
deity of comfortable romantic dreamers, clearly had a forbidding,
dangerous aspect.

I had long wanted to talk such matters over with others in the hopes that we might also sort out sexuality and its place in religion. I was, after all, an Episcopalian priest. I did not take my responsibilities lightly, nor did I want to be ordered what to believe. My excursions into territories other than church buildings had raised important issues. The idea that God intervenes to rescue people from catastrophes, or that images of Jesus appear in trees or on the doors of ovens, is clearly ridiculous, yet many millions of churchgoers still believe such things, just as they believed in "purity" and "evil." There were battles still to be fought and even after two thousand years it was obvious that Christianity still had a lot of thinking to do!

In the 1960s I had joined with clergy from other denominations hoping we might explore these matters. One such group was the Council on Religion and Homosexuality. But for nearly ten years, we had been clearing the air without coming to grips with the facts. The gay people present seemed always to be talking a different language from the others, who were too reverential, too hidebound. Perhaps we needed to talk things over on our own.

Making our way up Nob Hill toward the diocesan offices one spring day in 1972, John Williams, a fellow gay priest, and I discussed how we would build upon the work of the Council, and broach our demand that something more substantial be done and done openly to help end the ignorance that we were convinced existed throughout the church; to educate churchpeople and relieve not only gay churchpeople but gay people everywhere of the climate of fear in which they had to live. Suicide Prevention had been organized outside the church to help gay people and others in general. Now it was time to help churchpeople in particular.

The bishop, affable, friendly, and evangelically inclined, seemed to understand that some response to the increasingly obvious distress was called for. Moreover, the existence of same-sexuality was fast becoming a church issue of national dimensions, and San Francisco was a place where experiments in its resolution might be undertaken with success. On our way down the hill after our conference, we wondered at the support we had received. We had suggested a center of some kind where gay churchpeople, young and old, could gather in safety, perhaps invite others and offer counseling to those in trouble. We thought the new gay ghetto centered around Castro and 18th Streets might be a proper location. The bishop had been enthusiastic.

One of Peter's oldest friends, Ronald Bansemer, ran a real estate company in the heart of the Castro district. He and his business partner, Ray Herth, were both successful and generous. They also owned a small, pretty, nineteenth-century wooden frame cottage hidden behind the shop fronts only yards from the famous Castro crossroads itself. This cottage could not be seen from the street and was approached through a small white painted door squeezed between adjoining shop fronts and opening onto the narrowest of corridors; not much wider, in fact, than the required fire gap between the two buildings on either side.

This dark, forbidding alley opened out onto a patio behind the real estate offices, and behind this stood the cottage, fronted by a small wooden deck on which stood a potted palm. Coming from the noisy bustle of the street, it was a tiny oasis of quiet, ideal for our purposes. The cottage itself was also elegant, a small Victorian home, almost a doll's house, not much more than one story high and reached by six wooden steps leading up to the front door. It had been built in Gold Rush times when that part of San Francisco was still rural and undeveloped. Then when Castro Street had been commercialized the land in front had been sold for shops, and this was why the cottage sat behind them, a memorial to a forgotten age and safe from modern traffic only yards away. Through the front door of the cottage we found ourselves in a spacious living room leading to what was once a bedroom, and by a small corridor, to a well-equipped kitchen that looked across to the rear yards of homes on the next street.

Our friend then showed us a stairway leading down to a basement with a dirt floor. This, he told us, could be boarded over and made into a meeting room. The ceiling was easily high enough to stand up in and with new lighting might hold as many as fifty people. I noticed hooks on the walls and turned to our host. He grinned.

"We think the previous tenant was a secret leather man." We laughed, both thinking the same thought.

"S & M! Ha! Now that's really appropriate! We must keep the hooks! After all, Christians have been into sadomasochism for centuries!"

Our search for a place had taken several weeks. As with Suicide Prevention it had been difficult to find anywhere appropriate: basements, offices, small apartments, none of them really suitable. We wanted a private space, self-contained and capable of establishing its own identity. This cottage was ideal and our friends were prepared to let us have it for a nominal rent. Accordingly, notices went out immediately to all the parishes in the diocese announcing an organizational meeting for a new center for lesbian and gay churchpeople and their friends. It was not long before we also added bisexual, and later transsexual, people to our invitation.

The day of the meeting dawned. Knowing the hostility of gay people to the homophobic churches we did not anticipate much support from the Castro community even though we had pinned up notices here and there along the street and had also asked the local clergy to include our invitation in parish magazines. The congregation most likely to provide supporters was that of Grace Episcopal Cathedral, whose services we knew many gay men attended either because their own local parish did not welcome them, or because the cathedral congregation was usually large enough for them to remain anonymous. There was also the large cathedral staff of acolytes, many of whom were closeted gay men. Lesbians in the church, like women in general, were still not being given opportunities equal to those offered men, so we also hoped lesbians who still considered themselves Christians would turn up, too.

On the hard mud floor of the cottage basement we had lined up some rows of metal chairs, among them several from an old downtown movie palace. A pad of newsprint stood on an easel. In true democratic fashion we would write down whatever ideas the meeting might present. As usual at such foundational moments, a sinking feeling steals over the organizers, worried that the whole thing will flop. Although we were both convinced that "something" had to be done, we still did not know if this was the way to go about it. Few parishes had done anything about gay people, even though they had gay members in their congregations and often financially very generous members at that. There were also gay priests who surely should be taken notice of, gay youths, too, and even questioning children who were desperate for answers. But surely no less important was the great majority of heterosexuals in the church who were claiming that we should all be converted or condemned and expelled. There was no doubt that our very existence posed a serious problem, perhaps more serious than anyone realized. Nonetheless, would a place like this help solve the problem or exacerbate it? We couldn't tell.

There was a knock at the front door. Someone had managed to find their way down the dark narrow passage. It was a young woman. This boded well. Then suddenly, as if she had been sent on ahead to scout out the land, the dark mouth of the passage disgorged first a couple of men, then four more, then a group. Finally our friendly Realtors, who had been looking through their office window at what might be going on in their cottage, were astounded to see a great stream of people coming in from the street, young and old, men and women. Some wore leather and chains, some were in traditional hippie garb, some in fashionable rags. There were women wearing heavy boots who strode up the stairs as if to take immediate charge of the operation; there was almost every acolyte from the cathedral, and there were knowing teenagers in hopes of free handouts. Whether this curious crowd would understand what we hoped to do remained to be seen, but they seemed enthusiastic enough. Many knew each other from local churches and were eagerly admiring the house and its opportunities.

As they explored the rooms and made their way down the narrow staircase to fill the basement, it was clear there would be hardly room enough. Eventually, some sat on the stairs, while others stood around at the back or peered in from the rickety back door. Finally, not believing our luck, we called for silence, and like good churchgoers they sat obedient, waiting for the word.

We first explained our dilemma. Something had to be done, not about us but about the church. (This received cheers.) Many of us had nowhere to go. We wanted not so much a church of our own but a retreat from the streets where we would be unmolested by the police; an alternative to the bars; a safe house. (This also won immediate applause.) In this cottage we could offer refreshments, even cook a meal, talk about being gay and religious and help the churches understand homosexuality and see that we did not have two heads.

"And even if we do," cried a voice, "we mean them no harm!" More cheers.

We asked them: Did they think this was a good idea? Loud cheers.

"Get them off the sex kick and tell them about love!" called a voice from the back. Renewed cheering.

"That's right!" said a man in the front row. "They think we're sex mad. Our love is as good as theirs, maybe better from what I hear!"

We then reminded them that we had to be practical; that the rent was low but had to be paid. Could we raise enough money among us on a regular basis to keep the place open? This brought forth various suggestions, none of them likely to bear fruit. Local parishes were already strapped for funds. The Diocese might make a grant but not until authorized to do so at its conference still many months away. The national church could be approached for seed money, but even if the application was successful, the grant would not be distributed until after much paperwork and a year of consideration by various committees.

It is not often realized that, as my own years of work in public benefit corporations had already taught me, citizen groups have considerable financial power if each member will only pledge or guarantee small monthly payments. Public broadcasting, I told them, as well as

Suicide Prevention, had survived for years simply on the monthly contributions of their members. In fact, a dedicated membership was often the only way to persuade large donors that those who were soliciting grants had public support. The solution to our problem, I told them, was for everyone to pledge no more than a dollar a month. If we could boast a dedicated membership of a hundred, each contributing one dollar every month, this would mean more than a thousand dollars a year that the diocese or the national church might be prepared to match.

"Five dollars!" cried a voice. "I spend more than that on cigarettes!"

And five dollars it quickly became, thus guaranteeing a sufficient sum to keep the front door open, as well as to provide utilities and even food.

Two more important decisions remained for the meeting to make. What was the organization supposed to be aiming at besides being a place where gay people might find peace and quiet? Was it just for ourselves? Should we not use it to educate the church? And if such a program was possible, what was it to be called? The answers had to be reached in order, the purpose first and then the name.

Many suggestions flew back and forth as to why we had come together. That the cottage was a suitable safe house for gay people had obviously been agreed by acclamation; that we also had an appropriate mission was essential if we were to survive as a service operation capable of raising funds. But talk of "mission" brought immediate disagreement. Some of the more devotional participants had already talked in terms of the church's mission to the gay community, and of Jesus in the Castro as if our purpose was to convert gay people to Christianity and if possible to Episcopalianism. Others derided this as old-fashioned thinking.

"What d'you think's going on out there?" asked one leather-clad woman. "The churches don't want us! So who wants to join them?"

This managed to rouse some from the lethargy that usually accompanies discussion of money. It was also a critical juncture in the discussion and one upon which our hopes might easily founder. We asked the obvious question: if the churches were eventually to want us, would we want to join them? From the general, somewhat reluctant murmurs, it seemed the answer was a qualified yes. If that was so, we then asked, how could we show them that, indeed, we were not a threat? Or, better still, that we were an actual benefit?

Curiously, this caused many to shake their heads. Some, long devoted to traditional morality, became critical of other gay people

for behaving in ways that embarrassed the church and made it difficult for churchpeople to understand us. "Physical love is important,"
said one man, "but they don't like the way we make love. But I don't
like the way lesbians make love any more than I like the way heterosexuals make love, and they're in the majority."

"What's that got to do with Christianity?" another shouted.

"You tell me!" was the reply.

The argument went back and forth. At one point gay marriage was
proposed as one of the demands we might make upon the church at
large. If the church objected to promiscuity, it should logically permit
commitment. But maybe that was just a ploy on churchpeople's part,
a delaying tactic.

Eventually it became apparent to everyone that for gay people to
attempt to educate the heterosexuals in the church without also listening to the heterosexual point of view was doomed to failure, and
moreover that the question of physicality in lovemaking and its relationship to religion or moral theology was critically important. Someone also noted that Christianity had been founded upon the difference
between the body and the soul and the subservience of one to the
other, but that sex seemed to join them.

"So, if we do want to educate the church," asked John Williams,
"how do we go about it? What's our mission?"

People began calling out "purposes" that we scribbled on the pad
of newsprint standing in front of us on its easel, on which we had
recorded our discussion so far. Words like "peace," "unity," "marriage," and "integration" were proposed, but none of them proved
immediately acceptable because they were either too limiting or too
idealistic. For instance, an Episcopal gay organization known as
"Integrity" already existed. We needed something that smacked of
change. Without change, at least on the part of the church, we knew
our task would be insuperable. The more conservative members again
reminded us that gay people too might have gotten out of hand in
their new-found freedom, and that point of view also had to be reck-
oned with.

Finally, from the midst of a long list, only one concept seemed to
sum up the overall hope: reconciliation. It was, however, a concept
that remained unsatisfactory despite its long ecclesiastical history.
John Williams detested it. It might imply capitulation, and at best it
sounded no better than a political compromise. But it appealed to our
gathering and would certainly resonate well in church circles. With
any luck it might even open doors hitherto closed to us. As with "public" and "prevention," the meaning of such a word could be changed
by the use it was put to.

The name of the center derived from a plan that was later abandoned. Early on in the meeting there had been talk of a live-in manager. The cottage was, after all, equipped for dwelling and security would not be a problem. Accordingly, the first names suggested had the flavor of a parish house. "Gay Haven" was suggested but howled down as suggesting a bordello. "Episcopal Lodge" was rejected as more suitable for a motel. We cudgeled our brains, searching for a name that meant something harmless. Then came "The Vicarage," which it wasn't. And finally "The Parsonage," which seemed to have no pietistic or suggestive double meanings and enjoyed a long but simple history referring to persons of any gender. (It was later thought to refer to a Bishop Parsons, but that was not its origin.)

In the end, a live-in arrangement proved both inconvenient and at night too lonesome. We also needed the bedroom space for an office, and despite the advantages of twenty-four-hour coverage, it was not possible to find anyone who could easily move in an entire household and yet would not regard the daily coming and going of clients as an invasion of privacy. To replace this ideal coverage, we designed a day and evening schedule that retired and semiretired members could help maintain. They would manage the place and offer hospitality to whoever managed to negotiate the alley.

And so The Parsonage was born. Its role as reconciler seemed to satisfy more people than it irritated and our cottage was to function for more than ten years as both the haven it hoped to be and as a center for educating churchpeople about sexuality in general and homosexuality in particular. We painted the walls and we purchased furniture and carpeting and then invited the bishop to open it. It would mean a walk down the Castro among the leather queens and our rough, tough lesbian sisters! But he never hesitated. Wearing his cope and miter, he parked on a side street and paraded down the Castro in full fig, holding his crozier high all the way to the front door. The gay folk, crowding the sidewalks as usual, stopped, speechless. He waved. There was sporadic applause. At the corner of Castro and 18th Street, he was cheered. Was this the new look? The drags thought his outfit quite "divine"!

Through the alley, pulling his skirts from the dirty brickwork, the bishop clambered up the steps and came inside. Not surprisingly, a crowd had followed him in down the alley and pressed forward around the cottage. Lifting his crozier, he made a splendid speech, calling on the church to acknowledge our existence and absolve itself of its bigotries. He spoke of reconciliation with the church and dared to predict that one day she would welcome all kinds of people, regardless of their sexuality, into the family of Christ. There was then more applause until he lifted his crozier. The crowd, still not quite knowing who he was or what he was supposed to be doing, fell strangely silent. A few crossed themselves, some looked up to the blue sky above, as he blessed the cottage and the service of the Christian God. He then retired to bless the interior, room by room, in the Anglican manner.

Once exorcised of evil spirits (but not, we suspected, the ghost of the leather man) the cottage became hostess to all, with wine and cookies served on plastic trays. The following week, we all repaired to Grace Cathedral while an unexpected congregation nodded and smiled at us as they streamed into the massive dark interior. In the vestry the bishop and his ministers put on the scarlet and white of high holy days. The bell in the tower ceased tolling and we were ready. Led by the vergers, their silver-headed staves held high, we moved quietly into the nave as the organ burst into scintillating cascades of joyful music, its echoes reaching up and around the concrete buttresses and arched clerestories in the shadows of the roof.

After the vergers, in traditional hierarchical order came the choir, then the deacons, and at last deaconesses carrying the bible with its polished scarlet leather and pages shining with gilt. These, in turn, were followed by the ministers, then came the Parsonage, its two priests and its founding members, among whom was a young man named David carrying a tall stave from which floated a huge banner he had sewn himself from whole cloth. It carried a simple message: "Thank God I'm Gay," in stark white letters upon a purple ground. He carried it high, heavy though it was, and proudly. There was subdued clapping among the congregation as he slowly passed by them down the nave of the cathedral leading to the chancel, where the banner was taken from him and placed in a special rack. Then finally, walking slowly, searching the people round about for faces that he knew, came the bishop, solemn in his heavy robes.

We wondered at the numbers of men and women who were now suddenly prepared to support us in the safety of a church building, but not beyond its doors. In a supreme irony, it was as if the church, our principal persecutor, had once again become a sanctuary in the mediaeval sense; perhaps it had been one for some time without her acknowledging it. So many of those involved in church activities were gay and had remained hidden. The verger, diocesan officers, priests, half the congregation and the organist, together with a good number of every congregation in the diocese, were all gay. And in other denominations it was often the same.

The fact was, as we had been discovering for some time, and as Magnus Hirschfeld had pointed out so long ago, we were everywhere.

There was no occupation, no level of income, and above all no family where gay people, young and old, could not be found. The homosexual orientation was a fact of life. Only its condemnation, established by the very religious doctrine and dogma that we seemed now to be celebrating, had kept it hidden and ashamed. The contradictions inherent in such a marriage caused many an eyebrow to raise, and many to distrust what they regarded as a sellout either by the church or by gay people themselves. And at the national level, too, there were many for whom such support, given to such egregious sinners, smacked of a compromise made with the devil.

Nevertheless, we went to work. A team of lesbians rescued the foundations of our cottage, rebuilt the basement and laid an entire new floor. We received many donations of money and equipment; our volunteer treasurer worked long and hard to keep meticulous books. We devised elaborate training sessions for ourselves and educational workshops for churchpeople who either volunteered or who were designated by the parish priests to learn about those they did not understand and seemed so anxious to merely tolerate or dismiss.

Our own training sessions in listening and referring were organized and conducted by Thomas Tull, one of our members, himself a trained therapist. Since most of our members were Christians of one sort or another, many of them Episcopalians, this training included religious references and often began and ended in prayers. They also included sensual exercises in which, using lotion, we would massage each other's hands and fingers, something meant to release the sexual energy that sometimes built up between us. One purpose of such exercises was to enable us to learn how to relate to each other regardless of physical attraction. It was a curiously erotic self-discipline that we later discovered heterosexuals also found helpful.

The educational sessions we conducted for our heterosexual church visitors were more elaborate. Since they signed up from distant, often rural, parts of the diocese, we arranged for them to arrive either on Saturdays or in the evenings after their daily work. There being no parking at the Parsonage, their learning began even before they reached it, when they had to make their way among crowds of gay people of all sorts walking Castro Street. Few straight rural and suburban churchpeople had ever dared to visit this area, or wanted to. It was the classic irrational response: they didn't like faggots, and they'd never met a faggot because they didn't like them. They certainly met them face to face in the Castro.

After walking this gauntlet, they found our street door with its official Episcopal Church sign bolted to it, and maybe an advertising easel pointing the way in. They then had to make their way into the dark, narrow alley, seeming longer by night, when it was lit by no more than a single glimmering light bulb. Looking up, they could see only a slim wedge of sky between high walls which, as some told us, seemed to close in upon them like a trap. Wives clutched their husbands' hands as if fearing an immediate attack by voracious lesbians; husbands steeled themselves to ward off expected rape from sex-starved queers. Their lives in the protected isolation of safe suburban parishes had not prepared them for anything other than myths and horror. In view of our imposed and determined invisibility, it was not surprising that their ignorance produced such terrors, so that though they made it through, some were already pale and trembling when they arrived.

To their surprise, these initiates found themselves in a delightful courtyard before a pretty little cottage, its windows lit up warmly from within and often as not a jovial host standing at the door to welcome them. With what relief they climbed the steps and crossed the lintel into our comfortable sitting room! On the wall they even found a reassuring picture of Jesus at his most simpering, or perhaps a crucifix. How could they come to any harm, they thought, where such images were revered? Moreover, the men and women sitting around in comfortable chairs, seemed so ordinary, quite unlike the monsters they had warned their children about. Could these ordinary-looking people really be . . . ?

Losing no time, our volunteer chef quickly served them the supper he had prepared, which began with "Peace and Reconciliation Soup" concocted of seeds and vegetables each selected for their nutritional value and followed by a delicious tofu and watercress salad. To put them further at their ease, we talked banalities, asked them about their parishes, their families, and what the husbands did for a living. We knew well enough what the wives did—housework, laundry, caring for babies, and cooking their husbands' meals.

But then it was down beneath the floor by way of the rough wooden stairs! Fears returned. Our small talk had clearly been no more than a subterfuge, a deceitful seduction leading to orgiastic rites. Some, indeed, reported a not unpleasant frisson of anticipation! But no; here, too, there were bright lights, even a slide show telling the story of the Parsonage with pictures of laughing fellow parishioners, even of the bishop himself complete in cope and miter standing on the very steps they had only just descended and even blessing the very room they were sitting in! Were all these pleasant people also unmentionables? Surely not the bishop!

Besides suburban parishioners, the Parsonage also began to attract church dignitaries who flew in from Washington, New York, London, and even Australia. Once an actual papal delegate appeared, unsure of his role and determined not to betray himself in any particular. One morning a high ecclesiastic turned up from far away, tightly closeted and fearful of being identified. And a local vicar's wife asked to meet the women, since she too, she confided, was a secret lesbian.

In keeping with our announced mission, we also threw parties, so that often our little cottage became crowded with visitors. Some came directly off the street, others were invited by friendly clergy. Once the bishop came to visit when the place was packed with people—young and old, women, men, boys and girls, virtually all gay. There were community leaders, lawyers, social workers, businesspeople, aspirants for public office, and many who regularly attacked the church for its homophobic doctrines.

John Williams and I found the bishop looking rather lost among the general hilarity and told him we were honored by his presence. He nodded, pleased, he said, that it had all come together so well. You should both be proud, he went on, and then leaning nearer to me, he whispered, "I'm embarrassed. I've never had my sexuality questioned before." Everyone else was homosexual and he suspected some, at least, must have wondered about him.

"So now you know a bit of what it's like," I told him. "For us, I mean, living among the alien heterosexual majority."

A similar situation occurred when we found ourselves entertaining a representative of the FBI. He had come, he told us, on a friendly visit from a local congregation. A tall, handsome man who smiled at times but who seemed somewhat tongue-tied, he wanted to know what we did. We told him of our beginnings, showed him our slides, and described the various programs of outreach and education. And being determined to clear the air of myths, we asked him what he knew about homosexuals.

"How do you mean?" He seemed taken aback that we should reverse the questioning.

"Do you think we're subversives?"

He pursed his lips, unwilling, perhaps, to commit the Bureau without official permission.

"Some do. Yes, some do . . . and some are." He stared at us.

"Do you know any gay people?" we pursued, unwilling to let him off so easily.

He hesitated. "Yes," he admitted. "We know them."

This ominous response raised the temperature somewhat. I followed up with a favorite question.

"Perhaps it seems to you that we are really heterosexuals who are misbehaving?" It was more a statement than a question but one which usually managed to flush out the real reasons that underlay beliefs about us. "I mean," I continued, "maybe you don't think we are genuinely different, but just a lifestyle, as the press mistakenly calls it."

This seemed to stir him. "Well," he said with a dismissive shrug. "It's wrong, if that's what you mean."

"You mean illegal?" we prompted him. "Or what we *are,* is wrong, illegal?"

He began to look anxious. In acknowledging that we were not ignorant of why he was there, we were slowly forcing him to discuss the law that he was pledged to uphold.

"That too, yes."

"Why wrong, then? Because you, a 'card-carrying heterosexual,' as our friendly attorney calls himself, find our lovemaking nauseating, just as we find yours?"

He did not even smile. He did find it nauseating. He looked around him at the dark oak beams of the basement. Perhaps he noticed the hooks.

We pushed him. "Not something to make laws about, though, is it? Lots of things are nauseating. Were we in the majority, perhaps then we might legislate against your own lovemaking." These were hard words for him, though I remember our tone was gentle.

"The bible . . ." he began.

At that, we had him, in the same way we had once cornered the infamous state senator John Briggs whose California ballot initiative sought to fire gay schoolteachers. At the climax of a long debate on the air, I had forced him to justify his position and he, too, had invoked the bible. Homosexuality, he claimed, was against God's law. But the separation of church and state was on our side, and on that occasion Californians who had been hoodwinked by his rhetoric finally saw where such repressive legislation would lead, and voted the proposition down. The United States is not a theocracy. Now our FBI man too had betrayed himself.

We discussed the selective use of the bible, the injunctions against mixed fabrics, shellfish, and hats; went on to our view of what later was to be described as "homophobia"; and took him out to dinner to talk about love, for love, it seemed, is what he had quite forgotten.

One purpose of the Parsonage was to review the excuses that religious gay people used to explain why they remained members of institutions that vilified and condemned them, without hitting back. This was by no means an easy task, given the number of closeted gay clergy. These, for instance, continued to claim that all was well with the church and with Christianity while at the same time remaining silent about themselves for fear of their congregations (which showed, in fact, that their parishes were not so healthy, after all). These were, in effect, traitors to our cause and their double-dealing reinforced the evil they feared to condemn.

At the same time, it was becoming apparent that gays and lesbians themselves, devout or not, were often scarred by the oppression. We could not reasonably claim that homophobia was both an evil and that it had had no effect upon us, its sufferers. Gay people had been wounded, and it showed. Yet churchpeople now expected us to rise cheerfully from the ground and behave as if nothing had happened. So it is with racists who, on ceasing their oppression, believe nothing further need be done, when in fact they and their successors may have to spend generations clearing up the cultural and psychological catastrophe that generations of oppression brought about.

Those of us working at the Parsonage could also see that in their frustration many gay men had become addicted to sex, as others had to alcohol and other drugs. The Parsonage could offer no easy solution to such difficult illnesses, so instead we provided their sufferers with a place to meet. The cottage became crowded with self-help groups signing up for a nominal fee. These dealt with drugs, sexual obsession, and alcohol. Their members came in almost every day through our living room into the basement, where we would hear them sharing their lives and strengthening their determination to be free of whatever it was that held them in thrall. And it was as a result of this continuous activity and the obvious need of help that our board was willing to try another experiment. It was decided to invite clergy and congregations to seminars conducted by the manager-director of the Cauldron.

Seminars at the Parsonage did not aim to duplicate the experiences of the Cauldron's own clients, but the examination of the body and the critique of traditional doctrines of sex and sin that bodily desires and needs required was an important exercise leading to my own examination of existence, and one that seemed to be available only to gay men. As one of the local clergy reported, there was much anxiety in the diocese lest a Cauldron-style seminar require parishioners actually to engage in sexual activities for which they were not prepared!

For years, during similar discussions and meetings the Parsonage sought to push back such prejudices and fears not only in Northern California but in the Episcopal Church as a whole. Our members put forward motions in the National Convention before the House of

Bishops and the House of Delegates. The bishops, reluctant to divide themselves into liberals and conservatives on this or other issues such as the ordination of women, took conciliatory steps that the delegates from the parishes continued to refuse. One bishop told us he thought the reason for this was the fear our bifurcated social culture has of bisexuality and the blurring of gender. Certainly our existence within the church seemed to strike at centuries of moral teaching, a fact that made it difficult, if not impossible, for us to avoid questioning much else that the church stood for. It was already clear to me, for example, that I myself might well be on the way to abandoning traditional doctrine. I already regarded our public devotional stance as so much window dressing.

To this extent the Parsonage was indeed subversive, and our efforts at the national level were in vain. Had we been armed with the many refutations of modern church views on homosexuality such as the recent research into the "invention" of sodomy undertaken by Mark Jordan, our task would have been easier. But such work was way in the future.

We had, however, and at least for the moment, raised the level of discussion above the name-calling of uninformed bigotry, and for that a committee of the House of Bishops conferred upon our cottage industry a special commendation. For years it survived as a place where the question of homosexuals within a heterosexual church could be examined without fear of reprisals. Nevertheless, there were increasing signs of intransigence. An elderly church official attending one of our suburban parish meetings wanted Christ put back in the bedroom, and pointedly added, "Our bedrooms, not yours!" It was an impasse that was to become more and more unyielding as the gay community found itself face to face with the most horrific threat in its history.

CATASTROPHE

1979

*T*he monthly parties were not the only aspect of Parsonage life that was encouraging. The tables were piled with magazines, the shelves lined with books by gay authors, religious books, books on psychology and philosophy. The notice board displayed announcements and notices of meetings, concerts, and plays. Several elderly members died and willed us their furniture. Our newsletter was mailed to supporters all over the United States and even in other countries. Usually the front door on the street was propped or tied open for anyone to visit. Our members, trained and then officially commissioned by the bishop as "parsons," collected a useful list of referrals similar to that at Suicide Prevention for the homeless and those in trouble. We developed our contacts and we networked.

Our first intimation that something strange was happening outside in the Castro and Polk communities occurred at a party we gave after church one Sunday afternoon. Among those present were several young men who were living in a clergy house run by a priest who took care of hustlers and helped them obtain jobs to replace their prostitution. One of these youngsters made his way through the company, Coke can in hand, and introduced himself. He was angelic in the northern European tradition. A veritable Tadzio. Long blond hair framed a charming face and fell to strong young shoulders above a narrow waist. Large green eyes smiled at me from under long dark lashes. He held his head to one side in a seemingly habitual flirtatious pose. His voice was attractive, deep, street-wise. And several large discolored lumps rose from the ivory skin of his neck.

He did not know what was wrong with him, nor, he said, did the doctors he had been to. The lumps wouldn't go away and instead

were getting worse. They didn't help business. I wanted to comfort
him, tell him not to worry, but clearly something was wrong. Perhaps
he had mumps? No, it wasn't mumps. I saw his dilemma. Instinctively, those signs of ill health made one keep him at arm's length. His
family had long since given up attempting to make him over into a
heterosexual and he had eventually left home in disgust. What he
needed was nursing, or so we thought.

We then discovered that he was not the only one with this odd condition and that some infection, whatever it was, existed even within
our own tight-knit community. First Joe fell sick, then Bill, then others; others whom we had counted on to organize this program or that,
put out the newsletter, keep the house open. Such absences made the
organization creak and groan, placed additional burdens on the rest.
No one then suspected that whatever it was that was causing the trouble was lethal. Most of our members were young, in their twenties,
vibrant, energetic. In the Episcopal Church, women are traditionally
only helpers, second-class, a state of affairs that irrational thinking
and cruelty have fostered down the ages. But as our men fell ill, the
community was reinvigorated by our lesbians.

Once the word was out that the symptoms, the strange dark
patches, the lumps and bleedings, were not those of a temporary ail-
ment or even susceptible to modern drugs, but a lethal, incurable disease ostensibly affecting only gay males and contracted through intimate relations, the suspicion arose that we all would die, that no one
would escape. This dread grew stronger as first one friend, then
another, then several more, finally hundreds, began to vanish from the
scene. Later we learned that they had gone blind and died in agony or
madness; or they had simply faded away, mere skin and bone.

Slowly Castro's sidewalks were no longer crowded. The laughter
and noise of the bars took on a desperate tone. The self-help groups
attending our basement meetings increased in number. The city health
director demanded the closure of the tubs, which, despite demonstrations, fell one by one into bankruptcy.

The bishop's compassion for us at this time was earnest. Unable to
offer more than the traditional comforts of religion, he organized regular services of "healing" in the cathedral. This "healing," proffered
in the name of Christ, was intended to be a kind of spiritual panacea
for the ills not of the body but of the soul, no doubt including homosexuality itself. Indeed, an increasing number of Christians began
claiming that we were being judged by God for the sinners that we
were.

It was, and remains, a terrible time: a catastrophe of enormous proportions, like a war. Healing services were soon replaced by memorial services, first month by month, then week by week. There were more and more saddened, hopeless faces in the stalls and pews. The processions from the vestry, down the nave to the mournful strains of the great organ echoing in the concrete vaulting high above, took on a curiously universal quality: an endless funeral. The slow scrape of footsteps across the long marble steps and up toward the altar seemed to be inscribing the pain.

Most such services took place in the evening when the setting sun glowed through the stained glass, purple, blue, and scarlet. We remembered vigorous youthful faces, laughing in new-found love and identity, the happy toasts they gave each other, the hugs we shared as we threw off our chains of fear and rejection; the comradeship of belonging; the feel of their hands on one's shoulder, their smiles, their earnest talk in the evenings. But could the loss of these things be healed simply by coming to terms with the facts of life? We could not thank God we had survived, for we knew that in all likelihood the next memorial service, or the one after that, would be for ourselves. We gave thanks for our friends and colleagues, but to whom? To the Creator of this mess?

Anyone could see the Church did not have the answer. The age-old traditions that had held her steadily on course for two thousand years were creaking in every prayer, collapsing with every devotion that we uttered. In her present state she no longer made much sense. Even our very existence was beyond her. She was intellectually exhausted, surviving only on imagined capital.

Many younger gay men, when they first became too ill to live without help, left the city and went home, often to uneasy and "forgiving" parents whom previously they had not dared to confront. Others, on seeking help from home, especially if it was a fundamentalist Christian, Orthodox Jewish, or Catholic home, were rejected with contempt and died alone. Other young men, being at the onset of the disease more vigorous and essentially healthier, were able to sustain the ravages of opportunistic infections and often lived for some time, even years, seemingly capable of survival. Older men, sometimes weakened by a long history of alcohol or cigarettes, grew gradually more gaunt and exhausted by the month until finally they collapsed. Peter found himself nursing a handsome, athletic friend through a horrible travail of erupting organs, diarrhea, blindness, and incipient insanity. Some fell into their last awful stinking extremity in airplanes on the way home, some lingered on for weeks, doubled up, staring sightless at the wall.

No one seemed exempt except those who had been forever without sexual experience with someone else, and, for all we knew at the time, not even these. It was surely impossible, we told ourselves, that one could contract the disease merely by being homosexual, unless the very anomalous condition itself was somehow buried in our chromosomes and was part of what made us gay. Our one hope that this was not so was the continued health of lesbians.

Only after tests had been developed were we able to hope we might be spared. Yet even then the visit to the clinic was virtually one of despair. Many refused to be tested, fearing the results would enable the government or employers to segregate the sick from the healthy, making pariahs of the victims, outcasts, jobless, homeless: an invidious class system which, they predicted, might finally engulf us all. Yet one had to know. It was like a daily ache: am I doomed? How long do I have to live? The waiting for symptoms to express themselves was unending. Every bruise might be the beginning of the end. Even a cough was suspect. To wake feeling tired gripped the heart with sudden terror. Death had finally arrived and was already knocking at the door.

When we learned, finally, that nothing could or would be done, that there was no cure, that scientists and Ronald Reagan's regressive administration were dragging their collective feet, perhaps even wanted us to die, we could take no more. We had not released ourselves from silence and invisibility to be thus ignored. That our own government should by mere default bring into being the murderous doctrines of bigots and fools was outrageous. Accordingly, bold spirits in New York organized the AIDS Coalition To Unleash Power or "ACT UP," determined to force an unwilling, hostile heterosexual public to increase funding and the pace of research. Their message was "Silence Equals Death," as for us gay people, in one way or another, it has always done.

Meanwhile, in San Francisco churches and at others in an increasing number of metropolitan cities, prayer services and memorials continued. Nearly every community leader in the gay community died. Castro and Polk streets were emptied. Gay businesses closed, signs appearing in their doorways: "Owner deceased." Gay teens and young men disappeared, mostly already dead or dying. Eventually it was generally elderly gay men, some already on their way out, young ones who had been given up for lost, and our stalwart lesbians who could be found around the town.

When, finally, I went for my own test, I found myself among a group of other dejected, frightened men who stared at the floor waiting for the worst. We were given numbers by which alone we would later be identified. This was to protect us against discrimination by employers, landlords, and the government. A bright young nurse took my blood as I sat in a cubicle, my arm cushioned on the table before her. She was plump and motherly, and smiled reassuringly at me as she found the vein and carefully inserted the needle. She didn't speak. The dark blood flowed into the waiting tube. Was I even now observing my own death sentence insinuated among these corpuscles?

It took two weeks for the telltale evidence to express itself on the research dish or in the test tube. We were to call the clinic, state our anonymous number, and make an appointment. No results were given over the telephone or by mail. It was a Saturday morning, about eleven o'clock when I returned. The sky was grey and overcast as I walked slowly down the street. The bustle of Castro and 18th Streets fell silent behind me as I climbed three long wooden steps up to the waiting room and gave my number to the receptionist.

Three men were already waiting. There were magazines on the coffee table. The long fluorescent electric lamps above our heads buzzed threateningly . . . it was time they were changed. A number was called . . . no, not mine. One of the men, wearing jeans and a moustache, stood up, and without looking at the rest of us went through a misty glass door held open for him by a youngish man in a white coat, perhaps a doctor.

I found myself hyperventilating. Big breaths seemed to rise from my diaphragm and I forced myself to control them, to breathe sensibly. What was death, after all? All humans die. Moreover I had enjoyed some exciting times, met some extraordinary people. Suicide Prevention was still afloat, even flourishing. NPR was on its way; the Parsonage had been worthwhile, if unsure of its outcome; so maybe it might be good to go . . . That's my number being called . . . Stand up! Swallow.

I had not seen the previous client leave, so absorbed had I been in a vain attempt to think calmly. The thin, slightly balding young doctor did not smile as he sat down at his desk. I swallowed again. This was it!

"Before I begin . . ." He had a pleasant voice. "I'll tell you what we know about this disease."

Oh dear, a pep talk. I was going to die. What was he saying?

Yes, just what I had taught my own staff to say: ease in, line up the facts, then, when the anxiety has been allayed, talk business.

He told me about what they now assumed was a virus, how it seemed to be contracted, what they had found out so far. Then, as if it was an afterthought, he told me I had tested negative. I might live!

Still he didn't smile. I was to return in three months and be tested again. In the meantime, I was to use condoms for everything, not to engage in anal sex, not to kiss, not to exchange bodily fluids. So much was still unknown, he said, that we had to be careful. Even sweat was suspect. I left with enormous relief—similar, perhaps, to that experienced by soldiers who avoid the hail of bullets and make it to the next ditch. At the same time, I could see why others objected to the test. It could easily set people apart. Only the knowledge that the verdict was the result of sheer luck could prevent the insidious self-righteousness to which the healthy can be prone. When later I volunteered to test an AIDS vaccine at the National Institutes of Health, the doctors confirmed for me how insidious such selfishness can be, preventing even essential research.

And yet, whenever our parsons grew sick, we made visits to the hospitals where they were. It was quickly becoming apparent throughout the gay community that gay men were also nurturers. We took care of each other. A buddy system grew up rapidly, along with newly designed hospice services run by gay people and their friends. Peter joined in and cared for many until their end.

At Christmas and other holiday times, the AIDS wards in the local hospitals became the heart of the festivities. Gay acting groups, gay singing groups, gay clowns filled the hospital corridors with jokes and laughter. But above all, it was lovers who turned "transition," as we came to call death, into a time of peace. Few of those dying wanted to see the homophobic clergy, yet some who were young and facing their imminent end had little to help them through it and longed for security, even for the consolations of traditional faith.

The unthinking cruelty to which many of us were subjected was staggering. Some had to put up with antagonistic families or clergy who had called upon them to repent, to say it wasn't true; or who wanted to pretend that their son was dying of anemia or cancer. Others would subject their sons to verbal battery, crying that they were perverts even as they lay dying. Memorial services often had to be held twice, once for the family who kept the lies alive and refused to admit the existence of the gay lover or the gay friends, and a second time for the lover and the gay friends themselves, when the truth could be told and the loving relationships of the real gay family be recalled and honored.

Parents would steal household goods and savings even from surviving long-time partners, claiming it all belonged to his relatives. Parents would sometimes change the locks on house or apartment doors to keep the lover out, or threaten lawsuits to get back what their son

had shared even with a partner of many years. It was often dangerous
to get caught in the middle of such disputes, since the lover would
have little or no legal standing and might even be accused of alienating affection or of taking advantage of the illness to "steal" what were
his own belongings. Such battles might take place over the hospital
bed, with the dying man lying before them mute and horrified, unable
to speak for weakness, a tube down his throat, or from the sheer pain
of such confrontation.

Once when visiting the AIDS ward I came across a bed where lay
a young man burdened by intravenous drips and sweating profusely. He was alone, and as I went over to him he stretched out a
limp hand towards me. I peered down and recognized him. It was
David, who had carried the banner "Thank God I'm Gay" in our
cathedral procession. Surely I could weep for him, putting my arms
around his trembling body and kissing his brow and his cheeks.
"I'm so frightened!" he whispered. "I don't want to die." It
appeared his fundamentalist Christian family had written him when
he became ill, telling him not to expect their sympathy or presence.
In their view he now deserved to die and they would pray for his
soul.

"But all that's behind you," I said. "You remember the cathedral?
You were brave in the cathedral and we loved you for it. God does
love you. And we are your family." And as I lay my hand upon him
and blessed him, I wondered in my heart of hearts, what did it mean
to me? He had carried his banner so many times, in so many processions, and the message upon it rang true as never before. When next I
called, the bed was empty. He had gone in the night, his Asian American lover beside him, grasping his hands as if to accompany him into
the future.

Some families who discovered the truth about their sons were able
to change past judgmental attitudes in favor of continued love. But all
too many would not do this, and even when faced with these agonies
in their midst, turned their backs, ignoring them. What did they know
of such things? And, as they had told themselves time and time again
during similar catastrophes, "God's ways are strange." Perhaps their
meaning was that every cloud has a silver lining and that some good
can come even from the bad. But that their indifference, their callous
refusal to assist, could be justified by reference to a mystery, was difficult to reconcile with talk of love. Rather it was a reflection of what
they themselves would have done had they been God.

Such hard responses were in keeping with centuries of belief that
the soul was more precious than the body and that the chastisement of

the body was often good for the soul. Indeed, for people cruel enough to hold such ideas, the chastisement of those whom the church had already condemned to everlasting damnation might seem an appropriate corollary to such beliefs and one that might rightfully be imposed prior to Judgement Day, just as once it had by fire and gibbet.

The catastrophe of AIDS, which was already rampant among entire populations in Africa, now spread first to the blood banks where so many community-conscious gay men had donated their blood, then to those whose lives had initially been saved by that very blood and were now infected by it. It then moved from a few "needle" addicts into the addict population; then to women, their lovers, their husbands, or their babies.

Finally, but only after years of denial, this plague, as other plagues have done, brought home to everyone how all humans are at risk and dependent upon each other's health. The age-old paradox was fulfilled: after segregating themselves from those they despised, the heterosexual population had been forced back into acknowledging our presence. From being a few individual freaks we had then appeared to them as only a small group, finally a full-fledged minority, larger than they had ever realized. And as the disease identified some relation, or son of a friend, it finally dawned upon them that there were even more of us hidden away.

Doctors, conniving with parents ashamed of their sons, attempted to hush the death up by signing certificates that ignored the real facts. Marriages were threatened. Mothers supported sons against fathers who disowned them. Husbands, falling ill, finally admitted to horrified wives that they had slept with men. Local officials, bank managers, politicians, movie stars, household names of every sort, surreptitiously slid from public view and were no more heard of until they turned up in the obituaries. Some made statements before they left the limelight that there was nothing wrong; or "it isn't what you're thinking."

Finally there was no holding back the flood. From hundreds, the toll became thousands, then tens of thousands. Were all these people homosexuals? it was wondered in amazement. How could that be? Why hadn't they been told? Many, mostly in the uneducated rural South, convinced that knowledge was to blame, quickly voted to clamp down on sexual education. It was knowledge, they argued, that made people homosexual, spread disease, and shamed their families, just as knowledge always had. The gay young, those that were left, emboldened by scientific information and the growing awareness that we were an authentic minority, knew better. And when they fell ill their predicament quickly involved their families, spreading the word and raising the issue in far more compelling ways than in the case of older men who had long been dissociated from family life and were now dying alone.

At last, physicians, with their own vociferous gay contingent to deal with, finally took up the gay cause, albeit with rubber gloves, unable to dissemble any longer without endangering their pride or their professional livelihood. In fact, the Psychiatric Association, urged on by a handful of professional researchers such as Evelyn Hooker, had long been compelled to acknowledge that their earlier diagnosis had been wrong and that same-sexuality was not a mental illness after all.

As if not only to show that despite the catastrophe, a same-sexual orientation was a fact of life, but also to help end the notorious homophobia of the athletic world, a group led by Tom Waddell, a former Olympic athlete who was himself gay, organized the "Gay Olympic Games," a title that the official Olympic Committee, fearing bad press for themselves, immediately demanded be changed. Perhaps they feared that since so many Olympic athletes were gay, they would not know which games to attend!

Tom was tall, red-haired, a marvel of muscle and good sense. He lived in what was a former church with a companion, an artist. The old church building had been remodeled so that the living quarters were upstairs, leaving the congregational area to be used variously as a dance floor, meeting hall, and occasionally lecture theater. When we first met, he proposed that we should live together, he being attracted by my accent and I by his physical prowess. However, such superficial charms do not a marriage make and we went our own ways until he married a woman and raised a child before he also died. His Games have been an inspiration to all of us, raising our spirits, and making it obvious that homosexual men and women are as sound human specimens as could be wished for.

At the opening ceremony of the first Gay Games, gay athletes and their supporters, many of them actual Olympic competitors, arrived in San Francisco from all over the country and even other parts of the world.

"Muscles aren't as attractive as you'd think they are," a massive gold medalist shot-putter from New Zealand told me. "You know why I came out late? No one dared make a pass at me!"

He stood among a group of stalwarts each with great shoulders and splendid pectorals, while other groups milled around searching for their trainers: track stars from Sweden and Africa, hurdlers and long jumpers from Canada and Britain. Tom had opened up another doorway into physical reality. And in such often difficult ways, the movement for the rights of lesbians and gay people, so long building, continued to earn its laurels, and to make me to rethink what it means to be human.

THE DRAWING BOARD

1984–1998

After my explorations into the pluralism of bicentennial America, I was hired as a consultant by Nathan Shaw, who had joined the Corporation for Public Broadcasting to assist public television and radio stations around the country. This was financially helpful but intermittent work, and in between my consultancies I continued to broadcast. I became quite knowledgeable about the latest scientific developments, which often required detailed research. I was not encumbered with children and Peter was an independent spirit, so that I also had time to devote to a variety of other interests. I translated several ancient Greek plays and a couple of dialogues of Plato, adapting and dramatizing these as well as Tolkien's masterpiece *The Lord of the Rings* and several other English classics for general distribution. I was also given related acting contracts and assisted in the subsequent productions. I loved acting, and being increasingly avuncular, I found the part of Gandalf particularly enjoyable. Still available, these works have had success and garnered praise for over twenty years. What such creative activity contributed to my thoughts of souls and bodies, besides appealing to previously hidden dramatic leanings, I couldn't tell. Tolkien's Catholicism resonated with my priestly training, but his story seemed to me too strongly rooted in Zoroastrianism and inspired by the Second World War (during which most of the Hobbit saga appears to have been written) to do more than confirm my view that the Christian and similar views of existence as a divinely ordained battleground were as primitive as I now suspected them to be.

Indeed, by the mid-1980s I had become convinced not only that the Anglican communion in which officially I was still a priest, but Christianity in general and many other manifestations of religion were likely to be dangerously flawed, perhaps even built upon false or even fraudulent foundations. Religion seemed to be an expression of the widespread human need to make sense of the world around us, to gather our hopes, fears, and expectations together into a coherent, reliable structure. In this, religion is like philosophy, but according to our usages differs from philosophy in that it seeks to comprehend something other than the immediate material world—what philosophers since Aristotle have labeled metaphysics or "what comes after physics." It thus places a premium upon the belief in the soul as an immortal entity. Souls may belong to each human individually, or be collectively linked to an overall soul.

But by this time, I found I could no longer believe in souls. Personal immortality continued to have its attractions, but did not seem to me to match the facts. James Pike and my New York confidant had experimented with spiritualism, and no doubt Bailey Piers, had it still existed, would continue to echo with sailors' footsteps. However, I did not doubt the immense power of the human mind under certain circumstances to imagine, and perhaps even create and project, thoughts and images that would explain ghosts, spirits, and even "revelations." Eventually, I believe, we will learn how to control such inherent abilities. We already know, for example, that countless radio and television signals as well as cosmic and other rays pass through our heads all the time, and our consciousness perhaps lacks only a simple neurological mechanism to receive and understand them. One day we may even be able to process the thoughts of others at tachyonic speed. Perhaps, too, there are other universes, mirror images of our own.

But none of this adds up to an immortal soul for which there seems to be no other evidence at all. On the frontiers of theological thought there are those experimenting, as was I, with new ways of thinking about Christ and divinity that might not demand belief in a soul, but unless they were to do away with Christianity as we know it, I could not join them. The traditional progression of Soul-Judgement-Salvation seemed somehow inexorable, whereas I was now challenging my faith to make sense of the total dissolution of the human body at death and the reentry of its myriad parts and particles into the universe around.

Nor could I any longer believe in miracles like resurrection, ascension, and virgin births, nor in the essential elements of Christology and its theory (and it is only a theory) of redemption involving rewards and punishments in the hereafter. Nor did it seem possible that these essential components of traditional Christian faith could be newly interpreted to accommodate what we have now discovered about the universe without, at the same time, rendering them other than Christian. I did not doubt that these traditional beliefs "held together" or were consistent with each other. They are. Together, they make up a coherent doctrine, but one depending entirely upon faith, and not upon the facts of life as I had come to know them.

I had jumped onto the media bandwagon that had rolled in from the end of the nineteenth century, scattering absolutes in its path and breaking any number of traditional taboos, and I now found myself free of what I could only conceive to be a parochial, self-absorbed, and cruelly exclusive clique devoted to something which in fact did not exist. Its narrow views of the world, from which it excluded half of humanity and decimated the other half, were as mere peccadillos compared with the inherent falsity of its basic claim to explain existence.

Did I now immediately and officially declare myself apostate? I did not. Such a momentous step required as much time as I could afford to give. I had not thoughtlessly become a priest. Nor had I struggled all this way against my rising distaste merely to walk out overnight. I felt required to brood. Had I considered all the various points? Perhaps there was some flaw in my own argument similar to that which I thought I had discovered in the church's position. I met with other priests who also seemed in doubt but never dared more than academic ferment and wringing of hands. I needed someone to challenge me.

Many of my friends, gay as well as straight, had, like Peter, dispensed with religion long ago, instinctively and without a second's thought. I wished I could do the same. Peter had respected my beliefs and this too urged me to delay, but after thirty years together, we were growing apart. Who could abide a broody priest?

It was an increasingly sad and unhappy time for us, but new doors were already opening. For ten summers I had been on the faculty of the Communication Institute at Stanford University, when suddenly in 1984 I was invited by Martin Battestin to join the English Department at what should be the most celebrated university in America, the University of Virginia, founded by no less a person than Thomas Jefferson himself, the very man who, in his Statute for Religious Freedom, first established pluralism as an American virtue. The faculty were so fine that it had risen to be the top state university in the nation.

At first, as such offers usually are, it was a temporary appointment as a guest lecturer in their still undeveloped field of media scholarship. I thought I would return to California. I never did. It was as if a gauntlet had been cast before me that I had somehow taken up. I hoped to help organize the academic study of the modern media, but although the students welcomed me enthusiastically as "The Media Mind," my new colleagues were conservative and cautious. Even in 1984 it was to take us fifteen years to accomplish. Meanwhile, I found I had other fish to fry.

The Crescent is an Amtrak train that runs back and forth between New Orleans and Washington, D.C. Two hours before it reaches Washington, going north, it passes beneath a new-built bridge and roars to a halt beside what was then a semiderelict station serving the small rural town of Charlottesville, named for Charlotte of Mecklenburg, the wife of George III. It is also the location of a hamlet where Thomas Jefferson laid out and built a college, now a university, one of the three achievements of which he was proudest (the other two being the Declaration of Independence and Virginia's statute for religious freedom).

The original, idyllic campus, which Jefferson had described as an academical village, was at first scorned as a trendy experiment that would not last ten years and, even if it did, its buildings would collapse. But Jefferson knew what he was about. Built on two sides of a long open court around a terraced "Lawn" is a covered cloister entirely supported by 153 columns in white stuccoed brick. At the center of the walkway linking the two sides stands a rotunda with a surmounting lantern. Along the two sides of the cloister are the dark green painted doors to fifty student rooms, each with its own wood-burning fireplace, while ten magnificent Palladian homes or "pavilions" are carefully placed at regular but increasing intervals down both sides of the central Lawn. The whole is linked by the colonnaded walkway and an overhead balcony with simple decorated railing. Trees along two sides of the Lawn soften the classical lines, while behind the pavilions as many as sixteen formal gardens reach out to "ranges" of more individual rooms and smaller pavilions that Jefferson, who named everything, described as "hotels." Each garden is differently designed and set with beds, flowering trees, shrubbery, and elegant wooden seats. Today, the remainder of the university reaches across hundreds of acres into the surrounding countryside and contains residential colleges, dormitories, classrooms, laboratories, libraries, and two sports arenas. No architect has yet managed to match the original concept, though many have tried, with the result that the "grounds" abound in columns and temples. There is nothing else like it in all America. And it grew up in the heart of a land once given over to contradicting the very premises of freedom.

Educators are burdened by history. In the long story of civilizing influences, by which we must surely mean influences that encourage or enable us to live together happily and in peace without harming each other—in that history, the slowest influence to develop has been that of education. The value of sharing knowledge has often been denied or ignored, and the practice has been hampered and even suppressed. Knowledge, instead of being shared, has traditionally been withheld; information has been restricted, manipulated, or twisted to suit private or institutional ends, and each newly discovered fact has had to run a gauntlet of obstruction and denial, frequently never reaching those who would benefit from it. Priests, kings, and elites managed to keep humanity in general ignorance for thousands of years. Not surprisingly, the idea of public education for all was everywhere attacked again and again until well into the nineteenth century and, like female suffrage, was finally permitted by the wealthy and well-born males of the species only grudgingly.

As I had experienced years before in my confrontation with the Klan, nowhere was this sad vicious circle more apparent than in the American South. Southern landowners, their quasi-aristocratic families dating back to the earliest European settlements along the coast, took pride in their family connections, their possessions, and their plantations, worked first by "lower classes" who had no money of their own, and later by actual slaves, captives brought in from Africa and beaten into submission. For many generations these landowners spoke out against the industrial revolution in favor of a social system which cities of independent thinkers and public education for all would have blown apart. The poverty of the southern masses was thus deepened by the refusal to build more schools and even by laws actually prohibiting education.

In response, the southern poor found solace not only in simplistic, superstitious religion but also in a cult of the family, which, fed by class aspiration, assumed a pervasive influence reinforced by the very tyrannies for which it sought to compensate. At the top of the class system were those whose families could be traced back to original Virginian aristocrats. At the bottom were those in whose veins could be found even the smallest drop of African blood. The sectarian Christian preachers took over the pulpits of absent Anglican clergy, just as in our own time they have television channels, and adopted the cult of family as their own, reinforcing it with Pauline attacks on women's rights and differences in sexual orientation, both of which they regard as undermining patriarchy. The fact that both Jesus and the early church recommended the abandonment of the traditional family escaped them, as did the irony that cruel class structures are built up with family blood lines. Indeed, maybe this was precisely what Jesus meant and also why a family of friends and like-minded people is often more productive than biological relations who have nothing much in common except their basic genes.

So long as the South remained a rural enclave, such a regressive society appeared self-sustaining. In the War between the States, tens of thousands of southerners died to keep it alive. Genteel family hierarchies were enshrined; wives remained obedient; "niggers," "perverts," "faggots" and Jews were abused, tortured, or murdered. In the 1920s, the heyday of the Ku Klux Klan, sterilization was practiced in an effort to preserve healthy specimens and purity of race. Rural life, steaming in intolerable humidity, remained somnolent, stagnant, poor, ignorant, and fearful of divine wrath. Public schools, a burden on such a community, were discouraged by the rich as fomenting unrest or encouraging flight to the cities, away from the fields. New discoveries, new inventions, new theories being explored in the rest of the world, tended to pass unnoticed and unused. Complex laws and legal hurdles were put in place to prevent the lowest classes from voting or attending school. Delinquency, which naturally resulted from such widespread ignorance and suppressed energy, was dealt with not by improving education but by hiring more police and building more prisons. That the police, the courts, and the magistrates were often as ignorant and shallowly educated as those they were sentencing made southern justice a byword for cruelty and oppression. Fear and hatred of difference became endemic among those who stood most to gain by it.

Not surprisingly, the passage of the federal civil rights laws in the mid 1960s took as long as twenty years to take hold. Pockets of the Virginia Nazi Party under George Lincoln Rockwell were difficult to eradicate. During the 1980s, millions of southerners of all races, victims of overbearing preachers in churches and on television, were still donating millions of hard-earned dollars in the belief that they were saving their souls when, in fact, the money went to pay for the luxurious lives of the preachers themselves, who pranced, gesticulated, and wept their way into their trust, waving bibles and threatening with hellfire all who refused to accept Jesus and pay up. In the nineteenth century, evangelical revivalists, precursors of these televangelists, taking as their cue the glories of the newly explored American landscape, had offered the poor population a destiny born of an alliance among God, Man, and Nature. In their naivete, they assumed that God was Christian, Man was white and male, and Nature ideal for exploitation.

One forgets how strong the social pressure was in both Britain and the United States to conform to this Christian destiny. It was to be obtained by the subjugation of women, all nonwhite races, and all other religions. This was the dream (or the nightmare) that was still being preached (though more subtly) a hundred years later at the end of the twentieth century. As for variants in sexual orientation, which were not clearly identified until the end of the nineteenth century, they inevitably became a stalking horse for witch hunters, "born again," who added heterosexuality to the list of conditions for entry into their horrible Kingdom.

However, the neat, well-cared-for students drawn into the oasis of Thomas Jefferson's university were beginning to leaven this lump of ignorance by learning to analyze and critique their experiences and meeting others they never knew existed, such as atheists, homosexuals, Jews, and Muslims. Despite constant efforts by fundamentalist Christians and politicians to subvert the separation of church and state, the University of Virginia is not a Christian school and could not demand that its members adhere to Christian rather than rational community standards. This ensured that students would be challenged by arguments that shook their uncritical acceptance of propositions which in their homes had often been taken for granted. More importantly, such arguments had to do not only with theological matters but with the world in general.

The American university system is unique. Elsewhere in the world, education is structured so as to establish and maintain ruling elites, but in the United States, except in the private schools, it is intended to educate the entire population—a noble and magnificent goal, beside which the privileging of a self-serving minority, however benevolent, must surely pale. This difference is often forgotten in comparisons between the educational standards and achievements of various countries.

But there are weaknesses. During the twentieth century, no more than ten per cent of the fifty top American colleges required philosophy courses; only a third required natural sciences; and exemptions from requirements, once rarely granted, were frequent. Not that the course system is highly focused. Introduced to make a general liberal education possible, it is an alphabet soup, a smorgasbord of required subjects and "electives," a system partly dating from the freewheeling 1960s. It also shortchanges both science and the arts.

At many four-year schools, superior minds often excuse themselves from teaching so as to have time for arduous research resulting in books and articles for their colleagues to read. Among some faculties, a good income (once achieved), tenure for life at an early age that reduced the incentive to take risks, and hiring of spouses to match, too often have kept universities inbred, intellectually stagnant, and racially unbalanced. Similarly, "student self-governance," a popular theme among students and a system by which students inevitably propose their friends for top positions, enabled conservative administrations to avoid necessary changes under the spurious guise of self-determination. Indeed, Jefferson's university tried to change as slowly as possible and found it not too difficult to do so. It took many years before blacks and women were admitted. And much-touted "family values" still prevents gay couples from enjoying true equality.

I also discovered in this university, as in others, that subjects were often taught almost as in high school. Rows of desks and chairs, some even bolted to the floor, and a mass profusion of classes identified by a maze of codes, made faculty meetings seem like a strange numbers game. "202 following 384 when 295 was a prerequisite for 301? And what about 206? If we're going to have 180 and 165 it doesn't make sense for 207 in place of 302 . . ." The faculty pronounced these permutations with immense seriousness, as if careers, principles, and long-established theories depended on the result of such earnest deliberations—which, one later learns, they do. Old heads shook and nodded, young ones looked scornfully at each other, contemptuous of all minds that dared compete with their own. Voices became shrill with high disdain so that the air of intellectual self-importance within the room became almost palpable. Occasionally a woman, perhaps one of the new generation of feminists, would rise to her feet and slam her way out, angrily pushing past rows of knobby male knees as she went.

In several other universities I had already found that rules proliferate but conditional exemptions multiply, while courses or conditions must be satisfied before the course you really want to take is open to you. Prerequisites became more and more complicated: if this, then that; but not if the other; and then only when, so long as this, that, and the other are completed. In the American way, "inexorable" deadlines might always be appealed: one deadline for adding into courses; another deadline for dropping courses; yet another deadline for withdrawing from but not actually dropping courses; each action backed by a form, the forms carefully identified according to political protocol. At the University of Virginia, "Forced Action Forms," for example, which were required in order to change class assignments, were given a less offensive description because the name threatened to provoke charges against the administration for inciting sexual violence. Curiously, in this seemingly chaste environment, a public speaking course provoked hilarity among the secretariat by offering training in "oral competence," and being thought dangerously suggestive was altered accordingly.

Layers of administrative personnel functioning in the shadow of politically appointed "visitors" or trustees watched over the educational enterprise: proliferating provosts, vice provosts, and deans, each one monitoring the academic progress of hundreds of students; other deans in charge of housing, student life, student affairs, running the dormitories like holiday camps; each school within the same university using the same system but with different rules, different deadlines, different conditions to assess "good standing"; while among the students, fraternities and sororities often seemed beyond the control of anyone, throwing weekly parties at which alcohol consumption was high and sometimes lethal. Of these clubs, at least at Virginia, only special "service" fraternities with mixed racial and gender membership seemed to fulfill the Founder's expectations by volunteering their labor around the town wherever it might be needed. Residential colleges, organized at Virginia despite subtle opposition from pro-fraternity administrators, were also in keeping with Jefferson's dream. Designed to become enlarged families, they managed to encourage precisely the relationship between students and faculty that the fraternities for the most part had failed to achieve.

Once becoming a member of the faculty, and then a minor dean, I was soon caught up in the complexity of the academic obstacle course. It was like a minefield, yet seemed to serve some faculty as a stamping ground. Brains on the loose as it were, they enjoyed and indulged what to them were the fascinating vagaries of this entangled system, finding in each new knot a further challenge to their intellect and powers of decryption, so that when eventually they managed to establish a trail, they were as proud of the achievement as if it somehow added luster to their role as educators. In the same way, unable to see the wood for the trees, committees were encouraged to talk for hours without achieving more than the truly American satisfaction that absolutely everyone in the room had had a say. Hands went up and opinions were listened to regardless of their relevance to the task in hand. It was a way to ensure that decisions that had, in fact, already been arrived at by someone far higher up the ladder could then be implemented without complaint.

When electronic mail was made available, students and faculty alike spent hours typing out messages to each other and then replying to the replies or thanking for the thanks, in an endless ecstasy of logorrhea. I would receive not one or two but often forty or fifty messages every morning. So immediate was this electronic miracle that within minutes the entire faculty and hundreds of students might be in turmoil, all at their machines, furiously typing their opinions on whatever it was that had upset them. Indeed, the responses were sometimes so immediate that some must have spent all day at their machines, receiving and sending such messages. It was no laughing matter. One professor, inadvertently touching the wrong key, sent his private evaluations throughout the department, causing instant "page rage."

Years later, I still wonder at the trust that Americans put in such methods of mass production to educate the general population: students treated like automobiles; giant dormitories; organized eating troughs; warrens of classrooms; and enormous classes through which they are tracked and processed and propelled, until finally they emerge, scrubbed and glittering onto the surface of the planet.

At research universities like the one I now found myself in, the situation is exacerbated by the fact that the faculty are often more absorbed in their private enthusiasms than they are in students. "Students don't interest me," admitted one senior professor in a candid moment. And it was often difficult to involve professors in student affairs of any kind, even in the residential colleges designed for just such a purpose. Although professors claimed to be engaged in the task of education, all too often their teaching took second place to other work. "The moment I got tenure," one told me with a snicker, "I was never there"—meaning he repeatedly and successfully applied for foreign study, academic conferences in other cities, invited talks, and, of course, time with his family. When I became chair of the elderly Rhetoric and Communication Studies department, I discovered that some colleagues would cut their classes, handing them over to graduate students, or were even unwilling to teach undergraduates at all.

These were exceptions to the rule, but I continued to find examples of professorial absence from the field. Maybe it is at liberal arts colleges rather than at research universities that teaching is considered of paramount importance. At liberal arts colleges, I learned, the libraries were full of students all the year round and not only at examination time. Certainly the time that scholarly research demands is often overwhelming and the need to share one's findings and discuss them with others similarly engaged is essential, but a roster of celebrities is no guarantee that a student's education will benefit by their presence. One private university even took to advertising that at their place, contrary to expectation, top-ranking professors could actually be found in class. The faculty claim in self-defense that their primary interest among the undergraduates is in potential future graduate students who will follow them and take up research themselves. I certainly found that our graduate students and the brighter undergraduates were more interesting to talk to than typical undergraduates—how could they not be? But it is surely a mistake to privilege research over teaching. Both are arduous. Both are essential. Without either the educational enterprise would fail.

But I wondered at the desire to perpetuate ourselves. The teaching faculty of both state secondary and private high schools in Britain, I remembered, had the brilliance of mind and knowledge of their subject that, in America, was usually possessed only by university professors. At an angry meeting of graduate students demanding more support in their search for university jobs, I longed to tell them to teach high school where they were really needed rather than to seek the safe and relatively comfortable security of yet more private study. My conscience, on the other hand, reminded me how dependent my life and thinking had been on research rather than on the preservation of the status quo. I seemed to want to have it both ways.

Living as a Residential Fellow, even as my own professors had done at Cambridge, I also learned how respectful undergraduates were of us dons. And congenial colleagues who were interested in teaching often showed a far more tender regard for undergraduates and their work than did our tutors for any of us at Cambridge. Such a care surely springs from the parental sensibility, which somehow I seemed to share, though not so realistically, with those who were parents themselves. The married faculty could often discount the "postadolescent" behavior that I, an often lonesome bachelor, was likely to see through rosy spectacles. I began to care for the students almost as if they were my own children. Then, too, the naive simplicities of the young can be alluring. Heterosexual faculty would acknowledge being affected, as was I, by the unconscious sexual overtones inevitable in such a community. But sometimes I was very much moved by expressions of simple and long-lasting affection that were shyly and often offered me by the undergraduates—men as well as women. The sense of what one's students might or might not one day become is ever present. They told me of their hopes and confessed their fears and conceits. They became precious to me and once, when writing my diary of the time, I wept at what I was both enjoying and what I may have missed (until a visit to a married former student's home, beset with screaming kids, put the record straight).

I counted it an honor to have the responsibility of teaching and guiding young Americans. I flattered myself that in a way I fulfilled a role not unlike that taken on by the Greek Maecenas called upon to teach young Romans. I was several times reminded of the remark made by a BBC executive I had invited to address my class at Stanford University. He reported that he had been stunned by the beauty and the nonchalant ways of the gods and goddesses assembled at his feet. He wondered whether it was the food or the air that produced such splendid specimens. I suggested it might also have something to do with the United States Constitution.

"At the same time," I added, "let's not forget the description of Americans offered by the American historian, Henry Steele Commager. He called them 'careless.' They are forever moving on to something else."

Despite my enjoyment of teaching, it was as well that I had been invited to a place where research was considered important. I had set myself a difficult task: to examine my life and sort out the problem of existence; to add up my experiences and find a satisfactory solution to the various conundrums that had beset me over the years. The life of the mind was likely to be congenial to such an endeavor, and I was able to meet some of the best brains of America in the course of it, and among them some of the most congenial, openhearted, and generous men and women I had ever worked with. I already believed that problems to do with sexual orientation, like those to do with gender, race, and even differences in religious doctrine, would eventually be resolved. They provided, of themselves, no adequate reason for abandoning Christianity. I was no Jim Pike, jumping from denomination to denomination hoping to find a good Christian nest. And yet, denominational differences were immaterial compared with the fundamental question of existence itself, a question that was certainly not answered by Christianity even though *all* religious teaching must surely depend upon the answer.

However, before I could get to work, I found myself in the midst of controversy that I myself had unwittingly provoked. As an openly gay professor who was supposed to know something about the modern media as a means for distributing enlightenment, I was controversial in my own right. The life of the mind has traditionally taken Plato's approach to the world, dismissing the body and its senses, and dealing with life as an abstraction uncontaminated by emotion. In rejecting this bias I was not without allies. By the end of the twentieth century what came to be described as postmodernism had undermined and then exploded bedrock "objective" assumptions about reality into innumerable possible constructions. Young professors of all genders, encouraged by enlightened deans, were increasingly interested in this development. They were breaching age-old frontiers, blurring distinctions, and even invading and transforming language, that bastion of the literate, by means of images, nuances, and structures not acknowledged before. Words were taking on new meanings, sometimes opposite to the old ones. Culture itself was being picked apart and reassembled in ways that would have shocked thinkers of nearly every previous century. Nothing died or was abandoned, rather every detail was called upon to play new roles. It was as if the human brain, by ingesting quantities of material it had previously ignored or dismissed, had become more vigorous and robust.

The causes of such renewal were not far to seek. Ever since the cataclysms of the first half of the century, educators had been urged by one force or another to improve their product, to make their studies more relevant to the needs of their students, to burst the bubbles in which they lived and to streamline their institutions. But this had been a long, painful process. Many Americans had only reluctantly faced questions of racial inequality, women's rights, and homosexuality. University humanists who for generations had trod delicately around such issues found themselves confronted by the postmodernist insistence upon dredging up suppressed meanings and interests that were not supposed to exist, and linking subjects and ideas that hitherto were thought to have no relation with each other, such as phenomenology and cooking, or lesbians and literature. For a time, scientists managed to remain aloof on the grounds that they were practical people, but finally they too were engulfed in what turned out to be a heady deconstructionist brew in which feminism and sexual orientation were important ingredients. The advent of a "queer" spin to traditional ideas was yet another aspect of postmodern thought that fascinated the younger faculty.

Shortly after my arrival at the university I was invited to dinner parties that appeared to be taking place every night of the week. Of the various faculty members who were guests, nearly all were married men accompanied by their wives. I was repeatedly asked if I was married, and when I replied that I was not only a priest but had lived with the same man for nearly thirty years, I quickly became an object of peculiar interest. At the same time, several gay but obviously closeted colleagues warned me that if I persisted in rocking their boat I would do better to return to California. I was dangerous, and the price of their continued support and friendship was silence. I took no notice of this warning, abandoned my clerical collar, and continued to wear my pink triangle in my lapel. Things had gone too far to retreat.

I was nonetheless introduced to scholars who were either themselves clergy of one faith or another or who seemed to be regular churchgoers. We would talk together about this and that, but invariably the conversation would drift in the direction of the future of religion in general and of the Christian church in particular. The university being located in the heart of Christian fundamentalism, we would lament the rising number of our students who had, sometimes overnight, embraced a severely uncritical faith in the bible as the only word of God, a faith impervious to either reason or good sense.

The adherents of this lurking Christian fundamentalism, supported by bible-believing politicians, insisted that in attacking homosexuals they were supporting family values. They had little or no idea of what they meant by this. That there might be other kinds of families, or that homosexual people had families of their own, seemed not to have occurred to them. Love, too, was for them a very limited thing, confined and offered only by and to those like themselves; it could not be experienced by others. Sexuality for such people was accordingly a forbidden subject, to be neither researched, discussed, nor explained. And because it was the cause of both babies and Original Sin, sex was to be practiced only in secret and in a bona fide marriage bed, for the specific purpose of creating children who would carry on family bloodlines.

For those raised to honor the southern preoccupation with inheritance and the class structure that buttressed it, this virtual fertility cult of heterosexual parenthood and family ties was an obsession. Even the university, like the towns around, seemed replete with breeding couples. Were babies still the primary aims of southern society, just as weddings and grandparents were its perennial preoccupations? The iron hands of agricultural necessity, and a class structure dating from the first landings at Jamestown, seemed to hold not only politicians but even many of the intelligentsia subservient to preachers from the past.

THE MARCH

1987

Yet neither the mind nor politics can stay in the mud forever. The university, I discovered, was changing. My courses in media studies were being well received and gay students were organizing. Fraternity members who had been inclined to hurl rocks and abuse at the members of the Gay Student Union during their annual "public display of affection" had finally discovered that some of their own brothers were gay and stopped their harassment. A few openly gay students had also opened a Gay Helpline, the rules of its operation, I discovered, loosely based upon the rules of Suicide Prevention that I had worked out so many years ago in San Francisco. Two other links with my past were the fact that the president of the university in the 1920s had been the first chairman of what in America is still called educational broadcasting, and that there was already an annual exchange of Fellows with Downing, my own Cambridge college. I was being bound up, cocoon-like, in my own history. And now I had also taken up the challenge to work the very frontier described by Harvey Milk before he was assassinated.

Once declared, there was no going back. The appearance among the faculty of an elderly gentleman wearing a pink triangle had already given another professor to think. His children were now grown and he came to believe that he had missed out on the ecstasies of life. Like a ballet dancer, actor, or musician in whom the yearning for freedom to express himself had never died, he began to long for what he had never enjoyed. Moreover, he felt that his life had been a lie, and however painful it might be to his family, he was determined to correct the record and open all doors.

I was not unused to the predicament in which the closeted find themselves. One particularly eminent, long-married, extremely hand-some and nationally honored professor, since dead, was groping my crotch almost within hours of my being introduced to him. We were both now nearly sixty, but we managed to find time to get to bed, and though I was unable to perform, his continued approaches were flat-tering. But this other now newly aware colleague wanted more than surreptitious flirting, and invited me to join him in getting sexual ori-entation into the antidiscrimination clauses of the university. Such an act, he insisted, was what tenure was all about. I could not but agree with him. But though it was an essential step to take, it might also be dangerously divisive.

The faculty meeting at which we were to propose the motion was to occur in two weeks. The agenda was circulated and we immedi-ately detected a distinct cooling among our other collegial relation-ships. My colleague, burdened with familial responsibilities, was nonetheless eager to declare an orientation he now felt it essential to acknowledge publicly. In the face of an entire hostile institution it takes enormous willpower to stand firm. But he was a respected scholar who had won awards, and he was bold. We had no idea who our friends were or whether we had any, and certainly not how our motion would be received.

When we arrived at the large, ugly classroom in which the faculty meeting was to be held, we found it already crowded. More of our colleagues had turned up than had attended a faculty meeting in ten years. We were clearly in for trouble. The meeting was called to order, the minutes of the previous meeting were read, then we were invited to present our motion. A deadly hush fell upon the gathering. Those standing in the aisles, notebooks and papers stuffed beneath their arms or in piles at their feet, were clearly ready for a fight. Others sit-ting bolt upright in the wooden chairs, each with its writing arm folded by its side, stared straight ahead.

Our motion indicated that the time had come to acknowledge the necessity of equal treatment for gay and lesbian faculty; that conse-quently sexual orientation was no grounds for dismissal; and that the phrase "sexual orientation" should be included in an appropriate antidiscrimination clause added to the hiring policy of the College of Arts and Sciences, if not of the university as a whole. In a few succinct sentences and a level, reasonable tone, my colleague then explained why the change was essential both to attract distinguished scholars who might be lesbian or gay and to reassure existing junior faculty that if they were homosexual their sexual orientation would not be held against them when they sought tenure. I then rose to second the motion and it was opened for discussion.

Only two professors rose to speak; one seemed in favor, and the other argued that the clause was unnecessary. Why identify anyone? It was the usual ploy offered by closeted gays to maintain the status quo. The reason, we replied, was simple: it was precisely because certain groups suffer from discrimination. Only in an ideal world, where such injustice does not occur, would there be no need to recognize it. There were murmurs among the crowd, whether of support or not we were unable to tell. The motion was read again and put to the vote.

A curious hush settled upon the room. No one spoke. Some clutched at their coats or bags. Clearly everyone present felt the importance of the occasion.

"Those in favor of the motion please raise their hands."

A sea of hands rose up around us. It was a triumph.

Once this legal obstacle had been surmounted, another friendly professor was suddenly determined to go all the way and arrived at dinner one day with a young man he had met in a local mall. The attraction was shared and encouraged them to move in together. Thereafter I was regaled with interminable descriptions of each daily, sometimes hourly, orgasm. Clearly, sexual prowess need not necessarily diminish entirely with age. Certainly such liaisons occur among heterosexual professors, who are not unknown to find new lovers even among their graduate students. Within a year, yet another male professor had a seemingly permanent mate in a young black man who was deaf and partly dumb and who clearly adored him. They moved into an apartment in town but after a few weeks discovered their landlady to be an unrepentant racist.

"I notice you have a visitor," said she, one evening as the professor came back from conducting classes in Aristotle's rhetoric. "I don't permit niggers in my house," she went on, her face congealing into concrete.

The professor merely raised an eyebrow, drew himself up, and replied, "Is that so? Then we leave today and you may sue me for the rent." He had a strong case but no witnesses and in his earlier investigation of the local courts on behalf of his lover he had already learned how difficult it would be to get justice for a black man in that southern town.

Meanwhile, I had discovered a lesbian professor who also, she told me, thought "it was time to take a stand." She and her mate were hoping to conceive children by artificial insemination and could see that for them to obtain the social and health services offered to heterosexual families the traditional status of unequal spousal benefits would have to change.

Since a necessary preliminary to all change is the spread of accurate information, we offered to speak before the university staff and administration about what it meant to be homosexual. Once again we feared reprisals, since not only some university trustees but also many administrators and those responsible for support services were citizens drawn from the general rural community. News would leak out to locals who drove around with rifles and Confederate flags and might want to hunt us down.

But a crowd appeared, among them university accountants, gardeners, secretaries, maintenance crews, even police officers. It was a rerun of the Parsonage seminar. With as much good humor as we could muster we told them to be afraid of us no longer; that, as they could see, we did not have two heads; that we were not child molesters; and that when we made love it was much the same way as they made love, using similar dual-purpose organs. Their relief was tangible. They claimed, and for the most part we believed them, that they had never actually known anyone who was homosexual; since gay people had hid themselves, knowledge of that frightening and forbidden tribe had been confined to hearsay, rumor, and myth.

We also asked to meet the presumably heterosexual leaders of the student organizations who, likewise, admitted that they had always thought of us in a faceless way, which in turn had encouraged the fears they had of us. That there were actual professors who were homosexual made them question what they had been told. For here we were, living examples, and seemingly none the worse for it.

Finally, my lesbian colleague and I formed a Lesbian, Gay, and Bisexual Faculty and Staff Association, later to include both transsexuals and graduate students. Word was released among the few faculty and staff who had already declared themselves. With some misgiving (for everyone would, of necessity, be disclosing themselves publicly) we called a meeting in a small comfortable lounge in the Student Commons. Only a few supporters turned up for our first meeting, but as the year went on, the numbers grew. Newly arrived faculty from other universities asked to join, until within a year we had more than thirty members, including tenured, chaired professors and junior faculty still anxious for their jobs. The annual party to welcome lesbian, gay, and bisexual newcomers was held in the very pavilion whose foundation stone had been laid by Thomas Jefferson himself.

Our life did not immediately improve. In an irony not lost upon thinking people, a Republican state administration and judiciary riddled with fundamentalism invoked "family values" to take children from their gay parents, and deny spousal benefits to same-sex couples. Yet within a few years there were courses which included queer theory, the history of homosexuality, and the psychology of sexual orientation, and seminars on lesbians in film. We had expected few students to attend since some had been fearful of having the titles of these courses appear on their transcripts. But each class was crowded and waiting lists were lengthy.

And I had fallen in love again.

It was the evening of the day following the year's Commencement exercises. The beautiful Lawn had been a mass of some twenty thousand people, mostly parents and families, gathered to watch their children graduate. As was usual each year, the temperature had been in the high seventies with southern humidity to match, and the next was a day of rest. Everyone had packed and left for home the previous week, the graduating class returning with their parents only in order to "walk the Lawn" and receive their diplomas in the pretty gardens around the Lawn itself. The town and the university was therefore suddenly silent and I was already preparing lectures for the upcoming Summer Session.

There was a knock on my front door. Jehovah's Witnesses had been attempting to add to the number of the saved, and cursing the interruption, I put down my work on Documentary Form and Content and went to the door ready to argue from my privileged position of strength. However, it was not an aggressive proselytizer but a very sweaty young man in shorts and tee shirt who had clearly been out jogging. In the evening gloom I recognized him as the tall, handsome, dark-haired student who had once sat next me at a dinner party and spilt his glass of red wine over the white tablecloth. Clearly a klutz, for all his beauty.

"John!" I exclaimed. "What's up? What are you doing here? Are you in trouble? Or are you on a night run?" He was a swimmer and running was part of his training. The sweat was now running down his long brown legs. Perhaps he wanted a drink of water.

"You want some water? But you graduated. Congratulations! Come in . . . Sit down . . ." And I went to fetch the water.

I returned to find him sitting on the sofa, examining my notes. He grinned. Yes, he had graduated. He drank the water and asked why we were sitting on the sofa. I told him I was preparing my courses. He looked puzzled.

"But we shouldn't be on the sofa. We should be in bed!"

Breakfast the following morning was a continuation of this dream and so it remained. For a time we lived together, but he longed to escape the South and live in San Francisco. Later, after meeting his parents, who to my enormous surprise and relief told me they were as happy at our relationship as I was, we drove across the continent to California. Then back again because he didn't want to leave me. I was enchanted.

Universities are curious institutions. Isolated from everyday life by need and preference, their inhabitants are subject to the corrupting influences of student adulation and fear of intellectual contempt. Arrogance among the professors finds willing customers at the price of popularity upon which, nonetheless, the institution depends for its survival. Judgement, too, abounds. It becomes a habit. Grading becomes second nature: one's dinner gets a B+ depending upon the dessert; the coffee, a poor C; conversation, a B– depending on the quantity of information received; and even one's friends must remain in good standing with no more than one bad grade during the week and at least some hours of witty, acceptable discourse. Like most elderly lovers of beloveds younger than themselves, I was prey to such judgmental fears. John's attempts to allay my doubts of being good enough for him were reassuring only until I began to doubt again. I had incorporated society's ageism into my perception of the world. He, however, seemed unconscious of my flaws.

At the same time, he had also fallen in love with San Francisco, and wanted to live there. Knowing him for a free spirit, I aided his plan and kept up my spirits by enjoying the splendid environment. I was, after all, living in a pavilion at the heart of an architectural jewel, surrounded by youth and beauty of both mind and body, constantly renewed. Moreover, the number of students who were managing to throw off parental terrors was increasing. I learned that gay and lesbian coupling and uncoupling had been secretly taking place for years, giving grounds for a jealous suspicion among our heterosexual students that we were all enjoying passionate sex. No more so, in fact, than were they themselves. Many students, especially gay ones, remain virgins until they leave and throw caution to the winds.

Nonetheless, the canard that gay people are sexual beings while others are not was soon put to rest with an attempt in the university to outlaw widespread sexual harassment of women by straight men. This gallant effort was spearheaded by the director of Women's Studies. She drew evidence from universities and colleges nationwide demonstrating that the long-standing second-class status of the female of the species had enabled the males to assume and maintain unwarranted power and to hold and teach irrational theories about sexuality. Women and homosexual people were among their most violated victims. Even within a university setting, where intellect, reason, and levelheaded response to human relationships might be assumed to prevail, there was plenty of evidence that not a few heterosexual male faculty members, regardless of age, enjoyed pinching bottoms, clasping breasts, making lewd jokes, and inviting to bed those within their professional power. Despite myths to the contrary, gay men, it seemed, were not more likely to be attracted by youthful looks than were straight men. It was a telling indictment, but in response to the charges brought against them, the men accused women of inviting such attentions, perhaps even needing them. Some faculty had married their graduate students precisely as a result of such encounters. It was claimed that this was the Life Force operating to everyone's benefit even in the ivory tower. But that the ivory tower was in reality a whited sepulcher was quickly apparent. Once the men had been dared to defend themselves, molested students and wives with philandering or even battering husbands felt free to make complaints.

A new rule was proposed: office doors were to be left open during advising sessions; local coffee houses were declared off-limits to unrelated couples when one was an instructor; and for a time a pall of inhibition fell over all. One outraged professor described it as "the end of civilization as we have known it." Instead, the end of civilization was actually predicted by two fundamentalist professors of religious studies who lamented the existence not of sexual harassment but of same-sexuality and published a warning to the world in the *Wall Street Journal*. Meanwhile, the proposed new rule was stifled in favor of something less provocative and meaningless.

The attempt to end the harassment and molestation of women by heterosexual men had at least revealed the hypocrisy of attacking gay men as arch molesters. Heterosexuals were exposed as being far more prone to take advantage of women and girls than ever gay people were of those we admired. Yet I knew full well that as an openly gay dean, I walked to my lectures, advised my students, and when called upon made seemingly wise pronouncements, all the time being thought of as a suspicious character. Why, indeed, had this priest left his parish ministry? And why was he so interested in suicide, and the young?

At the same time, I felt far more secure than my heterosexual colleagues who, they would tell me when in their cups, were entranced by flirtatious nubile maidens. Indeed, women students who did not know I was gay, and how distasteful such machinations were to me, would pull up their skirts and thrust forward their breasts in hopes that, like Menelaos faced with his unruly wife, I would forgive them their peccadillos or maybe simply take them to bed. Had they only known it, they decreased their chances the further their skirts receded up their thighs and the more their bosoms protruded.

These were turbulent times. Secrets hitherto unspoken were being exposed. At the same time, I hoped, the human male was slowly learning to celebrate his own beauty and to reclaim the gentleness and delicacy he had once scorned as effeminate. The female, too, was learning to abandon the image of simpering hausfrau or genteel decoration. The ardent feminist and the angry queer were dismantling walls that once were thought to be impregnable. The new world they were creating would by no means be a uniform world, for men and women are different. With any luck, it might eventually become a world in which neither gender will use the other for its scapegoat.

I had in mind an ambitious program to study the modern media as a bona fide academic discipline in its own right. To do this required appropriate materials, and I also wanted to learn how educational institutions in other countries had attempted to come to terms with twentieth-century media technology. My work in this burgeoning area of the postmodern academy is yet another story, but while engaged in it I also kept my eyes open. In Moscow I came across two gay teenagers exchanging rings and planning their marriage. In Sydney, Australia, I was embroiled in an ongoing battle between gay organizations and fundamentalist churches. I found thriving lesbian and gay communities in Copenhagen and Berlin, and watched gay liaisons openly negotiated in Prague's Wenceslas Square. Yet the same old homophobia still existed in Britain, and I return to the States with relief—only to discover that back home as many as twenty-three of the United States were being cajoled into questioning the essential separation of church and state, attempting to restore Creationism to school textbooks, voting for censorship, burning unchristian books, and attacking rights of all kinds in the name of Jesus. Even at the University I found insidious regression. One Christmas Eve I was invited to attend a midnight mass in a local Episcopal church. Accompanied by an eminent professor and his wife, I sat and stood through the service and its carols memorializing the birth and death of Jesus. Then came the "Pax," the Kiss of Peace.

The vicar came forward to explain this significant moment in the ritual. He wanted us, he said, to take note of the official new prayer book, which enjoined the congregation and celebrant to turn and greet their neighbors in love and friendship.

A voice from right next to me exploded in the silence: "We don't do that sort of thing here!" An angry, frightened voice; a voice from the past. I was back in the heart of a conservative Christian country, raised on a daily diet of images, quotations, sound bites, and opinions reflecting a now-mindless religion.

My request to preach at a local Episcopal church was rejected out of hand. A local Catholic church withdrew its support of a church group helping patients with AIDS. Itinerant preachers, women as well as men, appeared on the grounds of the university handing out bibles or carrying large wooden crosses before which they stood, promising that hellfire awaited adulterers, fornicators, and homosexuals. Evangelists televised mass conversions while the screen listed those whom God hated, including "peterasts" (pet lovers?); local newspapers headlined lurid stories of child-molesting teachers and priests while the airwaves were filled with programs and commercials larded with happy heterosexual families and heterosexual couples kissing, fondling, hugging, being married, having sex.

It was as if each step taken toward sanity and rational behavior was accompanied by a slide backwards into further paroxysms of panic and paranoia. At a conference conducted by researchers hired by Parents and Friends of Lesbians and Gays (PFLAG) into the sources of hate in America, it was reported that most of it existed in the South.

All this time I had been gathering my thoughts together. I decided to abandon Christianity, to let it stew in its own juice. But in 1987, before I could take such a momentous step, John and I prepared to join the largest demonstration that homosexual people had ever conducted.

Accordingly, a contingent of gay students, faculty, and staff traveled across the rolling hills of Virginia by car and bus carrying just sufficient money and food for an overnight sojourn in the nation's capital. As the trees and fields swept by, it was enormously encouraging to know that there were now planes and buses, trucks and cars, arriving by the hundreds, each loaded with our brothers and sisters, our true families. At the university we had been living and fighting for our rights in a small country town cut off from the main stream—an oasis, perhaps, but nevertheless an oasis in the midst of rural deserts. For years our efforts had felt small and insignificant. But this time we hoped it would be different. We did not know what to expect, even though the event had been touted as the largest gathering of homosexual people in humanity's history.

We arrived in mid-morning at the National Archives museum and waited for John and others who had traveled with another contingent. The great grassy Mall that stretches from the Capitol on its hill all the way past and around the stately Washington Monument was already streaming with people coming in from every side. We munched cookies waiting for our mates. Finally, when some had arrived and the deadline was too close to delay any longer, we moved off, hoping the others would eventually find us under our university banner. Slowly we made our way toward the announced gathering place between the White House and the Washington Monument.

It was a splendid day. The sky, blue and bright, set off the many Stars and Stripes fluttering in the morning breeze around the Monument's great base. And as we came up the green slopes from which the obelisk, erect and proud, thrusts heavenward, we could observe spread out before us such a mass of people as few of us had ever seen. They reached down and across the meadows and on into the trees; they were crowded together, young and old, women and men, blacks, browns, tans, and pinks.

And from among this vast concourse rose flags and signs from every state in the Union: from Texas, from Michigan, from California, from Mississippi, from New York, New Hampshire, Vermont and Colorado . . . Several enormous stockpiles of wooden signs from the National Gay Task Force, from National AIDS Awareness, from ACT UP, from PFLAG, were being picked up and carried by the hundreds.

We gazed about, still hoping in vain to find our friends, but the swarms of men and women made it impossible to search them all. We joined the massing crowds where each state contingent waited to be called into line for the long march down Pennsylvania Avenue and on to the Capitol. Some youngsters had brought their parents or their parents had accompanied them as chaperons, to observe for the first time how many homosexual people there were in the world. These observers stood astounded in the midst of milling throngs of healthy, happy young men and women, none of them the warped, twisted, miserable folk of the past that the myths and stereotypes had promised. And this massive crowd represented only a small percentage of the total number of other homosexuals who could not afford to make the trip. There clearly existed in the United States not thousands, or hundreds of thousands, but millions of us, and if the multicolored flags of other nations were anything to go by, millions more all over the world.

They stood, these parents and friends, unbelieving, shaking their heads, mouths agape as they gestured, asking the inevitable question, "You mean . . . all these are . . . ? Oh my God! Oh my God! We had no idea!" Numbers mean little in the battle for truth; in the battle for existence they are very persuasive.

There was also another presence among us. Only a few weeks before, over the grass and upon the same vast acreage of ground where now we gathered in new hope, there had lain, line upon line, aisle upon aisle, the quilted memorials to our dead: the hundreds, thousands of loved ones who had succumbed to the plague of AIDS, so many that we, too, faced with such evidence, could only gasp in horror at the extent of the tragedy, at the enormous loss of leaders, mentors, friends, and lovers young and old which that great memorial quilt represented. We had walked among the all too faint echoes of their lives, woven or painted in ephemeral colors, perhaps patched with the very clothes they had worn or with some memento or picture, until, do what we could to contain our feelings, a great sob would finally rise up unrestrained at the extent of the tragedy.

We survivors, now gathering together, felt united with those who had gone. After centuries of denial and suppression we were announcing our continued existence. From now on ignorance of the facts on the part of heterosexuals could be considered willful. Further, given the high suicide rate among youngsters with no models, and claims by politicians that the number of known homosexuals is small and can be dismissed, the refusal of gay people to come out of the closet was increasingly inexcusable.

I found myself among a contingent of students from several universities, many lovers arm in arm. The march had already been proceeding for two hours before we were called into it, and as we slowly walked toward the turn into Pennsylvania Avenue the sun poured down hot and generous. It was difficult to believe I was still alive, surrounded by tens of thousands just like me, at the center of the New World. Demonstrations and marches by any number of special interests occurred every week in Washington, and presidents and congressmen had long grown tired of taking notice of their various demands. But I remembered the prediction that soon we would be an issue in every election in the country.

Only slowly did we move toward the White House, but it was now noon, and by long-announced agreement, the vast crowd, its multicolored banners waving gently in the breeze for more than a mile, fell suddenly silent. First individually, one by one, then in groups and finally like corn swept by an enormous scythe, we stooped, stretched ourselves out, and lay flat on the roadway.

For two long minutes we lay, arms and legs outstretched, head to toe, toe to head, all quite silent, in one vast concourse of mourning for our dead. The great sun overhead shone down upon us; the acrid scent of softening tarmacadam reached up from the roadway. Here and there a foot stirred, a bird chirruped in the trees above or across in Lafayette Park, and we remembered. We remembered their faces, their limbs, their joyful moments and their vitality. Once again we heard their laughter, their songs and wit (for so many of them were the wittier ones); we saw them in their favorite drag, in feathers, maybe, or trying to look tough and butch in their leather and chains; and try as we might we could not forget their final agonies. Two generations had gone before; more were on their way; now we marched for them, in their place. We were Out; we would never again be hidden or denied.

Slowly, with sighs as from a great rustling wind, we clambered to our feet, picked up the signs and banners lying by our sides, and continued to move forward, more silent now, more in touch with reality. And as if to remind us of this, we could hear great shouts and the crowd roaring just ahead.

We were coming up to the White House. To our left was the Park, to our right black uniformed guards and a police wagon with riot squads standing about. The march, now twenty or thirty persons wide, stretched endlessly behind and before us down towards the Avenue. In front, a roar went up, and the crowd in unison erupted into cries of "Shame! Shame! Shame!" We moved forward, everyone shouting. Beside the road, backing onto the Park, appeared a tall red banner held up by a small, rather pathetic, group of solemn-faced folk. On the banner was inscribed "The Wages of Sin is Hell." Other placards, more hastily made, were being held up: "Repent!" read one; "Homosexuality is an Abomination" and "Thank God for AIDS" read two others.

Suddenly a man ran out from the march as if to attack this group who stood their ground, seemingly prepared, if necessary, to face martyrdom at the hands of the ungodly. The police took notice, feeling for their Mace and clubs. Other marchers left the ranks to restrain their brother and bring him, protesting, back in line. I looked to the other side of the roadway where the White House now appeared, solemn, ornate and slightly fatuous in face of this massive outpouring of emotion. Was Ronald Reagan, the president, watching through that window in the upper storey? Or his son? Or was his son down here with us, disguised and incognito?

Slowly we moved on, past the Christians and down into the long stretch of the Avenue, I still looking around in hopes of finding my lost boyfriend. Far ahead in the distance, the Capitol building rose mistily into the sunshine on its massive base of steps and statues. The marchers, led by several rows of dying men and a few women trundled forward in wheelchairs, could now be seen moving toward it, a dark river above which fluttered the flags of every state, along with placards and banners of a hundred different organizations.

Suddenly I saw John, his face set and miserable. He was walking among the Californian section.

"You didn't wait." He said it brutally as I pushed towards him among the rows between us. He stared at me. For the moment he was inconsolable. I was, despite my age or even because of it, overwhelmed with guilt.

Although the march was far from over, with our arms about each other we made our way backwards, weaving in among a hundred other couples of all ages, between rows and lines that made way for us, passing through groups from Texas, Wyoming, Minnesota, Oregon, back past the Christians still being shamed, and finally joined an unnamed contingent of businesspeople, a mixture of old and young, men and women.

For a time we stood together on a grassy piece of park that gave us a view back to the White House and forward to the Capitol. The sun was already descending down the sky and long shadows reached out from the government buildings round about. But the marchers still filled the roadway in both directions. It was as if the long steady stream of humanity might continue on and never cease. Yes, we held each other close, kissed, made up. Were we not once again united with the world?

THE SOUP

1999

At the request of a small group of gay, closeted, Catholic and Anglo-Catholic undergraduates, I had for some years been celebrating a monthly Eucharist. They felt unwelcome at local churches and were unwilling to make a fuss about it. The service usually took place in someone's living room, just as it had done with the House Church, using household bread and a bottle of local wine. As time went on, I felt obliged to share with them my growing dissatisfaction with religion, and I could see this made them uneasy. When I finally decided that Christianity, being an exclusive religion, was essentially flawed as an explanation of existence, I was no longer able to say the words, honestly utter the creeds, or even bless them with sincerity. I told them why and asked to be excused. A few were adamant that my own personal beliefs did not matter. The priesthood was indelible. God had ordained me, and whatever I did, said, or believed thereafter could in no way invalidate my mystical power to change the bread and wine into the Body and Blood of Christ. It was the reverse of the impasse once faced by Reformers and Catholics alike when required to accept priests they did not like. But I did not now believe in my own ordination and could not bring myself to pretend that I did.

Then, in April 1992, my father died. Several visits to his seaside home in Britain, where he lived with his born-again second wife, had long since revealed his acknowledgment of my sexual orientation, for which his new spouse said I would be eternally punished. We had lived so long apart that at his death I was conscious only that my life's proscenium had changed. Perhaps, too, the stage itself had cleared, for I not only left the church but even began painting with splashes of color that my father would have despised as mere "daubs." I flew to

San Francisco, armed with a letter of resignation from the priesthood and requesting to be released from my priestly vows.

"Not," I told the Bishop, "because of the church's rejection of gay people, but because of the essential exclusivity which is at the heart of Christianity and of which such rejection is only one example. In time," I went on, "the church may accept gays just as it has accepted races other than whites and women, however half-heartedly. But what of Islam and Buddhists?" I didn't add that I also believed Christianity's understanding of existence itself was fatally flawed, but only that its acceptance of Jesus as divine and the only way to heaven was "a mistake." This seemed to sum up, as generously as possible, the long history of what had happened both to me and to religious thought itself. However, the Bishop clearly believed I would return to the fold and wrote that he would not act on my decision. "We are in for a long wait," said he. But I had done my homework and had finally made up my mind. Later the hierarchy would confirm my choice.

Despite their lack of knowledge, the ancient Ionian philosophers, with their belief in atoms and elemental forces, were remarkably daring. The people they lived among believed in gods, rewards, and punishments. Even since those times, speculation about existence has largely meant theories about the role of what was presumed to be divinity. Only a few names stand out as representatives of what has been a dissident minority. As late as the nineteenth century, A. R. Wallace and Charles Darwin's challenge to the doctrine of divine creation was considered outrageous. Even the iconoclastic T. H. Huxley could bring himself to admit only that he did not know what to believe. His coining of "agnostic," important step toward a new dispensation though it was, actually provided the pusillanimous with an excuse to withdraw from exploration. And in the United States, Darwin's discoveries were banned from the classroom even as late as the 1920s (and again in the 1990s). During the last century, indeed, it seemed as if the revolutionary work of Freud, Einstein, and the modernists might come to nothing. Only slowly did the new media of film, radio, the telephone, and the phonograph spread abroad the crucial facts of difference and variety, evidence essential for any change in attitude about the universe. Indeed, it had taken me long enough and even I hung back from doing the necessary research.

Life at the university threw into perspective all that I had gathered in my mental storehouse. I met many generous and wise colleagues who became close friends. Some, indeed, shared my growing unease with Christianity and religion in general, and were also sympathetic

with a view of the world as a cooperative enterprise. I wanted to reex-
amine what philosophers and other thinkers had to say about existence; to test their beliefs against what was still being touted as God's
Truth. A God worth believing in must be one of such compassion that
all is finally engulfed and transformed by it. But of our many imagined Gods, none has proved to be capable of the all-encompassing
unconditional love we would like to see. The Christian version as
described in statements attributed to both Jesus and Paul is so encumbered by Judgement that its much-touted benevolence is far from
trustworthy. Perhaps it is this which has made some posit an evolving
God, in whose evolution humans may have some, possibly crucial,
role. But even this meliorative idea depends upon the unreliable
progress of human affairs, and the successful consummation of such a
God must necessarily be as chancy as it is distant.

What seems to have provoked religions and philosophy to propose
their Gods is that things are not always what they seem. But this does
not really demand a divinity, except perhaps to the untutored mind. I
thought back to those I had known and admired along the way who
continued their religious observances seemingly without a second
thought, and wondered why. Had I missed something they had found?
Certainly, cultural influences are sometimes irresistible, but were even
great thinkers conditioned in this way?

There have been many explanations of existence, but even modern
theologians who treat us to a smorgasbord of alternative religious
views seem unable to draw useful conclusions from such variety.
Instead, they encourage us to wander toward whatever religion they
themselves happen to believe in. Modern philosophers, hurt by self-
administered battering over the meaning of words, and exhausted
from struggling in an intellectual swamp littered with deep, stagnant
pools of jargon and dangerous quicksands of unreliability, are still
unwilling to come to grips with ultimate questions and may even refer
us instead to science.

Scientists, however, seem lost for words. They present us with well-
argued hypotheses leading to apparently unambiguous conclusions,
only to beg off the search and retire into familiar holding patterns,
while we circle about not knowing how or where to land. Many such
experts, reluctant perhaps to abandon their upbringing and risk the
obloquy of their peers, their mates, or their employers, even continue
attending the church of their choice with justifications to the effect
that they are still agnostic and uncertain. I found this to be the case
with many of my academic colleagues and was reminded of the
scholar who, when asked if Mr. Jefferson ever smiled, replied "there's

no evidence" and was prepared to leave it at that. There may, indeed, be no evidence, but he surely did—just as a materialist hypothesis surely dispenses with divinity. You cannot have it both ways.

As a gay man with priestly training, working in a variety of settings, I too have sometimes been approached, especially by the dying, as one capable of answering questions about God. As a journalist, I was content to observe and take the words of experts more or less at their face value; as a priest, I seemed obliged to come up with answers that toed the party line. But as an educator I could do neither of these things. When all is said and done, students have a right to hear what you really believe, rather than what others may want you to think, or what the good book says, or what the administration hopes you think. This forces you to dig about for answers that will hold up under questioning and the disciplined scrutiny of colleagues trained to find flaws, poke holes, and detect contradictions usually without taking a position themselves.

Being gay, I was already primed to suspect that the traditional story of Creation was a contrivance to establish heterosexual hegemony, but also, perhaps foolishly, I had expected from religion the self-respect denied gay people by the rest of society. At the same time, I was privy to a variety of intimate experiences, familiar enough to the gay world but usually unavailable to most heterosexuals—experiences that seemed to strike deeply at our culture and to bring into question values which it has been the aim of most religions to establish and maintain.

In this account, I have tried to describe the pressures brought to bear by the culture I was born into and lived through and how they affected my search for a satisfactory explanation of existence. By choice, I came closer than most heterosexuals to many of society's outcasts and to those who have despaired to the point of suicide. Such desperation may be rare among those upon whom life has smiled, who have achieved what was expected of them, yet no one is altogether immune to the dark influence of such shadows, and it is often among the so-called successful that the unexamined life can find itself strangely irrelevant and wanting.

For important years of my life I also lived in fear, principally of heterosexuals. Though I knew about myself early on, and was never (or hardly ever) willing to deny what I was, my days and nights were always, and to some extent still are, burdened with accompanying anxiety. Consequently, I lived on several dimensions. At the superficial level I was a professional person, ostensibly a supporter of the structures in which I had managed to survive. Indeed, I was told I gave the impression of cheerful optimism. Yet from time to time, there would break in a darkened level of anger, induced not only by my fears but by the seemingly willful ignorance of others. It was an anger that continued to burn deep within me, and made me sometimes churlish, impatient, and even intolerant of inevitable gradualness in social improvements and understanding.

It was mostly held in check, this unrest, only by bitter experience that anger is counterproductive. It was also belied by demure, genteel behavior and appearance: a mask that enabled me to mix with the enemy. The legal crimes committed against gay people young and old because they love one another have been notoriously horrendous and are only slowly diminishing in number. Thus, at heart, I was shameless; for to be shameless under such a tyranny of gentility was to be virtuous; and in being so, to reach to the roots of our beings as organisms, which, contrary to what Plato and Christianity teach, need physical sustenance. We are chthonic, of the earth from which we are formed and re-formed. To deny this is to deny existence. To demonize those who do not deny it is not to escape this logic but merely to enact the brute in oneself. Being chthonic, earthy and intelligent at the same time, humans must select love or wither.

It is not surprising that Christian churches are encumbered with intellectual stagnation. Unthinking reliance upon fundamentalism or mere loyalty argues not merely apathy but atrophy. People need answers that exclusionary religions cannot satisfy, so that unless Christianity and other religions can manage to change themselves out of all recognition, we must and will do away with them. The argument that Christian theology, for example, has long been developing in such a way as to give more comprehensive, paradoxical meanings to God and the theories of incarnation and salvation, would seem hopeful. Yet if the historical content of Christianity is to be abandoned in this way, we should admit that it is no longer Christianity.

Gay people have an unusual perspective on religious claims to truth. Prison was once waiting round the corner; patrol wagons welcomed us and truncheons were unsheathed ready to brutalize all who expressed or admitted what they were. Churchgoing heterosexuals would never have permitted such treatment for long, yet their warped culture still elevates those who wish us gone. It has been to our enormous credit as gay people, as it has been to the enormous credit of African Americans and women, that we did not take to more than occasional violence rather than to peaceful means to redress our wrongs.

Such cultural criticism digs deep into religion and philosophy, making it inevitable that some new structure must eventually emerge, bringing in its train a new aesthetic and a morality based on love rather than on power. And all will benefit precisely because the gay predicament has discovered issues that the old world ignored but which are of concern to everyone, with religious affiliation or not, as physical beings with bodies and brains.

Philosophical and religious views of existence and of the universe are fast approaching each other and may eventually collide. In doing so, they may finally coincide. Indeed, the more determined philosophers are to declare themselves agnostic, the more ground they appear to give to the faithful. Conversely, the less the faithful insist upon dogmatic definitions of the inscrutable, the nearer they seem to approach the philosophically ineffable.

The scientists are alone in their methodical search for what are called facts. Many of them, unmoved by predictions that their task is hopeless, stoutly continue to nudge the frontiers of knowledge further and further forward into what for thousands of years has provided religious imagination with an open field. Searching through the shelves for the works of Kant, Hegel and Heidegger, Descartes, Hume and Dewey, we also come across slim volumes portentously entitled *Time* or *Being* or simply *God,* written by dead thinkers in their prime but long since forgotten. On taking them down we discover them to be more like commentaries on the works of the twenty-volume men whom they revered, even while other twenty-volume men (they are nearly always men) continued to pussyfoot around, expending their energies not on answers but on rival theories of knowledge. Regardless of science and the scientific method which has, in fact, expanded our knowledge, much effort and many lives have been spent discussing how we can say we know anything.

This search customarily begins with the classical enquiry into the difference between what seems and what is, and only later moves on to question (but not to refute) those who abandon reason for imagination dressed up as faith. Considerable energy is spent examining the concept of "truth," which seems to depend upon the meaning of words, or to stumble against the impossibility of agreeing about them. Inevitably, such thinking comes to a grinding halt or leads us back onto itself.

Significantly, the search for truth frequently invokes divine revelation, so that the presupposed existence of divinity permeates the entire enterprise, and hangs like a shadow over its conclusions, as if without its threats and promises moral chaos would inevitably result. Level-headed philosophers like Locke, for example, raised reason to her true place in human thought but ironically invoked revelation as his justification for doing so.

So perhaps we should not be surprised that many thinkers never get around to considering eternity, being distracted long before by problems of epistemology. Some, like Hume, edging in the right direction, nevertheless seem to yearn to return to the security and satisfaction of religion. They suffer from separation anxiety. Hume's character Cleanthes in *Dialogues Concerning Natural Religion* even quotes Bacon, who claimed that a little philosophy makes a man an atheist and a great deal converts him back to religion. Kant, too, raised by pietistic parents to revere their own simple faith, was ever grateful for it and felt constrained to present both sides of the argument for and against it in so objective a fashion that for generations his failure to take a stand was actually thought to have resolved the question.

Time and again, even our greatest minds revert to the beliefs they learned from their parents. Aristotle, with his microscopic eye, ends with his divine Mover who is unmoved by human affairs but finally responsible. So also the others. For Epicurus, God is an immortal blessed being, albeit in repose. Descartes thought God was an infinite, intelligent, all-powerful substance, to whose divine majesty he was devoted. For Hegel, God was an absolute spirit to which philosophy reconciles us. Locke affirmed his Christianity throughout his works, which are so spiced with references to "Our Saviour" that inevitably he finds even Christianity "reasonable." For Leibnitz, also, this is the best of all possible worlds because, he claims, God made it that way and cannot act contrary to the laws of logic. Fichte, too, assumes God exists even though only as an ideal. And even Tom Paine, a herald of the Age of Reason, begins with an article of deistic faith: "I believe in one God, he writes, and no more," thus saving his skin, but fatally undermining his argument.

For these thinkers, too much of their philosophies rests on the very idea of God to dismiss their easy acceptance of his existence as mere prevarication to get published or save face. Schopenhauer, another one who seems to have wanted it both ways, looked "Janus-like" towards both reason and faith, finally and pessimistically depending upon unreliable Will. And even Einstein, that scourge of traditionalists, went on enigmatically about an intelligence of such superiority that compared with it, all the systematic thinking and acting of human beings is an utterly insignificant reflection. Paul Tillich, theologian though he was, seems to have suspected the inconsistencies in such double-dealing. He thought one of the worst errors of theology was to make statements that contradicted the structure of reality, but could escape such an error only by redefining "reality" to suit himself.

Modern philosophers have tried in vain to disentangle these apparent contradictions. Wittgenstein finally abandoned theological speculation to metaphysics as being essentially undiscussable. Even Bergson, who had already hinted at a solution to the problem of existence, suggested it was a question without meaning, a pseudoproblem raised by a pseudoidea, then contradicted himself by proposing his *élan vital*, which, like Shaw's somewhat personalized Life Force, was supposed to oil the works and keep the universe running. (Not a bad idea if for Life Force we substitute Energy.)

By the end of the twentieth century, when it seemed that everything was being dismantled, philosophers found themselves reduced to pragmatic theories of contingency according to which certainty depended upon circumstance. Meanwhile physicists returned to the fray, and the ancient battle between science and religion was rejoined with self-appointed mediators on both sides either redrawing the frontier or redefining the terms of the truce.

Are physicists our hope? After all, they deal with life as it is rather than as we might want it to be. But even they hedge their bets. Some argue that the purpose of existence springs from an original explosion or "big bang," a form of "naive vitalism," susceptible to Bertrand Russell's distaste for the naive realist who trusts science but never finally abandons the insurance of a religious faith. Sartre, on the other hand, not a physicist but prepared to face the void, boldly offered to examine our fear of nonexistence and wrote at length on Nothingness without wholeheartedly commending anything. Even A. J. Ayer, like Wittgenstein and Russell, dismissed the idea of a Creator as vacuous, empty of meaning, and left it at that. For these later philosophers, existence would appear to be a chancy thing, a fluke—and a sad one, because according to their entropic point of view the universe will eventually resolve itself into a formless, silent entity without a future.

But the entropists forget eternity. Like those who argue that the chances of life elsewhere in the universe are so small as to be virtually nonexistent, they forget that eternity not only has time enough for even the smallest chance, but also resulted in ourselves. They ignore the very entropy from which the universe began before the "big bang."

Moreover, a desert from which all memory has been expunged because all movement has ceased is only the physicists' mathematical model, and mathematical models are curiously inept at describing reality. They depend upon the metaphor of figures and conclude with near-zero, nearly nothing. But "nothing" cannot by definition exist, and it is from this seeming black hole that we have arrived. The supposed desert of inertia ignores the fact that, according to its own equations, such an inauspicious end is likely to have had an equally uncompromising and inauspicious beginning, leading to the conclusion that the universe is an impossibility, which we know to be not true.

Some thinkers wishing to avoid the atheistic implications of what is often described as naive materialism instead prefer to argue in terms of abstract concepts (perhaps to avoid criticism from moralists who attack materialism as conducive to immorality). Heidegger, for example, though he wrote exhaustingly about Being, finally dismisses the issue of actual existence in a welter of complex tautological verbiage. William James, like a good American, tried to come to terms with and justify many differing, even contradictory, religious beliefs but ended up espousing what he described as a continuum in which spiritual feelings are evidence of a separate spiritual realm of existence. C. S. Peirce, a scientific thinker, demanded that the scientific method search for some external permanency, nothing human—and then, not surprisingly, pleaded to be permitted to attend church and enjoy the enlightened principles of religion celebrated at Easter and Christmas. Even Russell, who made it quite clear he did not believe in God, Christian or otherwise, nevertheless claimed that the big questions about existence lay outside the sphere of probable knowledge. John Dewey, however, like many others in the twentieth century, observing the endless rhythmic movements of belief and doubt, was a practical American. By means of what has been dubbed instrumentalism, he managed to clear away much unnecessarily complex thinking by establishing human experience as "reality." But then, so did Benedict de Spinoza, the much maligned Ernst Haeckel, and even some of the ancients like Xenophanes who identified God with Everything. (Which is perhaps what Tom Paine meant by cleverly suggesting that everything might be one enormous miracle.)

As they attempt to solve the problem of existence, many of these thinkers feel obliged to defend religion as productive of morality, as if immorality is inevitably consequent upon abandoning a belief in divinity. This has been an almost universal view of morality since classical times. Polybius, the Greek historian, believed, as did Cicero, that the masses can be controlled only by mysterious terrors and tragic fears, but in a perceptive caveat, goes on to add that educated people would not need religion to be well-behaved. Aristotle even recommended a phony war to keep the lower classes occupied. This view of the masses persisted even when reason took the field. Despite his trust in the binding force of the social contract, John Locke thought it "a plain fact" that unassisted human reason failed humanity in its great and proper business of morality. (As if the bloody battles between and among religious faiths had been a moral success.) Kant, also, liked to link religious principles and morality regardless of the consequences to reasoned thought. The nineteenth-century Victorian clerisy of scientists and intellectuals, faced with Darwin and unwilling to take a Nietzschean leap into atheism, often explored even pseudoreligions like spiritualism in desperate efforts to uphold Christian morality. Moral theologians and Christians in general continue to hold similar views. Other religions with their rewards and punishments give the question different slants but with similar ends in view.

The many modern apologists for a religious worldview, the mediators who, seemingly still uncertain, prefer to weave about among traditional theological ideas, actually confuse the issue. The world for these surviving agnostics remains a mystery; the illusion of an immortal soul is still unexploded; and the morality that upholds the status quo is still not discredited. And many of them are unable to rise above the two thousand years of acculturation that renders the very existence of gay people a moral offence.

References from many authors piled high on my desk. They dealt with differences between mind and body, mind and matter, the mind alone, the mind of God, God and physics, consciousness, the soul, the spirit; a long reading list of old, new, and the latest. Then it became time to take a stand, even though, as Machiavelli once remarked, there is nothing more difficult to carry out or more doubtful of success, nor dangerous to handle, than to initiate a new order of things. The enemy, he warns us, are those who profit by the old order, defenders of the New who are lukewarm, and those who would profit by it. The adversaries of anything new have laws in their favor, and humans do not truly believe anything until after they have experienced it.

Christianity, and for that matter religion as we have known it, is, it now seems to me, a dying thing, soon to be buried. The clues aren't far to seek, even though they have taken long to find. Slipping and sliding on greasy metal rungs high above the soaking pits with their lethal steel ingots; the blood-soaked beaches of Normandy; the bitchy drag queens of San Francisco; the NASA test tubes; the tubs; no one can be left out, everyone and everything must be included, or we return to past nonsense and iniquities. Feces, urine, rot, the myriad animalcules within the human intestinal tract, the planets and the stars, all are involved in an eternal recycling, an endless permutation adding up to more than the sum of its parts.

Eternity is the great fact of existence; it has no cause, it needs no explanation; and time is the measure of its endless exchange. The evidence for this is all around us. Despite the insults heaped for centuries upon material things by those seeking permanent perfection, the clues to our place in the universe surround us here and now. Their interactions, exchanges, permutations, and combinations occur continuously in a vast, and, to us, silent and unperceived totality of change; an eternally revolving parade reaching out in all directions. Nothing stands in its way, nothing can withstand its mighty force. Nothing is omitted and all take part. This is what religion has so far found indigestible. Theology has underestimated how horrible would be the very permanence and uniformity it would have us believe in.

It might be asked, if this is so, why not let things be? But life does not continue in the same way regardless of our explanation of it. Although the world does not stop and wait for us to understand it, false explanations of its meaning have caused catastrophe. We might conclude that when humans began to think, trying to make sense of things, we thought too much: invented answers that were too complicated, too cerebral, even fanciful. We didn't know, couldn't see, didn't have the tools. We came up with concepts like truth or even God, assuming they had substance or behaved just like ourselves. We weren't so much deluded as bemused.

Even now much is still unperceived or disregarded because the eternal and constant recycling of everything is almost undetectable. We can't hear the onrush of our neighboring planets. Most stars have held their places in the firmament unchanged for aeons. Our own sun, that boiling nuclear cauldron, shines down silently except to those listening in on radio telescopes.

To understand existence we must examine it in detail. Take water and fire, for instance. The ancients, simple folk we think, saw clues in them of greater things. But it is water that provides us with universal evidence of the endlessly recurring cycles of exchange. All the water on our planet is forever being recycled, and though it may take many forms and exist in many locations, from the ocean depths to the spittle in our very mouths or the interior of our body cells, it is always on the move. It moves slowly at the bottom of the ocean trench, faster when spat out upon the ground, and faster still when blown by gaseous winds in storms of rain and snow. It gathers in clouds to become whole vistas of undulating mountainous ranges or tenuous wisps merging and apparently vanishing as they warm or cool.

This flow of water that permeates our lives in such abundance everywhere is not always immediately available to us. Indeed, it is so often withheld from us that in times of drought, in desert sands, or whenever the supply is insufficient, we forget that it is present within our own bodies, in the leaves of trees, or as we now know, hidden within the very fibers of the clothes we wear or the chairs we sit in. Even rocks have been found to contain water.

Fire, too, as Heracleitus saw, is an example of the way exchange takes place. Flames metamorphose into a variety of substances. A burning house complete with the plastics, fabrics, and metal of its furniture and equipment can be reduced to heat, light, clouds of smoke, and a few inches of ashes on the ground. A burning forest and all that live there can be recycled into water vapor and gases hitherto held within the silica and cellulose envelopes of leaves, bark, branches, skin, and bones.

But of all the myriad transformations that occur from second to second everywhere, surely none is so readily apparent as those which go to form our own bodies with their daily ingestion and elimination of food and drink.

Unless we are the vegetarians that perhaps we should be, we select our hamburgers from our supermarkets, far from the plains and meadows, the execution troughs, and the slaughterhouses from which they came. Our teeth sink into the heated mixture of flesh, crushed bone, and perhaps spices; we chew and swallow, and the tasty morsel passes quickly down our throat into the cavernous stomach where it is digested by means of appropriate chemicals secreted from glands conveniently located here and there and which, in their own turn, have been built from this same process. Ten thousand tiny receptors lining the stomach immediately set to work absorbing the nutrients molecule by molecule—carbohydrates, minerals, sugars, oxygen, nitrogen, metals—leaving behind whatever has not been so reduced or has not yet found a suitable receptor.

After our meals we sit, usually undistracted by the quiet secretion of our gastric juices, the unfelt breakdown of tossed salad, wine, french fries, steak, ice cream, and coffee or soda into their constituent molecules. Two processes take place. The receptive cells lining the stomach each pass on their catch to the tiny tubules lined up beneath them, and thence the rich variety of elements are taken into blood corpuscles and other cells as they flow by under pressure from the pump-

ing of the heart. These elements—iron, sulphur, zinc, protein molecules (the list is printed on our food packages)—conjoin to form new
cells in muscles, sinews, eyeballs, tongue, ovaries, sperm, and brain.
This process is continuous. And continuous too is the careful sorting
out of molecules and red cell parts no longer wanted, discarded or
extruded from the walls of the intestinal tubes to join the unwanted
remains of dinner, the liquids in the bladder, then out along with
solids. And joining them, in the course of time, all the body's cells,
slowly, quietly, gently, move out once again into the wide world
which, in principle, they never left, to join the earth, the wind and the
rain, the animals and plants that feed on each other, and thence back
into more milk and hamburgers, vegetables and desserts.

These daily processes and functions are accomplished as silently as
if they did not occur, and the satisfaction in which they result we
describe simply as a good meal. What is important is that until our
own century this process was only mistily understood. We understood
still less of what our bodies consisted, or that they are subjected to the
passage of hundreds of electrical impulses, from cosmic rays to neutrinos, and nowadays to entire television programs in color and the
chatter of innumerable cell phones. Like other animals we took ourselves and our immediately surrounding environment for granted.

So slow, according to our limited perception, is this continuous
movement that the world along with our bodies seems to remain
unchanged. It is only as the changes accumulate that we can see that
we become other beings, no longer the same as once we were. In our
youth we quickly notice our increased size, our stronger limbs, our
improved sense organs, and, due to changes in the complexity of our
brains, we notice too, if we think of it, our enlarged understanding.

Meanwhile, the process of recycling continues unabated. Atoms,
molecules, whole cells are discarded by the millions on a daily basis,
minute by minute and second by second, to be replaced by others built
from the food and drink we ingest and the very air we breathe; food
and drink that are themselves products of similar processes in plants
and other animals. Molecules from the air we breathe come from the
breath of the dead. The odds that they will have once been in the
lungs of Jefferson or Jesus are very good, according to mathemati-
cians maybe as high as fifty-fifty.

As we grow older we see our bodies continue to change: first we
reach a high point in physical size and strength; then changes to our
skin and hair record the wear, tear, and stress of living on our planet,
its vicissitudes, its frustrations, its excitements, and its pain. We note
that cells have fallen away, and that changes that once seemed tempo-

rary have continued. Babies have sprung up overnight; young men and women betray signs of increasing age. Like the lengthening shadows as the earth continues its slow spin round the sun, or the birth of a chick from an egg, nothing stays the same. Change, as Heracleitus understood, is constant and time is indeed merely how we measure it. Were all things to remain the same, unchanged, static and inert, time would have no meaning, for there would be no differences to measure and no one to do the measuring. Speed up the process, and we would actually be seen to be a whirling mist endlessly joining and coalescing into clouds, meadows, flowers, fruits and vegetables, seas and rivers; we would fade into other humans as they are born and change. What we experience as our separate bodies are but flutters in an all-consuming, never-ending exchange.

And what of sex and love, those consuming passions without which we would not exist? Were there no sexual acts we would not propagate; were there no love, we would perish in a welter of our own blood. Our innate sexual needs drive our attractions, which in turn define our esthetic sense and bring us together regardless of established orientation. Our attractions, even those deriving from the epiphenomena of ideas, are necessarily all physical, operating within the complex structure of brain and body. There is no other process at work—none is needed; together these form the complex combinations of mental and sensual desires that we call love. Kindness is born of them, and sometimes pain. Their ordering is the supreme challenge of our lives. Essentially gregarious, we need each other. Fear of abandonment seems as likely to keep us together as does love.

The process continues and the conclusion is inescapable. Our existence is quite other than the fairy-tale sojourning of traditional religion. The total amount of chemicals, elements, compounds, and gases that make up a human body, including all its parts, may be weighed in a few pounds, but most of it is water—water from the skies and oceans. A quite small cloud, for example, may contain the same amount of water as that in a human body. The other chemicals could easily be carried in the hand: a pinch of this, a spoonful of that, a few grams of the other; all constantly being rearranged and passing into other things, just as plants use nutrients in a small amount of soil to grow their leaves and flowers. Each second of our daily lives measures this vast process of change and exchange. In the morning, we wash with water that once fell from the sky and will soon be taken up again, pulled from the ground by the warmth of the sun, drunk by cattle, absorbed into the cells of plants which in turn feed us, clothe us, and decorate our homes. Even stone and brick, two seemingly intransigent phenomena, grind very slowly into dust and soil, which in turn feed future plants, animals, and humans. Each footstep along a path removes a few molecules from the surface of the stone, just as the dripping of water will carry them away to the ocean and the thin layers of gases we call the sky. Even the stones underfoot, the metal of the pipes above our heads, the walls that surround us were carved, forged and built from rocks which themselves were forged in the sun along with the very atoms in our fingers.

Why are we at pains to deny all this? The denizens of the Cauldron learned to take it for granted. Astronauts survive because of it. Is it because, like other animals, we are oblivious to it; or because we have learned to be wary of our environment, to select what helps us and avoid what might cause us pain? Or have we been seduced into accepting an Ultimate Purpose dependent upon some hierarchy of existence in which everything is either "above" or "below" everything else in the order of things, including ourselves? But even the lowest of the "low," our feces, were composed not long before of the very food we originally, and with pleasure, regarded as nutritious. We despise them at our cost. These remains, ground up, squeezed together and gone over by a variety of digestive composites secreted from mucous membranes, and accompanied by tiny creatures discovered by scavenger cells far away in a difficult corner up some hidden tract, are all sent on their way, down and out to be recycled yet again.

This grand migration of parts leaves nothing behind. All is taken up by the surrounding earth, wind, and water to return again and again, for ever. Even energy is recycled, for what is everything but energy? Light, heat, and sound waves that accompany the exchange are either absorbed back into the planet or pass out into the eternal universe, to collide with other waves and particles. For we are each of us composed of parts that once were in the sun or formed the bodies of others, the dead, and of others before them: animals and plants, birds, fish, elephants, flowers, rain, snow, fire, rocks, and humans. These things and bodies are solids of our solids, flesh of our flesh, bone of our bone, lives of our life, just as we shall be of others still to come, we who are already made up of the dead. We are already resurrected life. And we enjoy a total "incarnation" and an immortality more complete than any yet imagined by religion. This grand and all-encompassing drama, this boundless totality, contains in its infinite care each tiny fraction of being, so that every particle, from photons of light to whole galaxies, has enormous significance for us, however we may describe their complexity: in classical or quantum mechanics, the constituents of our bodies, of our fingers and thumbs, tongues and organs, which at any one moment we feel to belong to us and to us alone, actually belongs to everything else, composed of particles that also belong to the chairs we sit in, the rains we shelter from, the grass we lie on, the flowers we pick; as well as the concrete under our feet, ground from rock; the sands melted into glass; the metal and plastics of machines; and whole cities all drawn from the very soil of the planet itself.

Only rarely are we made aware of these essential relationships. Only occasionally is the dignified passage of clouds moving silently overhead likely to remind us of our bathtub, the kitchen sink, or our urine. Daily practical needs require us to think of such phenomena separately, even though in doing so we mislead ourselves and distort reality. And being misled, we come to think and act as if we do not actively belong but instead are pilgrims. Nonetheless, we are in flux, all moving into and through each other in an endless marriage so tightly knit, in fact, that we can indeed claim to belong to everything and that everything belongs to us.

The neurological structures in animals, the nuclei of cells, the complex cortices in brains, also interact to produce molecular, atomic, or particulate patterns and electrical charges; these form memories, from whose complex structures come what we call ideas and theories and the imaginative fantasies that in turn provoke, inspire, and stimulate limbs and organs to form tools, build homes, design environments, create works of art, and develop civilizations. Art, poetry, the so-called life of the mind, whole cultures and all they represent, are far more than the simple sum of the parts they depend upon—just as the simple combination of oxygen and hydrogen gas, in appropriate parts, results not only in the otherwise unexpected state we call water but also in steam, ice, clouds, rain, mists, and snow. So too, photons of light, when intermixed and seen through a prism of mist or rain, produce the rainbow, which cannot exist separate from its parts.

Self-consciousness and even intentionality, seeming mysteries that to some suggest an immortal soul, are the artifacts of myriad signals passing back and forth between the two lobes and other parts of the brain in such variety, complexity, and speed that we experience yet a third entity, an epiphenomenon, the sense of Self. Though no more independent than any of its parts, it is nonetheless a flowering of the brain, dependent upon complex neurological workings of the brain, and perceived and remembered by the brain itself because formed from within itself, a constantly functioning continuum and presence that we call the mind.

Despite the dependence of the Self upon the brain, it would be misleading to say that we only seem to exist, for so long as the brain is functioning, the Self does exist as a real entity just as under somewhat analogous conditions a rainbow or a painting exists. Looked at in this way, everything is an epiphenomenon of one kind or another.

The loyally religious are suspicious of such phenomena as temptations to turn away from God and judgement, but the search for an explanation of existence is itself an artifact of our restive cells and even of particulate matter itself, not a measure of what mysteries are unexplained. The concept of peace and stillness in the afterlife thus seems to contradict the very nature of things, according to which even entropy is a phase of temporary rest rather than a state that is endlessly inert. And divinities and heavens are artifacts, reflections and repetitions of daily existence, rather than independent entities. It is the endless recycling that is existence, and true immortality.

And when we die, collapsed on the sidewalk, lying in a hospital bed, falling to our deaths in a plane crash, on the battlefield, at work or at home, we are already close to, surrounded by, enveloped, as it were, in immortality: sheets formed from the cotton of the fields or the wool of sheep; plastics boiled from minerals dug from the earth or the oil of ancient vegetation; concrete and metal poured from the rocks of the planet; all moving within the endless interchange from which our bodies are derived and from which others are already being born. Never does the process cease; never does it fail us. It is endlessly consoling and reassuring and far more reliable than the concept of Judgement Day, because we know it for a fact.

This recycling roundabout of an eternal soup has no beginning and no end. Religious people who claim to prefer a Beginning and an End forget that they too are stuck with eternity of one sort or another. Even Aristotle in his *Poetics,* caught up in a metaphor about wholes, thought that existence must begin and end, and Aquinas followed him. But logically, existence must be eternal—not the history and future of the Earth, of the Solar System, or of our own particular lives, but of all existence. The mean lifetime of protons may be not less than 10^{33} years, but for there to have been a true Beginning of everything before our time, and a true End of everything to look forward to, there must also have existed, and be going to exist, a state of Nothing. But in such a context Nothing is meaningless. It can neither lead up to anything nor follow anything. The word has meaning only relatively, within the context of existence, in the sense that there may be "nothing" in an empty bag. Even when particles annihilate, the total energy remains the same. It is a familiar story: by making words mean something other than what they do mean and attempting to make them say what they cannot say, we create a conundrum seemingly impossible to solve. Within the context of Existence, Nothing, as such, cannot exist, otherwise it would be Something. In its existential sense, it is nonsense.

In much the same way, perfection is a myth, its goal forever beyond our reach, yet forever leading us on with its impossible promise of completion. But completion has no chance of change. It can go nowhere. It has arrived and is static, paralyzed by its own achievement. All comes to a stop, and since we observe that change is eternal, completion becomes impossible. By using words like "perfection," we are led backwards into a religious quagmire, a metaphysical morass, because the word "perfect" usually assumes an End. And like belief in an immortal soul, it inevitably implies an afterlife complete with judgement, salvation, and the long history of unprovable, insubstantial theology.

Only if there were actual evidence—not just hearsay and imagination—that eternality is an impossibility, or that existence is part of a divine plan, would the concept of eternal recycling be untenable, and such evidence I could not find. Rather, the world and its universe, freed from imaginary distractions, now seemed far more vast than ever before. Each part enjoys an assured immortality of endless transfigurations, no less real because gradual and unnoticed. The shimmering, intangible consciousness of endless Selves within new identities fulfilled dreams once thought impossible.

Pain, suffering, and death are not thereby reduced. For our own sakes, we continue to work for their relief; meanwhile they remain facts within the process of existence. We may relieve our fears and agonies with dreams and fantasies, and perhaps this is the use of religion; but the facts remain and there are no other facts that I can see. However, like our triumphs and our ecstasies, the pains too are temporary within a reality whose profound and far-reaching extent can be a consolation.

Yet it is also true that the body's wants are with us every day. Our cells need comforting. And when variants or differences in sexual orientation, for example, are understood and are incorporated in the life of everyone (for sexual preferences will enrich experience); when gay children are raised to discover themselves and are permitted, even encouraged, as are heterosexual children, to fall in love with each other and express their love openly without fear, gay people will take their rightful place in life.

Such freedom and equality will come to pass, and just as the dead are incarnated in all of us, so we gay people will be in others still to come. Moralists who think they talk to God are people of the past. It is already time to be free of them. The endless process in which we find ourselves is not a procession toward some unearthly goal, despite the yearning in our cells to reach and reach. We are rendered rudderless by attempting to make sense of something that doesn't even exist. Christianity was not what you could call a hoax, though much of it was surely self-deception. We did our best with what meager facts we had. We built upon them, shored them up with theories reinforced with hopes and dreams. Then polished all their parts until they sparkled, blinded us.

But is it as simple as that, I wonder? On the other hand, it does take everything to achieve true simplicity. I am nearing my own dying time. I have seen much and traveled far; strayed, others would have said. My resignation letter was heavy with the weight of years. I must say, my soup solution, if it holds up, brings wondrous warmth—intimacy with the rest of existence in its variety; acknowledgment of ourselves as codependent with all else on our planet, indeed with the very planet itself; seeing in ourselves the constitution of the stars in their magnificence; all this is more than some romantic dream. It is a truth, and seemingly the only one. The saying that death brings release is also true. We know it does. We are not thereby denied dreams of endless pleasures and eternal joy, but such things must then depend upon the vastness, the grandeur of it all.

Meanwhile, we await the continued unfolding of the human brain, and my focus shifts to more immediate things. I think of my old loves: Peter ill, settled with another mate and warm and wanted once again. John digs and plants, making the planet beautiful with flowers. Our desires and interests had their way with us. Many friends have linked up with other dead and are already part of us, part of everything. As all of us have been and are, and you and I will be.

INDEX